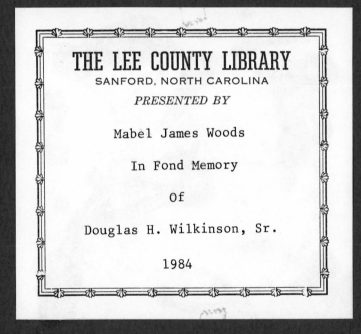

SOUTHERN BIOGRAPHY SERIES
William J. Cooper, Jr., Editor

The Percys of Mississippi

The Percys

LOUISIANA STATE UNIVERSITY PRESS
BATON ROUGE AND LONDON

# of Mississippi

POLITICS AND LITERATURE IN THE NEW SOUTH

Lewis Baker

Designer: Joanna Hill
Typeface: Linotron 202 Trump Mediaeval
Typesetter: G & S Typesetters, Inc.
Printer: Thomson-Shore
Binder: John Dekker & Sons

Publication of this book has been assisted by a grant from the Andrew W. Mellon Foundation.

Photographs for Chapters 1 through 10 are located in the Mississippi Department of Archives and History and are reproduced herein by courtesy of LeRoy P. Percy, with the exception of the photograph of Walker Percy in Chapter 10, which is reproduced courtesy of Jo Gulledge. Grateful acknowledgment is made to LeRoy P. Percy for permission to quote from the LeRoy P. Percy and Family Papers and the William Alexander Percy Papers, recorded on microfilm in the Department of Archives and Manuscripts, Troy H. Middleton Library, Louisiana State University. Permission to reprint excerpts from the Janet Percy Dana Longcope Papers granted courtesy of children of Janet Dana Longcope. Grateful acknowledgment is made to Farrar, Straus, and Giroux, Inc., for permission to quote from the following works by Walker Percy: From *The Last Gentleman*, copyright © 1966 by Walker Percy; from *Love in the Ruins*, copyright © 1971 by Walker Percy; from *Lancelot*, copyright © 1977 by Walker Percy; from *The Second Coming*, copyright © 1980 by Walker Percy. Grateful acknowledgment is made to Alfred A. Knopf, Inc., for permission to reprint excerpts from the following: *The Collected Poems of William Alexander Percy*, copyright © 1943 by LeRoy Pratt Percy; Walker Percy, *The Moviegoer*, copyright © 1960, 1961 by Walker Percy; William Alexander Percy, *Lanterns on the Levee*, copyright © 1941 by LeRoy Pratt Percy. Permission to quote from the interview with Shelby Foote by John Jones granted courtesy of the Mississippi Department of Archives and History. Grateful acknowledgment is made to the Mississippi Department of Archives and History and to the University Press of Mississippi for permission to reprint the interview with Walker Percy by John Jones, which appears in *Mississippi Writers Talking, II*.

LIBRARY OF CONGRESS CATALOGING IN PUBLICATION DATA

Baker, Lewis, 1953–
   The Percys of Mississippi.

   (Southern biography series)
   Bibliography: p.
   Includes index.
   1. Percy family.   I. Title.   II. Series.
CT274.P48B34   1983   929'.2'0973   83-7916
ISBN 0-8071-1102-3

To my mother and father

Contents

Illustrations

Preface

Will and Walker Percy have written extensively about themselves and their family, and any historian of the Percys who attempted to rival the grace of Will's *Lanterns on the Levee* or the insight of Walker's novels would face a formidable task. Fortunately, the present account finds its justification elsewhere, in the recent locating of the papers of LeRoy and Will Percy in the warehouse of the family's cotton compress at Greenville, Mississippi. This collection of some 8,600 letters, manuscripts, photographs, clippings, and other materials provides new insights into the ideas that guided the Percys' actions and the experiences that shaped their ideas.

Over the last four generations, the Percys' interests have shifted from politics to literature. However, the change has been gradual, and politics and literature, defined broadly, have operated dialectically throughout most of the family's history. The Percys' pursuit of what they have called "the good life" has been the common ground of their political and literary activities. I have borrowed the phrase because it offers a strategic ambiguity in that it can be applied to both material and spiritual well-being, the objectives of politics and literature, respectively.

The Percys' concept of the good life included an enjoyment of fine food and drink, travel, leisure, and elegance, as well as the spiritual luxuries of music, art, and literature. They considered all these things refinements appropriate to their stature. The Percys' idea of the good life also required a social setting to sustain it: an economy to provide them with pleasant material surroundings and a culture to furnish their minds in like fashion.

The Percys never forgot that their position carried with it certain duties to their neighbors. As their neighbors came to have less use for aristocrats, the political leadership of Colonel Percy and LeRoy gave way to Will's gentle moral guidance, and then to Walker's diagnostic novels. Thus personal sovereignty has gradually replaced sovereignty in the community, but the desire to experience the joys and responsibilities of the good life has endured.

Acknowledgments

My first thanks are to LeRoy Pratt Percy and the rest of the family, for letting me rummage through their warehouse and their past. Mary Lee Johansen did some rummaging of her own that turned up Will Percy's letters to her mother, Janet Dana Longcope.

I also owe a special debt to the late T. Harry Williams, who encouraged me to undertake this project and provided invaluable guidance in its early stages. Estelle Williams and the custodians of the T. Harry Williams Fellowship then gave me an uninterrupted year to complete the book, and more of an honor than they will ever know.

Professor Anne Loveland read several drafts of the manuscript and insisted on asking the right questions at each stage, whether I had an answer or not. Her patience and interest were invaluable.

Professors Burl Noggle, John Loos, William Cooper, Robert Becker, and Karl Roider of the Department of History at Louisiana State University all deserve my thanks, as do Professors Darwin Schrell and Lewis Simpson of the Department of English, and Professor Cecil Eubanks of the Department of Political Science.

Stone Miller and the staff of the L.S.U. Department of Archives and History were especially helpful in the process of organizing and microfilming the Percy Papers. Corrie Baker, Beth Paskoff, and the rest of the staff at L.S.U.'s Troy H. Middleton Library were also helpful in tracking down sources. Michael Gillette of the Lyndon Baines Johnson Library, John Jones, Michelle Hudson, and Dwight Harris of the Mississippi Department of Archives and History, J. G. Shoalmire of the Mississippi State University Library, and Mary Owens of the Washington County Library provided information and suggestions, as did Professors Robert Coles of Harvard University, John Gonzales of the University of Southern Mississippi, and William Bell of Mississippi State University. Brodie Crump of Greenville and Don Baker of Leland told me some good stories about the Percys. Ruth Davidson and Robin Ringo Martin of Dallas did the hardest job of typing.

I must also tip my cap to John Wallin and his boys of summer, who constantly reminded me that gentlemen and ladies still flourish. My wife, Dana Lee, made it all fun.

The Percys of Mississippi

Chapter 1

Colonel William Alexander Percy

The Percys Arrive

> *The great grandfather knew what was what and said so and acted accordingly and did not care what anyone thought.*
>
> Walker Percy
> *The Last Gentleman*

> *Those days you had to be a hero or a villain or a weakling—you couldn't be just middling ordinary.*
>
> Will Percy
> *Lanterns on the Levee*

Charles Percy came to the Spanish territory south of Natchez in 1776. He had left behind two wives, one in his native England, the other in the Bahamas, where he had sojourned only long enough to gather a cargo of slaves and a land grant from the Spanish government. In Mississippi he married again, to Susanna Collins, who settled him down and bore him six children. Their domestic peace was threatened when Margaret, Charles's English wife, showed up claiming the right of inheritance for Robert, her son by Charles; but a settlement was agreed upon and friendly relations established between Charles's two families. After Margaret's death, Robert accepted Susanna as a stepmother and settled nearby. Meanwhile Charles amassed a fortune growing indigo, and the Spanish, who called him Don Carlos, made him an alcalde, a magistrate, in the local government.[1]

But life in the New World was hard even for successful men like Don Carlos. His own ill health was worsened by the deaths of two of his three sons in childhood. When France declared war on Spain in 1793 Natchez became vulnerable to attack, adding an external threat to the anxiety he already felt about some of his neighbors. Charles Percy discovered that he was not up to living the life of Don Carlos. On January 31, 1794, he gathered several friends together to witness his will, and ten nights later he made his way through the darkness to

Percy Creek. In a remote spot where the water deepened, he tied a tin sugar kettle to his neck and threw himself in.[2]

Of Charles's three American sons, only Thomas George survived childhood in the New World. A bookish young man, Thomas G. attended Princeton, where he became a close friend of John Walker of Alabama. After college, Thomas G. settled next door to Walker on a plantation in Madison County, Alabama, and married Maria Pope, the sister of Walker's wife Matilda. Thomas G. was quite content to live the life of a gentleman planter. While Walker pursued a career as a senator, Thomas G. stayed at home tending his garden and accumulating a massive library. He did enjoy traveling, but unlike his father, he took his wife and family with him, and wherever he went he enjoyed himself immensely. From New York he wrote to Walker, "We have walked up and down Broadway & eke upon the battery & that many times & among crowds of well dress'd people, & been pretty well dress'd ourselves."

Aside from books and nature, the only thing Thomas G. took even half seriously was children. He described the birth of one of his sons as "the sudden appearance of a gentleman who though of Liliputian [*sic*] dimensions is thought to be of some consequence by certain people." He saw to it that his sons learned a profession that would enable them to earn a living independent of their inheritance. Two of his sons, John Walker and LeRoy, became doctors, and the youngest, William Alexander, graduated from Princeton and studied law at the University of Virginia for a year.[3]

After their father's death Walker, LeRoy, and William Alexander showed little inclination to practice the professions they had learned. All three, along with Walker's wife, Fannie, and William Alexander's new bride, Nannie Armstrong, moved to the land Thomas G. had left them in the Yazoo-Mississippi delta. They lived together in a drafty, rambling plantation house at Bachelor's Bend on Deer Creek, where the town of Leland now stands. Their inheritance was more than ample for their needs. The fine alluvial soil of the delta, deposited over the centuries by floods of the Yazoo and Mississippi rivers and fortified by the rotting debris of the hickory, oak, and cypress forests that stood above the swamps and bayous, was some of the richest cotton land in the world. It was, however, an inheritance that would have to be earned. Bear and panther roamed the woods; the ancient swamps were infested with water moccasins, malaria, and yellow fever. After the slaves had cleared the forests and drained the swamps, a way would have to be found to keep the perennial floods from washing away the work that had been done.[4]

Fannie and Nannie faced a comparable task. Both came from well-to-do families, and they now had to oversee the countless daily chores involved in running a frontier home and caring for the slaves, while maintaining the charm and grace that, as Will Percy wrote two generations later, determined "whether that world was delightful or vulgar." If there is a decorous way to shoo a skunk off the front porch, Nannie and Fannie must have discovered it, for they played their roles as successfully as the men. The Percy plantation became one of the most productive in the delta, and their home earned a reputation up and down the Mississippi for its gracious hospitality.[5]

The wealth that the Percys found in the delta's swamps gave them the freedom to live the good life that Don Carlos and Thomas G. had pursued. They were free to travel, to enjoy fine food and drink, to appoint their rustic surroundings with a touch of elegance. Socially, their wealth placed them above the criticism of the community and allowed them to advocate independent and at times unpopular positions without losing their neighbors' respect. Wealth also left the Percys the leisure to live the life of the mind, a habit that reinforced their already healthy tendency to follow their own course. They usually knew what they wanted to do, and their wealth allowed them to do it. Their sovereignty over their own lives was their key to the good life.

Thomas G. had prepared William Alexander well to live the good life of a successful planter, but he could not protect him from the rub that had plagued Don Carlos. William Alexander's prosperity won him the respect of his neighbors, respect that in times of crisis or disaster became the responsibility to lead. The crisis that drew him into public life was the election of Lincoln. He took to the stump to argue against secession and for the election of Judge Shall Yerger to represent Washington County at Mississippi's secession convention. Yerger was elected, but he was unable to restrain the other delegates as they rushed to make Mississippi the second state to leave the Union. Accepting the convention's verdict, Percy organized the Swamp Rangers, the first company of volunteers to leave the delta. After his men elected him a colonel he marched them to Grenada, where they became a part of the Army of Mississippi.[6]

In 1862 Percy was commissioned as a captain in the Confederate army and assigned to the staff of General John Bowen. As an inspector general, Captain Percy's duties included carrying orders to the line during battle. In his first major battle, at Iuka, he earned a reputation for his courage and coolness under fire from Union sharpshooters, who made a special effort to pick off officers on horseback. Percy remained on Bowen's staff throughout Ulysses S. Grant's siege of Vicksburg in 1863. During the siege Union troops blew up the levee at Yazoo Pass, flooding the delta. When Grant captured Vicksburg, Percy was transferred to the Army of Northern Virginia. With the levees gone, he left Mississippi not knowing whether there would be anything to return to after the war.[7]

Late in the year, Captain Percy joined the staff of General A. L. Long, commander of artillery for the Army of Northern Virginia's Second Corps, at Rappahannock Station. Once again Percy found himself in the path of Grant, who had come east for a decisive confrontation with Robert E. Lee. In May, 1864, Grant moved toward Richmond, initiating a series of battles that would last almost a year and encompass the most vicious fighting of the war. Percy fought at the first clash of the two armies at the Wilderness and raced with Lee's army to head off Grant at Spotsylvania Court House. At Cold Harbor, Percy saw seven thousand Union troops killed in half an hour, a mechanical slaughter that mocked the notion of war as a gallant fray. Percy's unit also took part in General Jubal Early's foray up the Shenandoah Valley which reached the very outskirts of Washington D.C. before Early withdrew. After General Philip Sheridan recaptured the valley for the Union, Percy was transferred to General Edward Alexander's First Corps Artillery. Only another transfer, this time back to Mississippi, saved Percy from having to witness Grant's final victory over Lee.[8]

Captain Percy spent the final months of the war as an assistant adjutant general on the staff of General G. B. Hodge, commander of the handful of Confederate troops still active in Mississippi. Percy spent most of his time trying to prevent desertions and keeping track of enemy movements. It was frustrating duty for a man accustomed to fighting, for Hodge's small contingent could do little to oppose the ever growing Union forces there. Percy was equally powerless to stop the obliteration of the few levees that still protected the delta. After Grant's capture of Vicksburg the levees had deteriorated through neglect, and when the river rose during the final year of the war, it washed away the dilapidated remains of the levee system.[9]

After the war Percy waded home through the soggy, abandoned fields of his plantation. Hundreds of delta families who shared his fate left their homes never to return, but Percy was too deeply enmeshed in the delta to sail away. His brother Walker had died during the war; his other brother, LeRoy, lay stricken with paralysis. William Alexander's first responsibility was to feed his houseful of women and children. Taking advantage of the education that Thomas G. had insisted on providing him with, he began practicing law in Greenville.[10]

Percy's legal practice thrust him into public life at a time when the delta was desperate for leaders. He was well cast for the part. Although he was only thirty-one, his silver hair and piercing eyes earned him the name "the Gray Eagle of the delta," while his dignified, martial bearing prompted his fellow citizens to call him Colonel Percy, the title he had enjoyed in the Army of Mississippi. His "promotion" was significant because the people of the delta, threatened by the river, the encroaching wilderness, and a triumphant federal government, put their future in the hands of those who had proven themselves in the war.[11]

The river loomed as the greatest danger facing the delta. Several planters wanted to revive the levee district established by the state legislature before the war. However, Colonel Percy knew that the old district was heavily in debt, and if it were revived, funds desperately needed for levee construction would be drained away by its creditors. To avoid this, Colonel Percy helped establish the new, unencumbered Board of Levee Commissioners for Bolivar, Washington, and Issaquena Counties. In 1866 Percy, Captain W. E. Hunt, Colonel F. A. Montgomery, and General Charles Clark asked the legislature to empower the board to impose taxes for levee construction. Perhaps fearing an attack if it refused such a contingent, the legislature passed an act establishing the Mississippi Levee District and granting it the authority to impose taxes and build levees in the three counties it encompassed.[12]

Unfortunately, the power to tax was useless as long as local planters had nothing to pay with. Colonel Percy solved this problem temporarily by persuading several planters to build levees and to accept bonds issued by the district as payment for their work; but the bonds would eventually have to be repaid. He realized that the levee district's tax base needed to be expanded: delta planters would have to reestablish their operations, and new settlers would have to be brought in. Only then could the district raise enough money to fight the Mississippi River.[13]

Like most men of his time, Colonel Percy saw the railroad as the key to economic growth. In 1870 he joined with several other planters to incorporate the Greenville, Deer Creek, and Rolling Fork Railroad, which its owners hoped would provide a means of shipping their cotton to market at Greenville. Two years later the Greenville, Columbus, and Birmingham Railroad hired Colonel Percy to canvass Washington County and drum up support for a subsidy to finance building a line from Stoneville to Greenville. During the canvass one planter told Percy, "We don't want them things in this county, killing the chickens and hogs and scaring the game"; but despite such opposition, the railroad received its bond issue and completed construction of the line.[14]

The railroads promised to bring new settlers to the delta, but their arrival would make little difference if the planters already there had been taxed out of existence. In addition to the new levee taxes, planters faced soaring property taxes imposed by state, local, and county governments. Many were unable to pay and forfeited their land, thus taking it out of production and further constricting the tax base. The delinquent tax roles for Washington County alone numbered over four thousand, and by the end of Reconstruction, over two million acres of delta farmland had been confiscated. Most planters, including Percy, blamed the rising tax burden on the corruption of the Republicans who controlled the state and local governments of Mississippi. Corruption was not the only cause of the increased cost of government, however, for public services were dramatically expanded after the war, to care for the black freedmen. But the planters saw the corruption. They saw themselves and their neighbors losing their land because of taxes imposed by representatives of the landless, and they decided to put a stop to it.[15]

Relying on the votes of the freedman majority, two black preacher-politicians had taken control of the Washington County government.

One of them, state Senator William Grey, was a staunch ally of Governor Adelbert Ames. Grey's local rival, chancery clerk J. Allen Ross, was aligned with Governor Ames's rival, James L. Alcorn. In 1873 the feud between Ames and Alcorn filtered down to Washington County, dividing the black vote between Grey and Ross and allowing the white planters to regain control of the board of supervisors, which controlled property tax evaluations and other local taxes.[16]

After regaining control of the board, Colonel Percy began working to ally local planters with the growing opposition to Governor Ames in other parts of Mississippi. In November, 1873, he organized a taxpayers' convention, which met at Greenville to adopt resolutions condemning the corruption of state officials and pledging to resist paying taxes through any legal means. The following January, Colonel Percy led Washington County's delegation to a statewide taxpayers' convention at Jackson and served on the resolutions committee of the convention. The convention issued a statement addressed to the people of the Union that described the conditions facing Mississippi taxpayers. The convention also established a committee to work with the legislature and governor to enact reforms.[17]

The leaders of the taxpayers' movement had little real hope of reforming Ames's government. Most of their energy was focused on unseating the legislature in the upcoming fall elections. In April a call went out for another statewide taxpayers' meeting in Jackson to organize for the coming campaign, and once again Colonel Percy called Washington County's taxpayers together to select delegates to this convention. The Gray Eagle urged cooperation with conservative elements in other parts of Mississippi, arguing that local corruption would end only after the downfall of the Republican state government that supported it. He urged the people of Washington County to work "in the spirit and with the earnestness which should actuate men suffering as we have." To do this effectually, he added, "we should define sharply the issues on which we propose to battle, and thoroughly organize our forces for action." When the convention met in August, Percy was placed on the platform committee, where he worked to insure that the issues of the campaign were defined sharply. As a member of the state executive committee, he also helped organize conservatives across the state.[18]

Colonel Percy's most important task in the coming election was to carry his own county. Thousands of newly enfranchised blacks had come to the delta after emancipation, increasing the area's representation in the legislature. If the Democrats were to capture the legislature, they would have to find some way to pry these black voters away from the Republicans. Percy's chance came in August, when the local Republican leaders had another falling out. Grey and Ross both wanted the lucrative job of sheriff. Grey announced that he intended to be sheriff at all costs, and claimed that Governor Ames would send a thousand troops to back him if necessary. Angered by Grey's threats, Ross urged the black voters of Washington County to support the Democratic ticket. Grey responded by urging them instead to load their shotguns. The result was a shoot-out in the streets of Greenville. Ross was killed, but Grey and his followers were routed by Captain William G. Yerger's hastily organized rifle company. Grey fled, and after a futile attempt to rally his followers for another battle, came out of hiding to withdraw from the sheriff's race.[19]

With Grey and Ross out of the picture, Colonel Percy put together a fusion ticket that included several black candidates for minor offices but presented whites for most of the important positions. Each side accused the other of trying to intimidate voters, but by Reconstruction standards the election appears to have been rather sedate. The split within the Republican party had neutralized the black majority in Washington County, and after the Kentucky abolitionist Cassius Clay visited Greenville and urged blacks to vote for the fusion ticket, there was little cause for the violence that accompanied redemption in other parts of the South. As the fusion party's candidate for state representative, Percy led his ticket to victory in the fall elections.[20]

The Democratic victory in Washington County was repeated across the state. When the new legislators assembled in January, they appointed Colonel Percy and four others to a committee to investigate corruption in the Ames administration and report on whether the governor should be impeached. The committee recommended impeachment on twenty-one articles, including abuses of the convict lease system and the pardon power. The house approved the committee report, and on March 14 Percy read the charges against Ames to the state senate. Ames resigned before the senate could try him, and senate president John M. Stone, a delta planter, became temporary governor. Mississippi was redeemed.[21]

With the state government under Democratic control, Colonel Percy made good his promise to clean up the corruption in Washington County. Following Ames's resignation Sheriff L. T. Webber had left the county for parts unknown. Judge C. C. Shackleford, another Republican appointee, had been refusing to hold court because he feared that Webber would be indicted. Once the sheriff was out of danger, Shackleford decided to convene his circuit court so that he could insure the acquittal of another Republican, a chancery clerk named Bolton, who had been charged with falsifying county records. Shackleford took up Bolton's case on the last day of his court's term and tried to ram through a verdict of not guilty, but the jury deadlocked. Hoping to save Bolton from having to stand trial under a new judge, Shackleford refused to adjourn his court. His obstinance angered the people of Greenville. That night they gathered at the courthouse to listen to angry speeches and then marched to Shackleford's house. When the judge refused to see them, Colonel Percy burst into Shackleford's bedrooom and warned him that if he did not adjourn his court immediately, Percy could not answer for the angry crowd outside. Shackleford hastily reconsidered and followed Colonel Percy to the courthouse to announce that the circuit court was adjourned. Bolton quickly left the county.[22]

Greenville's taxpayers gathered the following Monday to celebrate their victory over the Republicans. They adopted resolutions condemning Shackleford for allowing crime and corruption a free hand and declaring that "the thieves, vagrants, robbers and incendiaries, and their aiders and abettors in crime not yet in jail but still remaining in the community be . . . hereby notified to leave these parts and the quicker the better." With a sigh of relief the meeting further resolved that "we hail the coming of local peace and amity, of law and order, and are thankful that the final throe of our thraldom to misrule is over and that the sky of the future is clearing."[23]

Greenville honored Colonel Percy for his role in redemption by reelecting him to the state legislature in 1877. The following year his colleagues in the legislature elected the Colonel speaker of the house, and there was talk of his running for Congress. Such offices, however, held little appeal for the Gray Eagle. He had entered state politics only because he believed the Republicans were a threat to the delta and the good life it supported. With that threat eliminated, Colonel Percy de-

clined to stand for reelection after his second term in the legislature
and returned to Greenville. He served as a delegate to the Democratic
national conventions of 1880 and 1884 but never held another public
office.[24]

Colonel Percy's law practice kept him active in local affairs. As attorney for the levee board he lobbied ably for funding, and his knowledge of flood control made him a respected representative of the delta
at waterways conventions up and down the Mississippi Valley. When
the river rose in 1882 and other districts flooded, Greenville's levees
held fast, and the town gave Colonel Percy the credit. The Gray Eagle
also enriched the delta through his railroad accounts by seeking new
lines that would bring settlers to the delta and help planters market their crops. Percy was himself considerably enriched by these accounts, and his prosperity bound his family closer to the delta.[25]

Colonel Percy bound himself to the delta because of the good life it
promised. His neighbors respected and rewarded him because in crisis
after crisis, be it war, taxes, or high water, he put aside his private concerns to assume his public responsibilities. Each crisis faced successfully, each disaster averted, increased his prestige and, along with it,
his responsibility for and his stake in the welfare of the delta. The
Gray Eagle had come a long way from Percy Creek to arrive in the
delta.[26]

Chapter 2

LeRoy Percy

LeRoy Percy

*The next generation, the grandfather, seemed to know what was
what but he was not really so sure. He was brave but he gave
much thought to the business of being brave.*

> Walker Percy
> *The Last Gentleman*

*He suffered like a god that had no part
In its creation, but was resolved—how madly—
To make it over, if not beautiful,
Tolerable at least and roomed for men.*

> William Alexander Percy
> "Enzio's Kingdom"

*I guess a man's job is to make the world a better place to live in,
so far as he is able—always remembering the results will be in-
finitesimal—and to attend to his own soul.*

> LeRoy Percy, quoted in *Lanterns on the Levee*

Colonel Percy's family life was as fruitful as his career. He and Nannie
had two daughters, Fannie and Lady, and three sons, LeRoy, William
Armstrong, and Walker. All three sons inherited the Colonel's courage
and flair for politics. LeRoy, the eldest son, born November 19, 1860,
also inherited his father's love of the delta. He stayed in Greenville
and assumed his father's role of community leader, while Willie and
Walker left to pursue successful legal careers in Memphis and Birmingham, respectively.[1]

After attending Greenville's public schools young LeRoy entered the
University of the South at Sewanee, Tennessee. He got his first taste of
politics when he successfully opposed the establishment of Greek fra-
ternities at Sewanee, by arguing that they were undemocratic. LeRoy
graduated in 1879 and returned to Greenville to read law in his father's
office. He could not have picked a better place to become familiar with

the issues and people of the delta. Levees, railroads, and cotton were topics of daily concern, and his father's partner, Judge William G. Yerger, had political connections that matched Colonel Percy's. The young man learned the interests of the delta and made them his own.[2]

LeRoy's thoughts were not entirely of the law and the delta. He spent his evenings courting a beautiful blond French girl named Camille Bourges. Camille's father, Ernest, had been a cotton factor in New Orleans. When the price of cotton went up following the war, Ernest bought the Woodstock Plantation and moved his family to the delta. When prices fell, Ernest was forced to sell out and move into Greenville. His wife, Marie Camille Generelly Bourges, was the daughter of a prominent New Orleans family, and Ernest's setbacks did nothing to shake her faith in her own claim to aristocracy. She considered LeRoy, like the delta, a bit wild and raw, and objected to her Catholic daughter's marrying an Episcopalian. But Camille preferred the handsome young Sewanee man to her other suitors and finally won her mother's approval for the match.[3]

Shortly after announcing his engagement to Camille, LeRoy went off to the University of Virginia Law School to prepare himself to support a wife. Anxious to return to Camille, LeRoy lived off campus, away from the distractions of student life. On one occassion, however, his inability to resist a good fight lured him into campus politics. One Saturday afternoon several drunken students had gone to the circus, only to be thrown out when their applause for one of the show girls became overly enthusiastic. The students returned to the campus and met that night to decide how to answer this affront to their dignity. LeRoy had not gone to the circus, but he joined the faction that favored returning and fighting it out. Future president Woodrow Wilson, a student at the time, led the faction opposed to fighting. Wilson delivered a temperate, literary, and completely ineffectual speech, and a brawl would probably have followed had it not been for Red Echols, another student. Echols had seen a student killed with a tent stake in a similar fight a few years before. He had also seen the crew of this circus and knew that the students "were in for the worst licking that a bunch of men ever had." Hoping to impress his fellow students with the gravity of the situation, Echols drew his pistol and laid it on a table, urging all who were willing to return to do likewise and vow to "shoot and shoot to kill." At that, LeRoy's supporters quietly slipped out of the doors and windows.[4]

By concentrating on his studies LeRoy was able to graduate from law school in only one year. He returned to Greenville and read law in Judge Yerger's office until November, when he passed his bar exam impressively, prompting one of his examiners to predict, "He will stand fire." Starting out as the junior partner in his father's firm, LeRoy struggled for two years to establish himself well enough to support Camille. Finally he realized that he would never make that much money, and he married her anyway on December 9, 1883. Shortly over a year later they had a son whom they named William Alexander, after Colonel Percy. Delighted, the Colonel teased his in-laws by predicting that his grandson would become the first American pope. Mrs. Bourges's reaction to this remark has not been recorded.[5]

Fortunately, LeRoy's law practice grew apace with his family. In 1884 the delta's northern counties established the Yazoo-Mississippi Levee District. Aware of what Colonel Percy had done for the southern delta's Mississippi Levee District, the board members chose LeRoy to be attorney for the new district and to represent it at flood control meetings and conventions across the country. LeRoy's new position increased his contacts among flood control proponents and expanded his knowledge of the technical side of flood control, thus binding his career to the delta's major concern, the levees.[6]

Colonel Percy died in 1888. The delta mourned the loss of one of its most forceful leaders and looked to his eldest son, LeRoy, to take his place. After his father's death LeRoy took a larger part in local politics by becoming chairman of the county Democratic Executive Committee. His continuing partnership with Judge Yerger also kept LeRoy in touch with state politics. When a convention was called in 1890 to rewrite the state's constitution, Yerger led the delta representatives who opposed disfranchising Mississippi's black voters. Yerger was hardly a champion of racial equality, but he realized that the delta's power in state politics rested on the black vote, which was firmly controlled by white politicians like himself. Politicians from other parts of the state resented the delta's use of this power to secure disproportionate funding for its schools and to block the prohibition legislation favored by white hill farmers. As C. Vann Woodward put it, the issue behind black disfranchisement was not white supremacy but "which whites should be supreme."[7]

Yerger and his allies were only partly successful. The convention agreed to continue distributing school funds on the basis of total, rather than white, enrollment. Since few blacks attended schools, this method of allocation insured that the delta would continue to receive more funds per actual student than other parts of the state. But the convention also adopted what became known as the second Mississippi plan, a new set of voting requirements that included a poll tax and a literacy requirement, both designed to discourage blacks from voting. Also, the white counties received more seats in the state legislature. This dramatic change in the political balance of power forced delta politicians, including young LeRoy Percy, to adopt a new approach to statewide politics. Henceforth the delta would be a minority section with an overriding special interest—the levees.[8]

The importance of the levees was underscored again in 1890 when another flood inundated Greenville. The next year, the levees of the upper district broke at a point that had been thought impregnable. An investigation revealed that the break had been caused by incendiaries, most likely levee workers angry at not having been paid. To prevent such an occurrence in their district the Mississippi Levee Board established the Levee Guard, and LeRoy did his part by becoming a captain and leading the armed patrols on their rounds.[9]

The major problem confronting LeRoy and others interested in better levees remained the lack of an adequate tax base to pay for them. During the 1880s the delta had grown dramatically. The population had increased by half and the amount of land in cultivation had nearly doubled, but much of the area remained a soggy wilderness. LeRoy, like Colonel Percy, saw the railroads as the solution to this problem. In 1892 the Illinois Central Railroad bought out one of LeRoy's largest clients, the Louisville, New Orleans, and Texas Railroad. The Illinois Central had increased its business in Illinois by helping farmers settle along their line. Hoping to do the same in the delta, its officials retained LeRoy's firm to advise them on local conditions and develop a settlement policy suitable to agriculture in the delta. Like his work for the levee board, LeRoy's association with the Illinois Central allowed him to help develop the delta while advancing his own career. During the next decade, much of the land owned by the railroad was sold to planters and put back into production, thus widening the base of the levee districts.[10]

A serious threat to the levee system arose from within the levee board itself in 1894, when forty thousand dollars was discovered to be missing from the district's funds. The secretary-treasurer was General S. W. Ferguson, an old friend of the Percys and several board members. Ferguson had been given the job because he needed it, even though he had no aptitude for accounting. Trusting in their friend's integrity, board members John Casey and Johnson Erwin insisted on a thorough audit, which they believed would clear the General of any wrongdoing. That night Ferguson left town and fled the country, leaving his friends to face an outraged citizenry. Yerger and Percy were especially criticized when it was discovered that they had inadvertently allowed Ferguson's bond to lapse, leaving the district uninsured against the loss. In August the levee board held a public meeting in Greenville. The members admitted that they had been careless and promised several reforms aimed at making the operation of the district more business-like. The board's actions indicated that it was properly chastened, but it was too late to repair its damaged credibility. Aspiring politicians throughout the delta smelled an opportunity to take control of the board and its lucrative patronage.[11]

Incoming governor Anselm J. McLaurin was in the best position to take advantage of the board's vulnerability, for he controlled the appointments to it. "Old Anse," as he was called, was not a man to neglect opportunity. He used the Ferguson affair as an excuse to ignore the advice of LeRoy and other levee experts, and filled the board with political hacks who had supported his candidacy for governor. LeRoy was infuriated. The Ferguson affair had underlined the danger of making appointments to the levee board for personal reasons. Funds for levee building were simply too scarce to be wasted through either corruption or incompetence, and LeRoy suspected Old Anse's men of both. In a public statement LeRoy, Judge Yerger, Charles Scott of Bolivar County, and Murray Smith of Vicksburg charged that McLaurin had "desecrated" the governor's office by having "McLaurinized" Mississippi. Not surprisingly, the new board decided not to retain Yerger and Percy as their attorneys.[12]

The rivalry between LeRoy and McLaurin carried over into the delta's congressional election of 1896, when Old Anse announced he was backing Andrew H. Longino, an advocate of free silver. LeRoy supported the incumbent of twelve years, General T. C. Catchings. A portly, heavy-jowled man whose rare speeches bored even his supporters, Catchings compounded his unpopularity by favoring the gold standard over the more popular free silver position. But within this porcine monument to phlegm lurked a keen mind familiar with every aspect of flood control. As a senior member of the House Committee on Rivers and Harbors, Catchings made sure that the delta always received its fair share of federal appropriations for levee construction.[13]

Like Catchings, LeRoy supported the gold standard but considered the issue insignificant compared to the need for continued levee appropriations. LeRoy knew that free silver had strong popular support, so to neutralize the issue, he published a letter from Catchings promising that if reelected, the congressman would obey the will of his constituents and vote for any silver bills presented to the House. Eighteen years before, Colonel Percy had abandoned free silver to preserve Democratic party unity, which he considered vital to the survival of the delta. Sensing the shift in the political winds, LeRoy took a new tack, but his destination remained the same.[14]

The Democratic nomination, which was tantamount to election, would be decided by a convention of delegates from each of the district's counties. But in most counties the delegate selection process was followed by cries of fraud and foul play; thus when the convention met in Greenville, rival delegations representing Catchings and Longino appeared and demanded to be seated. Fortunately for Catchings, three of his supporters, LeRoy, Charles Scott, and Pat Henry, constituted a majority of the five man executive committee that would decide which delegations to seat. After a long day of debate failed to settle anything, the executive committee voted to seat the crucial pro-Catchings delegation from Bolivar County, thereby insuring the General's renomination. This high-handed action angered Longino's delegates. They bolted the convention and threatened to split the party until James K. Vardaman, the young leader of the Longino faction from LeFlore County, changed his mind and led his delegation back to the convention. Their solid front broken, the other Longino delegations slowly straggled back to watch Catchings be nominated. The convention then elected a new executive committee that, not surprisingly, included both LeRoy Percy and James Vardaman.[15]

The next year the worst flood in the delta's history roared down the Mississippi River. Floodwaters submerged all but the highest points and damaged several levees, leaving the delta unprotected against another rise. While the levee boards raced against time to repair the damage, McLaurin turned down their request for convicts to help in the work. Catchings, on the other hand, did his part by guiding a Senate investigating committee through the stricken area. His efforts were rewarded when the committee recommended a special appropriation to repair the levees.[16]

The flood of 1897 confirmed LeRoy in his belief that levees were more important to the delta than the silver issue. Accordingly, as the next congressional election approached, he offered a trade to one of McLaurin's lieutenants, Lorraine C. Dulaney. If McLaurin would appoint Judge Yerger to the Senate seat about to be vacated through Edward Walthall's retirement, LeRoy would support a free silver man for governor in 1900. LeRoy also told Dulaney that this would probably be Catchings' last term and that, if it was, he would support a free silver candidate in the 1900 congressional election, "provided they would name good men, not McLaurins, for the places." Dulaney reported LeRoy's offer to Walter Sillers, one of McLaurin's aides. Sillers met with LeRoy a few days later, but he was unwilling to go along with the plan unless Catchings would withdraw from the current congressional race. LeRoy refused even to consider deserting Catchings, and the deal fell through. McLaurin's aides met in Greenville a few days later and endorsed Pat Henry for the congressional nomination. Hoping to avoid another split convention, the executive committee scheduled a primary for July 11 to decide between the two candidates. Henry was delighted, for he was a far better campaigner than Catchings.[17]

As the campaign wore on into summer, tempers on both sides grew short. When C. E. Wright, pro-Henry editor of the Vicksburg *Daily Dispatch* attempted to speak to Catchings in the street, the General ignored him. Angered by this affront, Wright hit Catchings over the head with his umbrella. This proved to be a mistake, for Catchings took the umbrella from Wright, poked him with it several times, and then mauled him with his fists. After the crowd separated them, both men were arrested, placed under a peace bond, and released.[18]

General Catchings was less dangerous behind a speaker's podium than he was with an umbrella, and so he left most of the campaigning to LeRoy. On June 10 LeRoy debated Pat Henry at a picnic and barbecue at Hollendale. Henry began by hammering away at the free silver issue, but LeRoy interrupted him to point out that Catchings had voted for the silver legislation presented to Congress during his last term. Forced to retract his claim that Catchings had opposed this legislation, Henry next tried to explain why he had supported Catchings in the last election but was now running against him. He claimed that he had supported Catchings only after the General promised to support free silver. But LeRoy was ready for him again. He produced the letter that Catchings had written promising to vote for silver legislation, and another letter showing that Henry had thrown his support to Catchings before the General's letter was written, not after.

Unable to make silver the issue, Henry attacked Catchings' record on securing levee appropriations for the delta. This was a mistake, for LeRoy was intimately familiar with the levee system and legislation pertaining to it. He answered Henry's charges by simply listing the special appropriations Catchings had guided through Congress and then comparing the delta's levees with those of other states, leaving his opponent buried under an avalanche of statistics. Then, dripping sarcasm, LeRoy told the crowd that he was unsure how Henry intended to get a silver bill through a Republican Congress but that he suspected it might prove harder than Henry imagined.[19]

To counter LeRoy's success at the Hollendale picnic, Old Anse himself took to the stump at Indianola on the Fourth of July. When he discovered that LeRoy was in the crowd, however, McLaurin decided against speaking for Henry. Instead, he spoke for three hours on the blessings of free silver, sprinkling his discourse with what one reporter called "a few jokes and anecdotes of doubtful age and obscure application." His speech completely ignored the congressional race and had little impact on the crowd, most of whom wandered off to gaze at the steaming barbecue. Finally several of his listeners shouted at Old Anse to sit down and shut up so that dinner could be served. After dinner Colonel James D. Thames repeated the charges that Henry had made against Catchings, with LeRoy again interrupting to correct his dates and figures. Then LeRoy and several other Catchings supporters made short, humorous speeches designed to appease the free silver men in the crowd. The Indianola picnic was another clear victory for Catchings.[20]

The primary was held a week later. Early returns showed that Catchings had carried LeRoy's home ground, Washington County, by 461 votes, and had run even with Henry in the rest of the district. However, returns from Issaquena County, a McLaurin stronghold, were slow coming in, prompting rumors of illegal voting there. When the returns did come in, they gave Henry a majority of 300, a remarkable total, considering that two years before there had not been 300 people in Issaquena eligible to vote, much less registered to do so. Nevertheless, the Vicksburg *Daily Dispatch*, its editor still smarting from the thrashing Catchings had given him, accepted Issaquena's returns. With Henry still trailing, the *Dispatch* turned to Coahoma County, where two rival Democratic factions had existed since the split at the convention two years before. By throwing out the returns from the Catchings faction in Coahoma and counting the returns for Issaquena, the *Dispatch* calculated that Henry had won by 4 votes. When the Catchings press charged that the Issaquena returns had been doctored, Henry's supporters claimed that large numbers of Republicans had voted illegally in Washington County. The returns from Washington, however, were not out of line with the number of voters in 1896 or the census figures of 1890, and unlike the Issaquena returns, they had been counted in public.

So in spite of the primary, the district executive committee would again have to decide the congressional election. When the committee met in Greenville on July 20 to certify the returns, Colonel Thames tried to set up a subcommittee to investigate the returns, but LeRoy would have no part of it. He demanded an immediate public investigation by the entire committee and challenged Henry's men to substantiate their allegations. Unable to furnish evidence of illegal voting, Thames sought a delay, but LeRoy insisted that the committee remain in session until the election was settled. Thames gave up, and Catchings was unanimously declared the party's nominee. The same returns showed that LeRoy had been reelected to the district executive committee.[21]

The election was not a complete success. A majority of the new executive committee were anti-Catchings men. As it turned out, however, this made little difference, for the General had had enough. Tired and disgusted by the charges made against him during the campaign, he confessed that he had "felt most keenly the shafts of venom which have been plunged into me," and announced that this would be his last term.[22]

Catchings' retirement announcement did not settle LeRoy's feud with McLaurin. In 1899 Old Anse was elected to the Senate. When the Democratic state convention met to choose a new governor, LeRoy introduced a resolution charging McLaurin with nepotism and intoxication. But Old Anse controlled the convention and was able to have Andrew Longino chosen to succeed him as governor. LeRoy had denied Longino the delta's congressional seat three years before, and the new governor repaid him by having legislation passed that reduced the delta's share of the state's school funds.[23]

Longino angered LeRoy again in 1902 by refusing to call a special session of the legislature to rewrite Mississippi's insurance laws. The insurance companies claimed that the decision of the Mississippi Supreme Court in the case of the *Hartford Insurance Company* v. *D. J. Schinkler* had made it impossible to continue writing fire insurance on cotton. Worried by the prospect of their cotton disappearing in an uninsured blaze, planters and factors from across the state gathered in Jackson on July 2 and urged Governor Longino to call a special session to consider the insurance companies' requests. At the convention LeRoy was appointed to the special committee to study the feasibility of repealing the valued policy clause, contact legislators to find out if they would vote for this change, and report to the governor. Finding most legislators indifferent to their cause, the committee urged the governor to call a special session anyway so that they could explain their position. Longino refused, arguing that a special session would be too expensive. When the cotton was picked that autumn, the fears of the planters and factors proved well founded. Insurance rates soared, and many factors could not find enough insurance at any price. Seeing a golden opportunity for fraud, swindlers descended on Mississippi, selling bogus insurance that lacked funds to pay claims.[24]

Longino's refusal to call the legislature into special session may have cost him a hunting trip. In November, President Theodore Roosevelt and Stuyvesant Fish, president of the Illinois Central Railroad, came to the delta to hunt bear. LeRoy was included in the President's hunting party, but Longino, who had originally been invited to join them, was somehow never informed of the exact date or location. Fish was probably as delighted by this oversight as LeRoy, for Longino had raised the tax valuation on the Illinois Central the year before. While the hunters feasted on wild game, Longino's supporters ate crow. The Jackson *Daily Clarion-Ledger*, which supported the governor, contradicted its own earlier reports by denying that Longino had ever been invited. The *Clarion-Ledger* served its readers sour grapes for dessert, claiming that the site of the hunt was inhabited only by aged bear that no true sportsman would shoot.[25]

The President's party camped between the bayous and lagoons along the Sunflower River, in country covered with cane and briars higher than a man's head. The bear shared their swamp with deer, turkey, and wildcats. And Holt Collier. Collier was a professional hunter who supplied the railroad's crews with fresh meat, and no one hunted the Sunflower without him. The colossal Negro knew where the bear were and had a reputation for killing them with his bowie knife. Collier placed Roosevelt where he could have the first kill, but by the time the dogs ran a bear past his spot, the President had moved. Collier was determined that Roosevelt take the first bear, and refused to be frustrated by the President's poor judgment. He followed his yelping hounds into a shallow lagoon where they had cornered a small black bear. Collier hit the bear over the head with his rifle, tied a rope around its neck, and invited Roosevelt to shoot it. Roosevelt refused to shoot a captive animal, of course, but he and the rest of the party had several more sporting chances during the next week.[26]

LeRoy's quarrel with Longino expired with the governor's term in 1903, but his feud with Old Anse McLaurin raged on. McLaurin sat out the August primary and then threw his support to Judge Frank Critz in the runoff. Critz was opposed by James Vardaman, the newspaper editor from Greenwood whose defection had broken the unity of the anti-Catchings forces in 1896. Vardaman was among the first delta politicians to see that the new primary laws and the disfranchisement of blacks made it imperative to seek popular support in other parts of the state. Vardaman did so with a vengeance, using the race issue to appeal to Mississippi's white hill farmers. Vardaman opposed education for blacks because it unfitted them for picking cotton, and in one speech he openly approved of lynchings.

For LeRoy, however, the levees were still the most important issue in the delta, and he had seen the kind of men that McLaurin and his supporters had appointed to the levee board in the past. He decided to support Vardaman, explaining that he was "a lifetime resident of the Delta, thoroughly cognizant of the paramount importance of the levee question."[27]

LeRoy's support proved crucial in the runoff. With it, Vardaman carried several counties in the delta that Critz had won in the first primary, and captured the nomination for governor. Vardaman repaid LeRoy by replacing Longino's appointees to the levee board with Dr. J. T. Atterbury and other men acceptable to the delta.[28]

LeRoy did not comment on, either in public statements or his correspondence, Vardaman's racist rhetoric at this time. However, delta planters generally took a more businesslike approach to the race issue than did most Mississippi farmers, and LeRoy probably shared this attitude. Mississippi's woods were full of hill farmers who spent one month a year rounding up blacks to pick their cotton, and the other eleven hatching schemes to ship them all to Africa or Saint Louis. In the delta, on the other hand, the shortage of year-round agricultural labor was one of the chief impediments to economic growth, and the planters knew it. Blacks received better treatment and wages in the delta, and consequently they moved there from other parts of the state. Farmers in the rest of the state reacted to this trend by running labor recruiting agents from the delta out of town and forbidding blacks to leave the area during cotton picking season. Colonel W. J. Ferguson of Hinds County told a reporter that if all of the blacks left for the delta, he would follow them there. "I am not going to live where there are no niggers," he declared. "I've always been used to having them to catch my horse and black my shoes, and I'm going to have at least one of them around the place if I have to follow them all the way down into Africa."[29] Most farmers, however, were not this willing to admit their dependence on blacks. Voting for Vardaman gave them a means of publicly denying that dependence. LeRoy probably feared that Vardaman would convince Mississippi's blacks that they were not needed and frighten them out of the state, leaving the delta bereft of labor.[30]

While LeRoy understood the delta's dependence on black labor, he hoped that an influx of white settlers would eventually end it. LeRoy believed that in the long run, only white settlers could replace the blacks who were emigrating to the North, and he knew that in the short run, there was plenty of work for whites and blacks. LeRoy used his positions on the board of directors of the Southern Railroad and as attorney for the Illinois Central to encourage immigration to the delta. Stuyvesant Fish of the Illinois Central was especially interested in helping because he knew that immigration would increase his railroad's business in the delta. LeRoy corresponded with Fish on conditions facing settlers, advised him on ways to encourage immigration, and helped set up the Roundaway Plantation, a model farm built by the railroad in Coahoma County.[31]

LeRoy also used his partnership in the cotton factorage of Messrs. O. B. Crittenden and Company to encourage immigration. In 1897 Crittenden and Company leased the 11,000 acre Sunnyside Plantation, located across the river from Greenville, from the estate of the late Austin Corbin. Corbin had imported 125 Italian families to farm Sunnyside, but malaria struck in 1897, and by the time Crittenden and Company took over, only 30 families remained.

LeRoy had little hope of replacing the Italians with black tenants, so he decided to give Corbin's experiment another chance, this time using his experience as a planter to avoid the mistakes Corbin had made. More Italians were imported, and credit was extended to those who needed it to establish themselves. LeRoy was careful to enlist settlers from the northern, agricultural provinces, rather than from the cities. Competent managers were brought in to instruct the settlers on the peculiarities of cotton planting, and the more experienced Negro tenants were scattered around Sunnyside to provide an example. LeRoy also made sure that proper sanitary conditions were maintained to prevent another outbreak of malaria.

LeRoy's new tenants at Sunnyside prospered impressively. Unlike his black tenants, the Italians preferred to rent the better, higher priced land. Using the intensive farming techniques they had learned in Italy, entire families worked the fields from sunup to sundown, six days a week, from March through December, and their diligence paid off in bigger crops. They also grew their own vegetables and paid close attention to their accounts at the company store and to the price of cotton. This thrift allowed most of them to pay off the expense of immigrating by the end of their first year.

As the Italian population at Sunnyside grew to five hundred, LeRoy brought more of the plantation under cultivation. Other planters noted his success, and Italian settlements began to dot the delta. Pointing to the Italians' greater productivity, LeRoy argued that they made better tenants than blacks. He told the *Manufacturer's Record* that "if the immigration of these people is encouraged, they will gradually take the place of the Negro without there being any such violent change as to paralyze for a generation the prosperity of the country."[32] Although the number of Italians remained relatively small, their success suggested that they might someday solve the delta's labor shortage.[33]

LeRoy also enlisted the aid of Stuyvesant Fish and the Illinois Central in bringing Italians to the delta. Fish preferred bringing in small, independent farmers rather than tenants, but LeRoy and Charles Scott of Bolivar County convinced him that this was impracticable in the delta, because farming there required a large capital investment in warehouses, gins, and other equipment. Fish contacted the commissioner general of immigration and offered to take any immigrants "whom you do not know what to do with." Fish also persuaded Italian ambassador Baron Edmondo Mayor Des Planches to tour the delta as the guest of the Illinois Central and see the conditions awaiting Italian immigrants there for himself. LeRoy, Charles Scott, and other leading planters entertained Planches during his tour and made sure he came away with a favorable impression of the delta.[34]

Many Italian officials did not share Planches' enthusiasm. An epidemic of yellow fever in New Orleans in 1905 revived their fears that the delta's damp climate was unsuitable for Italians, and led emigration officials in Rome to begin pointing their charges toward Texas. The Italian government was also alarmed by reports that delta landlords were cheating their tenants by charging excessive prices at the company store and paying less than market value for cotton. Several investigations cleared Sunnyside of such charges, but other landlords may have used the same sharp practices with the Italians that they sometimes used with their black tenants. Such treatment hurt the pride of the Italians even more than it did their pocketbooks, for they regarded blacks as their inferiors and bristled when local whites treated them like Negroes. As Senator Augusto Pierantoni of Italy wrote, "Italian feeling rebels on hearing that our peasants are compared to Asiatics or Negroes." After 1905 the Italian government began placing as many obstacles as possible in the path of emigrants headed for the delta.[35]

LeRoy was determined to remove these obstacles. In February, 1907, he asked Baron Des Planches to help him bring over more Italians to settle on his 3,200 acre Trail Lake Plantation. LeRoy assured Des Planches that Italians settling at Trail Lake would receive the same fair treatment that the ambassador had observed at Sunnyside. He also had the tenant contracts used at Sunnyside translated into Italian, hoping this would lessen the Italians' suspicions. But Luigi Villari, the Italian vice-consul at New Orleans, continued actively to oppose LeRoy's efforts. Villari began demanding that Italians seeking to send money home to bring their relatives to America come to New Orleans and swear to an affadavit. When this proved inconvenient, as it usually did, he diverted prospective immigrants farther west. LeRoy tried unsuccessfully through intermediaries to have this policy changed. Finally he went to Washington himself for several interviews with Ambassador Planches, who promised to take the matter up with his government and the consul at New Orleans.[36]

While in Washington, LeRoy also tried to remove the obstacles to Italian immigration established by the American government. Pressured by labor unions and urban reformers, Congress had forbidden American corporations to contract for labor in foreign countries. This policy hampered planters trying to import agricultural laborers, so LeRoy drew up a share contract that was permissible under the law because it involved no wages. He explained the contract to the commissioner general of immigration and won his stamp of approval. LeRoy also had lunch with President Roosevelt and probably used the opportunity to suggest that the government investigate Sunnyside and then remonstrate with the Italians for their attitude toward it.[37]

Unfortunately, LeRoy's discussions with Ambassador Planches failed to soften the attitude of the Italian government. In October

LeRoy wrote that it was still doing everything possible to discourage immigration to the delta and that he had given up on solving the labor problem with Italian farmers. Replying to a request for information from the New Orleans consul, LeRoy wrote, "I have been the recipient of nothing but hostility and antagonism on the part of the representatives of the Italian government, and for that reason, as you can readily understand, I take no interest in furnishing data to its representatives."[38] LeRoy continued seeking what Italian farmers he could get, but he gave up on working with emigration officials to import large numbers of them.[39]

The final demise of the Sunnyside experiment came at the hands of Mary Grace Quackenbos, attorney for the Justice Department. LeRoy had wanted the government to investigate Sunnyside in order to reassure the Italians, so when Quackenbos arrived, he instructed his managers and bookkeepers to cooperate with her completely. He wrote a friend that "if she doesn't admit that she has seen the most contented and prosperous colony in the South I shall be surprised."[40] But Quackenbos proved to be full of surprises. Following her divorce, this wealthy New York philanthropist had begun investigating peonage cases for the Justice Department. When she came to Sunnyside, she had already earned the censure of the Tampa Chamber of Commerce for publicizing unsubstantiated peonage charges there. After talking with her, LeRoy's enthusiasm for the investigation waned. He sent her on to investigate Charles Scott's Italian colony at Rosedale, but warned Scott that she knew nothing about planting and was full of impracticable ideas.[41]

LeRoy's apprehensions were confirmed when Quackenbos' report led the Justice Department to seek an indictment against Crittenden for violating the federal peonage law by holding tenants at Sunnyside against their will. As Crittenden's attorney, LeRoy knew that there were no grounds for an indictment, but he feared that even unsubstantiated charges might frighten prospective immigrants away from the delta. After the government failed to get an indictment, LeRoy returned to Washington and asked Roosevelt not to publish Quackenbos' report until a thorough investigation could be made. Roosevelt agreed, but on the way home LeRoy angered the President by attacking Quackenbos in the New York *Herald*. Attorney General Charles J.

Bonaparte was already angry at LeRoy for going over his head to Roosevelt, and somehow the report was leaked to the press. Several muckraking articles appeared purporting to expose the corruption at Sunnyside. LeRoy sought retractions from several newspapers but found them uninterested in stories of prosperous farmers. He finally gave up, writing to one muckraker, "We shall not trouble you further in the matter, and regret that we made the mistake of supposing you were a reputable newspaper correspondent, instead of recognizing the fact that you were merely a common, cheerful, and industrious liar."[42] A later congressional investigation failed to substantiate any of the charges made in the press, but the damage had been done. The Italian colony at Sunnyside lingered on, but LeRoy's dream of populating the delta with Italian farmers was finished.[43]

Compounding the delta's labor problem was the arrival of an unwanted immigrant, the Mexican boll weevil. Weevils began spreading across the South from Texas around the turn of the century. LeRoy saw them coming, and feared that their arrival would trigger a panic that would be more harmful than the insects themselves. "One great danger to be guarded against," he warned, "is the stampeding of the negro labor. This would bring about all of the loss that the weevil might ultimately cause, and could be fully as difficult to remedy."[44] To head off the weevil and its attendant panic, LeRoy diversified the crops grown at Trail Lake and experimented with weevil-resistant strains of cotton. He also urged other planters to do the same, and helped get a government center for weevil research established in the delta. Thanks to such precautions, the weevil did less damage there than in other parts of the South.[45]

Another threat to the delta's labor supply proved harder to control than the weevil. With his term as governor expiring in 1907, Jim Vardaman decided to run for the Senate. His opponent was John Sharp Williams, Democratic minority leader in the House of Representatives. Hoping to offset Williams' popularity among Mississippi's hill farmers, Vardaman waged a campaign of vicious racial rhetoric complete with accounts of blacks raping white women. LeRoy criticized such tactics harshly, warning that they would frighten blacks out of the delta.[46]

LeRoy's preference for Williams over Vardaman went deeper than his concern for his own and the delta's economic well-being. LeRoy's thought was strongly imbued with the economic outlook of the Gilded Age, but he never forgot that prosperity was only a means, albeit a vital one, of supporting the customs and values that his family associated with the good life. LeRoy was a gentleman, and Vardaman was not. LeRoy was appalled that Vardaman would spin his lurid tales of rape in mixed company. "He brings the shame of Southern women before a great audience," LeRoy wrote, "and depicts in vivid colors those things which we scarcely whisper to our wives at our own firesides, because they are so revolting to every instinct of decency."[47]

On the other hand, John Sharp Williams' credentials as a southern gentleman rivaled LeRoy's. Like LeRoy, Williams was a successful planter and an Episcopalian educated at Sewanee and the University of Virginia. In political matters Williams professed to be a follower of Thomas Jefferson and had even kept alive another time-honored tradition of southern statesmen by getting into a fistfight within the halls of Congress. LeRoy and Williams also shared a favorite pastime of southern gentlemen, sipping bourbon. Williams once visited LeRoy after Mississippi enacted prohibition. Chippie Strauss, LeRoy's secretary, was sent out to find a couple of quarts to celebrate the visit, and upon returning he complained that the bourbon had cost him twenty-five dollars. "Ah," drawled John Sharp, "at last we've found a place where they appreciate the true value of liquor."[48]

LeRoy also actively supported the candidacy of his friend Charles Scott for governor. Scott's platform included a state program to encourage Italian immigration. Jeff Truly, McLaurin's candidate for governor, attacked Scott by suggesting that the immigrants were members of the Mafia. Then, following Vardaman's example, Truly called for a redistribution of the state education funds that would bar blacks from public schools. As the campaign approached its climax, LeRoy decided to publicly challenge Vardaman's and Truly's racism. Early in May he delivered a speech to the Mississippi Bar Association in which he argued that blacks should not be barred from public schools.[49]

LeRoy's speech was the product of three concerns: paternal sympathy for blacks, interest in the delta's prosperity, and the desire to preserve southern morals and values. He argued that during slavery each black had a master to protect him and that "in freedom, you cannot, through the helplessness of ignorance, make him the slave of every white man with no master's protection to shield him." Furthermore, LeRoy warned, barring blacks from the schools might drive them from the state. He agreed with Vardaman that the South should not rely on the Negro for its long-term prosperity, saying, "There is not enough of him, and what there is, is not good enough." But he knew from his experience at Sunnyside that replacing blacks "with white men, possessing the potentialities of citizenship," would be a lengthy process, and he did not want to trigger a black exodus before another source of labor could be found. LeRoy also argued that the education of blacks was necessary "for the preservation of the manhood of the South, its high ideals, its lofty character." Ignorant blacks, he pointed out, could be easily cheated, and therefore they should be educated to avoid tempting planters and merchants into dishonesty.[50]

LeRoy's mixture of moral and economic arguments for black education was more than an attempt to appeal to different elements in his audience. The rich cotton land of the delta made paternalism profitable, for the most successful planters were those who could attract the most labor to their land. LeRoy's lucrative law practice made it easier for him to treat his tenants well in the inevitable lean years and in turn made the good years even better. He believed in doing right and being pragmatic, and the wealth of the delta's land made the two compatible.

LeRoy's speech was widely reported across the country. His friend J. M. Dickinson of Chicago sent a copy of it to the President, and Roosevelt was so impressed that he had it published in the *Outlook* and called LeRoy "a splendid fellow." Several northern newspapers and magazines commended the speech, but it probably had little effect on the election in Mississippi.[51]

LeRoy spent the rest of the campaign marshaling support for Scott and Williams in the delta. Scott's chances in Washington County were threatened when his kinsman, Frank Scott, announced that the levee board intended to collect back taxes on cotton there. LeRoy defused the issue by leading a taxpayers' meeting composed mostly of Charles Scott's supporters which blocked the plan to collect the taxes. LeRoy, however, doubted that Scott could win the election. "I am a little skeptical," he wrote privately, "about Mississippi electing a gentleman governor." LeRoy expected Edmund Noel to win, because "Noel is a canting, narrow, small board Baptist."[52]

LeRoy also tried to coax Vardaman into debating Williams at a

United Daughters of the Confederacy barbecue in Greenville. Varda-man had already debated Williams at Meridian and lost. He may also have remembered hearing LeRoy defend Congressman Catchings at such affairs ten years before, and wondered just whom the UDC intended to barbecue. Vardaman declined the invitation, so LeRoy made sure the entire county knew that he was afraid to debate Williams.[53]

The results of the August 1 primary were mixed. Scott failed to make the runoff, in which Edmund Noel was elected governor over Earl Brewer. Williams defeated Vardaman, but by only 648 votes. Appalled that the race had been so close, Williams refused to attend his own victory celebration. LeRoy was more philosophical about the election results, calling them "gratifying because they might have been, and threatened to be, so much worse." Williams had, after all, been elected, and LeRoy preferred Noel to Brewer for governor, even though "he is no shining intellectual light."[54]

After the election LeRoy went to Memphis, where he heard President Roosevelt address the Deep Water Way Association. From there, LeRoy went on to Lake Jackson, Wyoming, to hunt elk and cinnamon bear. In December he returned to the east to deliver an address on levees to the National Rivers and Harbors Congress, meeting in Washington D.C.[55]

LeRoy's concern with flood control led him back into state politics when he urged Governor Noel to appoint Dr. J. T. Atterbury to the levee board. LeRoy charged that the other candidate for the board, E. N. Thomas, was in debt to J. B. Watt, president of the Bank of Washington in Greenville, and that if appointed, Thomas would use his influence to have the levee board's funds deposited there. Since Atterbury was a director of the rival First National Bank, LeRoy urged the governor to sponsor legislation requiring the board to deposit its funds in the bank that would pay the most interest, so that the whole issue could be removed from the political arena and the most competent men appointed to the board. But Thomas had supported Noel in the second primary, and the governor appointed him to the board. LeRoy suspected that Thomas was being rewarded for his support, and told Noel, "I thought you were good enough to beat Brewer with, and I still think so, and that is all you are good for."[56]

Shortly after lambasting Noel, LeRoy was angered by the state legislature. He had been working for over a year with government engineers and levee experts, drawing up plans for the Black Bayou Drainage District. The proposed district would not have affected LeRoy's property, but by opening up thousands of acres to cultivation, it would have benefited the entire delta by expanding the tax base. The state senate killed the Black Bayou bill, prompting LeRoy to write a friend that "tin horn politicians and natural obstructionists and kickers got in their work before a red neck legislature and killed the bill."[57]

In May, LeRoy's control of Washington County politics was challenged when E. N. Thomas launched a campaign for the chairmanship of the county's delegation to the upcoming state Democratic convention. Thomas hoped that winning the chairmanship would vindicate his appointment to the levee board. LeRoy also saw the election as an opportunity to be vindicated by the voters. He headed off Thomas' attempt to strike a deal with Charles Scott and then thoroughly trounced Thomas at the county convention. LeRoy wrote his brother Walker that the election had been "the culmination of the fight that the small fry had been making on me for several years, until they had acquired a very magnificent idea of their own importance and political acumen." Pleased by the convention's outcome, he added, "I think it had a very fine educational effect on them."[58]

While solidifying his control of Washington County, LeRoy was also improving his relations with the McLaurin clan. By 1908 he and Camille were seeing members of the McLaurin family socially, and later that year LeRoy wrote President Roosevelt asking a favor for Senator McLaurin. LeRoy also helped L. C. Dulaney, a longtime McLaurinite, establish a meat packing plant in Greenville. The reason for this rapprochement was simple—Jim Vardaman. LeRoy knew that Vardaman would challenge McLaurin when Old Anse ran for reelection to the Senate in 1911, and as he wrote his old friend Captain J. S. McNeilly, "I can't get up any interest in making a fight on Anse for Vardaman. Between an ornery scrub and a spectacular ass there is not much room for preference."[59]

LeRoy knew that all too often such choices were the very stuff of politics. His integrity and his mutuality of interest with the delta prevented him from using his political influence for personal gain at the public's expense. He was, however, willing to work with less scrupulous men in order to retain that influence, and he would have traded votes with the Devil if he thought it would strengthen the levees. Le-Roy described his own activist ideal of citizenship in a letter of praise to Theodore Roosevelt, written as the President was preparing to leave office. LeRoy commended Roosevelt for what he had done "to arouse the American people to a sense of civic duty, to make them feel that they were part and parcel of the government, and responsible for it, that the poor had a right to demand its protection, and that the rich were amenable to its laws, and that both, regardless of poverty or wealth, were entitled to be dealt with fairly. . . . You, by your individual efforts, have brought about a moral awakening to the duties of citizenship that was sorely needed."[60]

The active civic involvement that LeRoy ascribed to Roosevelt had also inspired his own career as a lawyer, planter, and politician. The Percys' land, their reputation, their fortune, and their fate were in the delta, and LeRoy's forty-nine years there had tightened the bond. He had devoted himself to the delta's interests because the delta promised him the good life. When he succeeded in making it "a better place to live," he discovered that the "moral awakening to the duties of citizenship" was the good life.

Chapter 3

Camille Percy

The Senate

Three days before the Christmas of 1909, Anselm J. McLaurin died at his home in Brandon. Old Anse would have chuckled all the way to his grave had he known that his death would throw a match into Mississippi's political powder keg. Governor Noel avoided the stampede of candidates aspiring to serve out the remaining half of McLaurin's Senate term by quickly appointing Colonel James B. Gordon as McLaurin's temporary replacement. Gordon was a seventy-year-old Confederate veteran who would spend most of his time in the Senate composing poetry. By appointing him, Noel avoided showing preference for

any of the serious candidates and left the selection of the new senator
to the legislature that would meet in January.[1]

Jim Vardaman was the clear front-runner in the Senate race. His
close loss to John Sharp Williams had proven that his racial slurs and
neopopulism appealed to the voters. But Vardaman was more popular
with the people than with the politicians. When the legislature met,
he had more votes than any other candidate but lacked the necessary
majority.

The majority of votes in the legislature was scattered over a large
and fluctuating field of candidates. None had a statewide following
comparable to Vardaman's, but each commanded a potentially crucial
bloc of votes. The early front-runner among these opposition candidates was Charleton H. Alexander, a prominent attorney from Jackson. Alexander was popular because he had sponsored Mississippi's
prohibition act. Frank Critz and Representative Adam Byrd each controlled part of the now broken McLaurin faction, while former state
senators John Curtis Kyle of Sardis and C. C. Dunn of Meridian, and
Representative William D. Anderson of Tupelo, commanded local factions scattered across the state. None of these men could win the Senate seat on his own, but if they held their supporters in line they could
stop Vardaman.[2]

Stopping Vardaman was LeRoy Percy's major objective. He went to
Jackson to size up the situation and then returned to Greenville to talk
the matter over with his family and friends. Charles Scott had been
expected to enter the race as the delta's candidate, but his poor showing in the recent gubernatorial campaign suggested that his support,
even in the delta, was questionable. LeRoy, knowing that the delta
must be united if Vardaman were to be stopped, decided to enter the
race himself.[3]

LeRoy was in an excellent position to unite the delta behind his candidacy. He had consolidated his control of Washington County at the
1908 county convention, and Charles Scott's endorsement assured
him of the support of the delta's leading planters. Furthermore, with
Old Anse gone, the McLaurin faction was leaderless, and LeRoy's connections with the younger McLaurins and L. C. Dulaney enabled him
to pick up support from his old enemies. If LeRoy could hold this coalition together, he could help stop Vardaman, and perhaps even become Mississippi's new senator.

LeRoy returned to Jackson on January 1, bringing Camille, their son Will, campaign manager William Crump, and supporters J. T. Atterbury and state representative Van Boddie with him. They set up their campaign headquarters at the Edwards House, where most of the opposition candidates were staying. LeRoy's brothers, William Percy of Memphis and Walker Percy of Birmingham, joined LeRoy in Jackson and went to work lining up support for their brother.[4]

LeRoy was not the only candidate whose first priority was stopping Vardaman. The White Chief, as Vardaman's supporters called him, had angered the McLaurin clan by reforming the convict lease system, and had frightened others with his denunciations of blacks. Furthermore, Vardaman was the front-runner, and so it was natural for the other candidates to unite against him. Representatives of the candidates opposing Vardaman set up a steering committee to coordinate their strategy. The committee agreed that no one would drop out of the race until it was certain that their candidate's votes would not go to Vardaman. They also decided to follow precedent by calling for a Democratic caucus to choose a candidate rather than allowing it to be fought out in an actual legislative session. Since virtually all of the legislators were Democrats, the caucus' choice would be decisive. More important, the caucus could adopt a secret ballot that would neutralize Vardaman's popular support.[5]

When the caucus convened on January 6, anxious spectators overflowed the capitol gallery and crowded onto the floor of the legislature. Vardaman's supporters opened with a gambit designed to break precedent and establish an open ballot. Knowing that this would be voted down if presented openly, a Vardaman supporter moved that the caucus adopt the rules of the house of representatives, which included an open ballot requirement. The opposition caught the trick and tabled the motion.

The candidates then addressed the caucus. Vardaman spoke first, balancing his denunciation of blacks with appeals for prohibition and for regulation of trusts. LeRoy countered Vardaman's appeal for progressive support by endorsing the National Democratic platform, which included several reform measures. Then, swallowing hard, LeRoy sought to broaden his support by praising the late Senator McLaurin.

After the speeches the caucus took three ballots. The number of votes needed to nominate fluctuated around 85, depending on how many legislators were present. Vardaman received 71 votes on the first ballot. Meanwhile the opposition candidates jockeyed for position, hoping that a strong showing would create a bandwagon effect for their candidacies. Alexander led the opposition candidates on the first ballot with 24 votes, but on the second ballot LeRoy pulled ahead of him with 28 votes. LeRoy slipped to 26 votes on the third ballot, barely retaining his lead.[6]

The caucus continued taking three inconclusive ballots each night. LeRoy and Alexander exchanged the lead until January 12, when LeRoy broke away from the pack with 31 votes, and Representative William Anderson edged ahead of Alexander into second place. Anderson's surge continued the next night, when he tied LeRoy for the lead on one ballot before falling back into the pack.

By January 25 Anderson's campaign had peaked and begun to sag, so he withdrew from the race. Anderson's withdrawal was the first test of the steering committee's strategy, and the results were encouraging. The secret ballot made it impossible to tell precisely where Anderson's votes went, but Vardaman received no more than a couple of them. Alexander gained the most, with Percy, Byrd, and Kyle also adding slightly to their totals. Emboldened by their success, the following night the steering committee tried withdrawing another candidate, Adam Byrd, on the first ballot. LeRoy did well among Byrd's supporters, many of whom were former McLaurin men. He polled 38 votes, more than any opposition candidate had previously posted. When Byrd rejoined the race on the next ballot, LeRoy's total fell to 32, only 5 ahead of Alexander.

Byrd's temporary withdrawal was partly a response to increasing pressure, both within and outside the caucus, for a resolution of the deadlock. On January 28 Byrd tried again to break the stalemate, this time without notifying the steering committee of his plans. Byrd called on the caucus to adjourn *sine die*, which would have thrown the election back into the legislature. Byrd's resolution threw the caucus into turmoil; order was finally restored when Van Boddie shouted down his fellow legislators in a voice that was heard by passersby in the streets. After Senator Washington Gibbs explained the effect of Byrd's resolution, it was tabled. The opposition candidates were not willing to risk electing Vardaman in order to break the deadlock. They did inch closer to a decision on the evening's second ballot, when Frank Critz, another former McLaurinite, withdrew, scattering his six votes among Vardaman's remaining opponents.[7]

Byrd was not the only candidate who felt the strain of the caucus' war of nerves. The next day Vardaman tried to break the opposition apart by charging that railroad and corporate lobbyists were in Jackson working against him. By failing to mention any names, Vardaman probably hoped to provoke suspicions and perhaps accusations among the opposition. LeRoy called Vardaman's bluff by demanding the names of the lobbyists involved. Vardaman never produced them, and his attempt to disrupt the opposition failed. In fact, his charges may have given his opponents the one thing they needed to beat him—a leader. By replying to Vardaman on behalf of all of the candidates, LeRoy set himself in the forefront of the opposition and focused the attention of the caucus on his candidacy.

LeRoy's candidacy remained the center of attention when B. T. Hobbs, editor of the Brookhaven *Leader*, charged in his paper that one of LeRoy's aides, Frank Cannon, had plied Representative Walter W. Robinson with so much whiskey that he had become sick. The next night Cannon went after Hobbs in the lobby of the Edwards House but pulled back when Hobbs drew a pistol. Cannon was later vindicated when Robinson admitted that Percy's aide had only fetched him a doctor after Vardaman's homemade, rotgut whiskey had made him sick. In addition to keeping LeRoy's name in the papers, the incident revived the flagging public interest in the caucus. Hearing that liquor was being served in Jackson, people from all over the dry state headed for the capital to join the party.[8]

The rumors of flowing liquor also helped the prohibitionist Alexander. He made large gains the next two nights, pulling even with LeRoy and vying with him for the lead on each ballot. On February 4 the steering committee tried again to break the deadlock. The four leading opposition candidates—Percy, Alexander, Byrd, and Kyle—gathered their supporters together in the Senate chamber at noon and explained their plan. The legislators were to choose one of the four candidates to withdraw from the race, and all four had agreed to accept their decision. It was a dangerous game for LeRoy, because as the front-runner his elimination would help the other candidates the most. But his campaign manager, William Crump, had conducted an informal poll and found that LeRoy was the second choice of most of the legislators favoring other opposition candidates. LeRoy knew that this was one occasion when he did not want to draw attention to himself, and simply told the meeting that he would abide by its decision. Alexander, on the other hand, tried to use the meeting to drum up support for his own candidacy by appearing magnanimous. He spoke eloquently of his own willingness to withdraw for the common good, and much to his surprise the legislators took him up on his offer. LeRoy's major opponent among the opposition candidates had dug his own grave.[9]

Rumors of the meeting spread through Jackson during the afternoon. When the caucus met that evening, the galleries were packed with spectators anxious to see whether Vardaman could attract enough of Alexander's supporters to win. The steering committee's strategy was vindicated when Vardaman added only four new votes. LeRoy picked up several, boosting his total to 45, and Kyle moved ahead of Byrd with 25 votes.

Worn down by the war of nerves and perhaps running short on whiskey, the caucus adjourned for a week while the legislators headed south to the Mardi Gras in New Orleans. Upon their return an end to the caucus seemed imminent. Vardaman surged to 78 votes the first night back, and then to 79 the next evening, only 7 short of a majority. LeRoy kept pace with him, posting over 50 votes on several ballots to easily lead the opposition candidates; but finishing second would be small consolation should Vardaman win a majority. The next night, February 11, a dark horse headed the White Chief off at the pass when house speaker Hugh N. Street resigned his chairmanship of the caucus and entered the race. Street's candidacy further divided the opposition forces, but he also picked up substantial support from Vardaman's ranks and reduced his tally to 63 votes.[10]

Street's candidacy gave the opposition candidates time to unite behind LeRoy, who by now was clearly their only chance to beat Vardaman. LeRoy bided his time, giving the other candidates a long week to firm up their control over their supporters. On February 22, he told William Crump, "Let's put it to the touch." The opposition candidates were called together, and all agreed to withdraw in LeRoy's favor.[11]

Again Jackson buzzed with rumors. Spectators packed the capitol building that evening to see whether the withdrawing candidates could hold their supporters in line. Vardaman was there, pleading with and cajoling legislators, trying to scratch up the handful of votes he still needed. LeRoy was there, too, watching as the other candidates announced their withdrawals, waiting to see if his gamble would pay off. Finally the caucus took its fifty-eighth and final vote, and Mississippi had a new senator—LeRoy Percy, by a slim margin of 87 votes to 82.[12]

LeRoy made a brief acceptance speech and returned to the Edwards House, where the victory celebration lasted far into the early morning. At 6 A.M., those who had gone to bed were awakened by two brass bands leading a trainload of shouting Percy supporters from the railroad station through the dew-damp streets of Jackson to the Edwards House, and the party was off and running again. Later that morning LeRoy boarded the train to Greenville. Upon his arrival that evening thirty thousand well wishers from all over the delta greeted him with cheers. Cannons were fired, and a torchlight parade escorted him to the Opera House. LeRoy had remained quiet amid all the celebrating. Now, at home, surrounded by his friends and family, he stood staring at the floor, overwhelmed by their affection and loyalty. Never before had he felt so completely a part of the delta. He refused to make a speech, and instead simply thanked his friends as best he could.[13]

LeRoy knew that the fight against Vardaman had only begun. The day after LeRoy left Jackson, Vardaman addressed a rally of his own supporters, repeating his charges that unfair means had been used against him in the caucus and pledging to unseat LeRoy in the next year's primary. Before leaving for Washington, LeRoy sent out a few letters trying to line up support for the coming election, but unlike the flamboyant Vardaman, he was virtually unknown to voters outside the delta.[14]

LeRoy and Camille sailed for Washington on March 9 and arrived just in time to relieve the beleaguered Senator Gordon. The aged Confederate colonel had been flabbergasted by what he considered the Senate's radical disregard of the Constitution. When his colleagues allowed him to occupy the Senate Chair for a session, Colonel Gordon commemorated the event with a poem:

I've been chased by Yanks, and I've suffered for sin,
And I've writhed in my bed in terrible pain,
But if God forgives me for where I have been,
I promise never to sit up here again.[15]

LeRoy was no happier in Washington than Senator Gordon had been. Bold and intimidating in a courtroom or caucus, LeRoy was shy at social gatherings and slow to make new friends. Fortunately Camille was there to drag him from one entertainment to the next and smooth his way into Washington's social life with her vivacious charm. Despite Cam's efforts, LeRoy felt cramped in Washington. He found it hard to get any work done, and caught himself thinking of home.[16]

Quite a few people back in Mississippi were thinking of LeRoy, too. Vardaman's supporters continued to echo his charges of foul play at the caucus. Their complaints remained unfocused until late in March, when Theodore G. Bilbo, one of Vardaman's supporters at the caucus, appeared before the Hinds County Grand Jury at Jackson. Bilbo told the grand jury that L. C. Dulaney had given him five hundred dollars to vote for LeRoy. Unacquainted with Bilbo's character, the grand jury returned an indictment against Dulaney for bribery. Dulaney's trial was delayed by a change of venue, and in the meantime the legislature decided to investigate the charges of corruption at the caucus. Van Boddie and LeRoy's brother Willie presented LeRoy's case, and both the house and senate reports cleared him and his supporters of any wrongdoing. Nevertheless, Bilbo's lurid tales of paid hostesses dispensing liquor and valises full of corporate money in Jackson hotel rooms filled the pages of county weeklies, provoking moonshine-sipping Baptist hill farmers to call down the wrath of God upon the Percys. Whether or not they really believed that Dulaney had offered Bilbo the money, they hated LeRoy because they knew he had the five hundred dollars.[17]

LeRoy saw the whole sordid affair as an attack on his honor. He returned to Jackson breathing fire, and in a speech before a joint session of the legislature challenged Vardaman to let the voters judge the candidates for themselves. LeRoy proposed that the primary scheduled for 1911 be moved up to November, 1910, and promised to resign immediately if Vardaman beat him. LeRoy knew that his challenge was politically foolish, for he needed all the time he had to overcome Vardaman's popularity. But when his honor was involved, LeRoy could be resolutely impractical. Vardaman pounced on LeRoy's offer, only to have the state Democratic Executive Committee pull the rug from beneath his feet by requiring that all candidates entering the special primary take part in a series of debates designed to quickly acquaint the voters with the issues. Vardaman had seen LeRoy dissect opponents in debate and knew that appearing on the stump with him was the one way he might lose the election, so he backed off and began making plans for the next year. Finally, against LeRoy's wishes, Governor Noel announced that he would not appoint Vardaman even if he defeated Percy, and the plan fell through completely.[18]

Immediately after his speech to the legislature LeRoy returned to Washington to speak against a provision of the Payne-Aldrich Tariff that called for an investigation of cotton prices over the last ten years. LeRoy told the Senate that for years, pools and trusts had kept the price of cotton depressed by flooding the market with phantom cotton futures. Now, he charged, the price of cotton had risen and these speculators were in a bind because they were going to have to pay a fair price to farmers to fill their futures contracts. LeRoy believed that the speculators wanted an investigation to discredit those who held the futures contracts, so that the speculators would not have to honor them. LeRoy suggested that if the government wanted to investigate something, it should look into "the nefarious rules of the New York Cotton Exchange." LeRoy thought that the Republican majority's hostility toward farmers made such an investigation unlikely, however. As for Congress' threat to intervene now on the side of the trusts, LeRoy told his colleagues that the farmer "might well offer up the prayer that the old Negro did in the bear fight, 'Oh, God, if you won't help me, don't help the bear.'"[19]

LeRoy's excoriation of the cotton trust made him sound almost as progressive as Vardaman. Noticing this similarity, LeRoy had his speech issued in Mississippi in pamphlet form. But his brand of progressivism differed significantly from Vardaman's. LeRoy was closely attuned to the economic interests of the delta's wealthy planters, while Vardaman better understood the needs of Mississippi's hill farmers. Furthermore, Vardaman's progressivism was essentially religious: the White Chief told his supporters that they were the repository of moral virtue and that the corruption of the wealthy—in this case, delta planters—caused their poverty. Vardaman had supported prohibition ever since it became popular in his home county early in his career, and he had been born again at a large revival shortly before the 1908 election. This religious brand of progressivism was popular with Baptist hill farmers and became irresistible when in his political sermons Vardaman used blacks as a symbol for unbridled lust.[20]

LeRoy's progressivism, on the other hand, was secular in nature and relied primarily on economics for its analytic framework. Like Theodore Roosevelt, he wanted an honest-broker government that would police business practices in order to help businessmen create a prosperous, efficient paradise on earth. Roosevelt recognized their similar viewpoints and wrote LeRoy, "You don't know how glad I am that you are in the Senate." LeRoy's brand of progressivism was shaped by conditions in the delta, where the rich potential of the soil depended for its fruition on government appropriations for levees and drainage. His job as a senator, he told the voters, was not to deliver harangues on the race issue, but to secure as large appropriations as possible for projects that would aid Mississippi's economy. The secular nature of LeRoy's progressivism did not preclude morality; in fact, it emphasized it, for honesty was essential if government were to be efficient. He had learned this lesson from corrupt levee boards that endangered the delta's very existence. Whereas LeRoy's morality was stoic, emphasizing duty, self-discipline, and integrity among the community's leaders, Vardaman's morality was reformist, seeking to save men from themselves through legislation like prohibition.[21]

Although LeRoy sometimes opposed expenditures as an undue expansion of the government's powers, he always supported appropriations that would benefit Mississippi. In June he spoke against a bill to establish postal savings banks, warning that this would lead the government further into the banking business than it belonged. His primary reason for opposing the bill was probably that it would remove badly needed investment funds from the delta. In the same speech, he chastised the Senate for cutting appropriations for the Agriculture Department, levee construction, and rural mail delivery while wasting money on useless military expenditures. Rather than spending money on "barbaric force," he argued, the government should devote itself to promoting "peace happiness and prosperity."[22]

When LeRoy returned to Mississippi to campaign, he found that most voters cared little about his positions on issues. What they wanted was a show, and on July 1 they got one. Provoked by Bilbo's taunts, LeRoy agreed to speak at a rally at Lauderdale Springs, in the heart of Vardaman country. Expecting a fight, LeRoy's brother Walker, his son Will, and several friends, all well armed, accompanied him into enemy territory. Walker thought that the best way to deal with Bilbo would simply be to kill him and be done with it. He told Will this, causing LeRoy's pale, poetic son to spend the night before the rally standing in front of a mirror practicing with a pistol, so that he would not forget to release the safety if there were a shoot-out. The next morning Walker spotted Bilbo eating breakfast in the hotel restaurant, and in a booming voice announced, "I think I'm going to kill that little son-of-a-bitch sitting over there." Walker knew that no gentleman would allow such a remark to pass and expected to shoot it out with Bilbo then and there. Bilbo, however, was not concerned with what a gentleman would do, and continued staring down into his oatmeal, frustrating Walker's plan. Bilbo understood the Percys' sense of honor well enough to use it to lure LeRoy into the hill country, but he would have considered it foolish to act on such a premise himself.[23]

Bilbo regained his voice that afternoon at the rally. His brother, J. T., brought a group of his friends over from Meridian, where he had spent the previous day exhibiting a two-headed, eight-legged pig. Quickly taking the measure of his audience, Bilbo repeated his charges of corruption at the caucus, throwing in enough dirty jokes to keep the crowd's attention and eventually working it into a frenzy. Sensing the crowd's hostility, LeRoy's handful of local supporters advised him to cancel his speech or confine his remarks to some innocuous subject. But LeRoy was there to answer Bilbo, and answer him he did. He began slowly and calmly, explaining that he had entered the Senate race only to stop Vardaman. When LeRoy mentioned the caucus, the crowd interrupted him with catcalls. Provoked, LeRoy told them that he had no doubt that liquor was consumed at the caucus, because he had seen Bilbo drinking Percy liquor on the night of his victory. With this, the crowd began shouting for Vardaman. LeRoy returned their insults and demanded silence by the fire that flashed from his steel gray eyes. Seeing that "he was going to finish his speech or die in the attempt," most of the crowd quieted down, but a few continued to scream for Vardaman. Finally Captain Hunter Sharpe leaped onto the platform and told his neighbors that they were about to be quiet, one way or another. Sharpe was a crack shot, and the crowd became silent as they tried to remember just how many men the captain had killed. LeRoy resumed his denunciation of Bilbo, calling him a moral degenerate, a liar, and practically everything else short of Walker's more concise description. The crowd knew courage when they saw it, and LeRoy ended his speech to deafening applause and cheers.[24]

LeRoy had agreed to speak with Bilbo only to prove that he was not afraid to face him. That done, he refused to speak with him again. Bilbo suffered no shortage of targets for his slander, however. He called John J. Henry, former penitentiary warden, "a cross between a hyena and a mongrel . . . begotten in a nigger graveyard at midnight, sucked by a sow and educated by a fool." Henry caught Bilbo on a train and pistol-whipped him, putting him in a hospital for a week. When Bilbo insulted state senator Wash Gibbs, the "War Horse of Yazoo" took the gold headed cane presented to him for helping rid the state of carpetbaggers and cracked it over Bilbo's skull, sending him sprawling into a gutter. Gibbs's admirers replaced his cane with one inscribed TO W. D. GIBBS FOR ONE BROKEN ON BILBO'S HEAD.[25]

Meanwhile, LeRoy moved south and west from Lauderdale Springs, continuing his campaign tour deeper into Vardaman territory. On July 4 he spoke at Godbold Wells and was again heckled. He demanded of the crowd whether they believed legislators had been bought at the caucus, and when the hecklers replied that they did, he asked "what kind of cattle they thought these representatives were to be bought and sold on the hoof." The Vardaman press jumped on this remark and charged that LeRoy had called the voters cattle. For the rest of the campaign, LeRoy would be greeted by hecklers bearing signs labeling themselves cattle and rednecks, and wearing the red neckties that symbolized the growing class consciousness of Vardaman's supporters.[26]

LeRoy knew that there was nothing he could do to overcome the voters' resentment of his wealth and aristocratic bearing, but his sense of duty made him go on with the campaign. Late in August he wrote Camille that "Vardaman's whole campaign is built on lies—but that doesn't argue that it will not win." LeRoy's old friend Captain Mc-Neilly had urged him to accept defeat, but as LeRoy wrote Camille, "My friends would not understand it, and I can't afford to forfeit their respect and esteem—better to drink the cup to the dregs. If we were only a year younger," he added wistfully, "a lost year would not matter so much." Being away from Camille was the part of campaigning Le-Roy found hardest to bear. A week later he wrote to tell her that he must continue campaigning through September in order to catch the large crowds that would gather for court days, but he promised that "some day this cruel war will be over and then we will try to pick up the broken threads of our lives . . . and if we can come out of it in good health, with honor, and not a [sic] bankrupt I will be satisfied."[27]

Despite his weariness, LeRoy spent the next three months on the campaign trail. He was heckled frequently, but even when he was not, his speeches did him little good. On October 31, he addressed a large, sympathetic audience at Jackson's State Fair Grounds—a well-behaved audience his son described as what one would expect at a Yale-Harvard football game. Free of interruptions at last, LeRoy told his audience, "The questions which confront your Representatives and Senators are, in the main, business questions. . . . At the risk of being a trifle tedious, I am going to give you a few illustrations of the questions which arise in Congress." Compared to Vardaman's flamboyant, utterly quixotic demand for the repeal of the Fourteenth Amendment, LeRoy's discussion of rural free mail delivery and the eradication of cattle ticks was more than "a trifle tedious."[28]

LeRoy returned to Washington in late November, while Dulaney was still being tried for bribery. During the trial someone noticed that the bank notes Bilbo claimed Dulaney had given him at the caucus had been issued after the caucus was over, proving beyond doubt that Bilbo was lying. In December the jury, which included six Vardaman supporters, acquitted Dulaney.[29]

Back in Washington, LeRoy devoted much of his time to the massive report being prepared by the Joint Committee on Immigration, work for which his experience at Sunnyside had prepared him. He took time out from his committee assignments to address two issues left over from the Civil War and Reconstruction. LeRoy opposed the Sulloway pension bill, a proposal to increase the pensions of Union veterans of the Civil War, because he believed its main purpose was to keep these veterans voting Republican. He also spoke out against the proposed seventeenth amendment, which called for the direct election of senators. LeRoy was not opposed to senators being elected by the people, but he objected to that wording in the amendment which took the control of these elections away from the states and placed it with the federal government. LeRoy feared that even the possibility of the federal government's intervening in southern elections in order to allow blacks to vote would fuel the flaming racial rhetoric of demagogues like Vardaman and weaken the position of southern moderates.[30]

Vardaman opened his campaign on February 24, 1911, with a speech to a large crowd at Jackson. Confident of victory, the White Chief reiterated his hodgepodge platform of progressive reforms and racial slurs, and played down his controversial positions. He campaigned very little after this, preferring to let his supporters, including Bilbo, attack LeRoy for him. They kept LeRoy on the defensive throughout the campaign by adding new charges to the old complaint of corruption at the caucus. LeRoy was attacked for opposing prohibition, for bringing Italians to the delta, for hunting and playing cards on Sunday, for representing the black Knights of Pythias Lodge in a lawsuit against the white lodge of the same name, and for being a tool of the railroads. LeRoy answered the charges. He produced letters of support from clergymen to vouch for his morals, pointed out that he had helped enforce the prohibition laws after unsuccessfully opposing them, cited legal files to show that he had acted against the interest of the railroads when he thought they were wrong, and reminded voters that he had resigned his attorneyship upon his election. His denials, however, were seldom circulated widely, and even when they were, there was nothing LeRoy could say to refute what lay behind them—the fact that he was a wealthy corporate attorney and planter with little sympathy for the religious zeal and malignant racism of Vardaman's supporters.[31]

While LeRoy was in Washington, his son, Will, and campaign manager, William Crump, ran his campaign. They secured endorsements from John Sharp Williams, Governor Noel, and Charles Scott, as well as from several candidates for lesser offices and the scattered remnants of the old McLaurin coalition. Wherever there was local support, they established Percy organizations, and they took special pains to place LeRoy's supporters on as many Democratic county executive committees as possible. Crump and Will also kept the newspapers supporting LeRoy informed of his activities; and they circulated countless pamphlets and letters explaining his positions on the issues, often by giving them to drummers, who distributed them to customers as they wandered the state selling their patent medicines and sewing machines.[32]

LeRoy returned to Mississippi in March and campaigned relent-
lessly until the election. He crisscrossed the state several times, speaking at Ruleville, Antioch, Bogue Chitto, Purvis, Woodville, Fulton,
anywhere he could find an audience. Some days he spoke two or three
times, often from the back of a train or standing on a wagon. He told
the voters that he was not corrupt, that Vardaman's proposals were
nonsense, that being a senator involved more than making flamboyant
speeches. LeRoy maintained a constant air of optimism, even though
he knew he had no chance of beating Vardaman.[33]

Some of LeRoy's speeches were joint appearances with Charleton
Alexander, who had entered the Senate race the year before. Alexander
had been LeRoy's strongest rival at the caucus until the other candidates selected him to withdraw, and he had escaped most of the
charges of corruption that dogged LeRoy's campaign. At first, LeRoy's
managers welcomed Alexander's entry into the race, hoping that he
could win votes from Vardaman that LeRoy could not reach and then
perhaps swing those votes to LeRoy in a runoff. As the August primary
drew near, however, Alexander shifted some of his fire from Vardaman
to LeRoy, probably hoping to get into the runoff himself. Alexander
posed a serious threat to Vardaman because he was an ardent prohibitionist, but he was a poor speaker, and by the end of the campaign the
Vardaman press had managed to link him to the caucus.[34]

Whether LeRoy spoke alone or with Alexander, Vardaman's supporters continued to heckle him. On June 23, at Rose Hill, LeRoy invited a
group of hecklers at the rear of the crowd to come to the front and face
him with their charges. They refused, and when Deputy Sheriff Foster
Rounds went over to quiet one of them, another slipped up behind and
stabbed him twice in the back, seriously wounding him. During the
final month of the campaign LeRoy concentrated more and more on
this and other violent incidents, blaming them on Vardaman's lawlessness. Hoping that he, rather than Alexander, would get into the runoff,
LeRoy also began telling audiences that only his own election would
vindicate the proceedings at the caucus. William Crump sounded a
similar theme, telling the press that Vardaman's only chance to win
the election was to see that Alexander got into the runoff against him.[35]

As it turned out, neither LeRoy nor Alexander would face Vardaman
in a runoff. The White Chief polled an overwhelming majority over
both candidates on August 1. Vardaman carried 74 of Mississippi's 79

counties, collecting 79,000 votes to Alexander's 31,000 and LeRoy's 21,000. Bilbo was elected lieutenant governor by a similar margin, and most of the new legislators were Vardaman men. LeRoy had been clearly and completely repudiated by the voters.[36]

LeRoy's defeat was not an isolated event. Poor white farmers across the South were in the process of transferring their allegiance from the old Bourbon aristocracy to a new generation of plebeian leaders. Vardaman, along with Pitchfork Ben Tillman of South Carolina, Tom Watson of Georgia, and later, Huey Long of Louisiana, rode this wave of revolt to power. LeRoy tried to hold back the tide and was overwhelmed.

LeRoy knew that his defeat was part of a general revolt, but he could not help taking it as a personal rebuke, and he continued to act as he thought his honor demanded. Two days after the election he stood with his friends on his front lawn and announced that he would resign his Senate seat before the legislature met, so that it could appoint Vardaman, the people's choice. LeRoy added only one qualification, saying that he would not allow his supporters to change his mind but that further abuse from Vardaman's supporters might. In a letter to John Sharp Williams, LeRoy explained that even though he had been released from his earlier pledge to resign by Vardaman's refusal to debate, he still thought it was the proper thing to do. He added, "You will, and Vardaman may, understand what I meant by the possibility of being swerved by abuse. If he values this unexpired term he had better understand it."[37]

LeRoy was right in predicting that his friends would try to dissuade him from resigning. Governor Noel telegraphed as soon as he heard of LeRoy's decision, and followed this up with a letter urging LeRoy to retain his seat while his supporters tried to convince Congress not to seat Vardaman. Dunbar Rowland, director of the Mississippi Department of Archives, agreed, writing LeRoy that "there are times when I believe in war to the hilt, not for personal reasons but for the sake of principle. There are legal barriers to this man's occupying a seat in the Senate, and you as an able and astute lawyer should know how to find and apply them." Scores of Mississippians urged LeRoy to remain in the Senate as long as possible, as did the New York *Evening Post* and several other newspapers across the nation. Many of LeRoy's colleagues in Congress also hoped that he would change his mind and keep Vardaman at home as long as possible. John Sharp Williams was one of the few who agreed with LeRoy's reasoning, and he wrote from Washington that he was the only person there who did. But LeRoy would not be swayed by his friends. Exhausted by the campaign, he, Camille, and Will left the letters to pile up on his desk and sailed for Greece.[38]

LeRoy's friends could not dissuade him from resigning, but as he had warned, his enemies could. While LeRoy was in Europe, George Creel, a reporter for *Cosmopolitan* magazine, came to Jackson to muckrake LeRoy. Creel, wined and dined by Vardaman's supporters, carefully recorded all of the charges made against LeRoy during the campaign. Then, showing the same regard for the truth that would later distinguish him as the head of America's propaganda agency during the First World War, Creel packed all of these charges into an article without bothering to mention that most had already been proven false. The article appeared in October, before LeRoy returned to the country. In the interim, LeRoy's brother Willie sent letters to many of LeRoy's supporters, asking whether they thought that, in light of the article, he should reconsider his decision to resign. Governor Noel again led a host of supporters who thought LeRoy should remain in the Senate, and by the time LeRoy returned to Greenville late in October, his desk was covered with letters urging him to reconsider. This time, even John Sharp Williams advised LeRoy to at least delay his resignation until the Senate could investigate Creel's charges.[39]

LeRoy was not anxious to use Creel's article as an excuse not to resign. When he left for Europe, he had hoped that his public career was over. His financial affairs had deteriorated because of neglect, and more important, as his brother Walker wrote, "His natural pride made him rebel at the prospect of sitting for a year in the Senate feeling that he did not have the people of his state behind him." On his return from Greece LeRoy told reporters he would make no statement on the matter until January, when the legislature would convene. His indecision vanished when he learned that Vardaman had endorsed the article and that Creel had gotten his material from Vardaman's aides. Early in November LeRoy decided to serve out the rest of his term.[40]

Rather than waiting until the legislature convened, LeRoy decided to make his announcement in the Senate. On December 12 he declared that Creel's article had made it impossible for him to resign. He denounced Creel and *Cosmopolitan* owner William Randolph Hearst in scathing terms and then warned the Senate what to expect from Vardaman by reporting some of his cruder homilies. LeRoy refused to ask for an investigation of his election because doing so, he said, would insult the integrity of Mississippi's legislature and courts. If the new, pro-Vardaman legislature really believed Creel's charges, he added, they could ask the Senate to investigate the caucus.[41]

LeRoy's speech angered Vardaman's supporters in the legislature. Anxious to see the White Chief in Washington, they passed a resolution calling on LeRoy to resign. As LeRoy predicted, however, they were not angry enough to ask the Senate to investigate their charges concerning his election.[42]

LeRoy's decision to remain in the Senate proved far more important to the delta than he had anticipated. In April the Mississippi, Ohio, and Missouri rivers overflowed at the same time, producing one of the worst floods in recent memory and leaving hundreds of thousands of people throughout the Mississippi valley homeless. LeRoy immediately introduced a bill empowering the secretary of war to spend $1.5 million at once to prevent further damage to the levees. When opposition to this plan arose, LeRoy buried his opponents under an avalanche of statistics. The bill was passed, providing desperately needed emergency funds. As the floodwaters slowly receded, LeRoy turned his attention to preventing a recurrence of such a disaster. Working with Senator Joseph Ransdell of Louisiana and the delta's congressman, B. G. Humphreys, LeRoy persuaded Congress to raise the annual appropriation for levee construction from $4 million to $6 million. Humphreys later attributed this increase to George Creel.[43]

LeRoy also took an active interest in his committee assignments. As a member of the Committee on Interoceanic Canals, he opposed a plan backed by American shipbuilders to violate a previous agreement with Great Britain by restricting traffic in the Panama Canal to American ships. His assignment to the Immigration Committee led LeRoy to support a literacy requirement that he hoped would restrict immigration. LeRoy, having given up his hopes of populating the delta with immigrants, believed that eastern cities were being harmed by an influx of immigrants larger than they could absorb.[44]

As a lame duck LeRoy was free to defend unpopular positions whenever they appealed to him. He voted to sustain President Taft's veto of an act that would have made it illegal to ship liquor to states where prohibition was in effect, such as Mississippi. When a Mississippi labor union censured him for voting against the eight-hour day, he wrote back that he had voted for other labor legislation in the past, such as workman's compensation, and couldn't care less whether they censured him. Furthermore, he warned them, he had no intention of blindly following their dictates, and if they were represented by someone who did, that man would be either a fool or a coward. LeRoy also spoke at some length opposing an act to forbid certain types of speculation in cotton futures, an act favored by most farm organizations. LeRoy told the Senate, "I do not believe there has been six hours' intelligent consideration of this subject by all the farmers' unions in the United States in a quarter of a century. I have no desire to belittle the accomplishments, whatever they may be, of these unions. If they have wrought great good, they have done it by stealth." LeRoy enjoyed insulting the farm unions so much that he had five hundred copies of his speech printed and circulated as a pamphlet.[45]

LeRoy was at his best as a lame duck because it was then that he was free to act on his view, inherited from his father, of what a senator should be. LeRoy believed that a senator's duty was to inform himself more thoroughly on issues affecting his state than his constituents could, and then to vote for their best interest, whether they liked it or not. This conception of his duty prevented LeRoy from supporting popular reforms and weakened his campaign against Vardaman.

Ironically, though, it was Vardaman's charge of corruption that lost LeRoy his Senate seat. Ironic, because honor was the cornerstone of LeRoy's conception of a good public official. Honor, he discovered, was a tricky business involving both integrity and respect, respect being the public recognition of integrity. Until the election, integrity and respect had gone hand in hand, but after, their paths diverged. The difference between inner integrity and public respect was the secret LeRoy discovered at the heart of dishonor.

It was a secret that meant little in Greenville, for there he was still honored. His friends were still there, and his farm. His bird dogs yipped impatiently for cold winter dawns filled with dove and quail. Most important, Camille was still there, a year older, and still the prettiest girl in the delta. Together they began to pick up the pieces of their lives.

Chapter 4

Will Percy

Will Percy

That's the queerest chicken ever hatched in a Percy brood. There's never been one even slightly like him, insofar as I know.
                                                    LeRoy Percy, on Will Percy

I became intolerably religious, going to early mass at the slightest provocation, racking my brain to find something to confess once a month, praying inordinately and fasting on the sly. It was infinitely trying to the family and so unexpected, so unlike anything in the case-history of any recorded member of the clan, French, English, or Scotch. I just couldn't help it, it was a violent attack, perhaps I've never fully recovered.
                                                    Will Percy
                                                    Lanterns on the Levee

The father was a brave man too and said he didn't care what others thought, but he did care. More than anything else, he wished to act with honor and be thought of well by other men. So living for him was a strain.
                                                    Walker Percy
                                                    The Last Gentleman

William Alexander Percy was born to LeRoy and Camille on May 14, 1885. Even as a young child Will was sensitive and intense, and he displayed natural artistic talents and a strong religious impulse that were abnormalities in his family's history. Before he was old enough to enter grammar school, Will attended mass daily with Camille. Afterwards, they often visited his Bourges grandparents, where Will amused his aunts and grandmother by acting out ceremonies that he had seen in church. His musical talent was awakened early by his Grandmother Percy's piano playing. When Will surprised his family by tapping out Lohengrin's "Wedding March" with his fingers, his Grandmother Bourges gave him a toy piano, and his Aunt Nana later gave him lessons. Religion and art were considered the provinces of women, and Will's proclivities for them made him the delight of his grandmothers and aunts.

At seven Will was enrolled in a local school run by the Sisters of Saint Rose of Lima. Under his teacher Sister Evangelist Will's religious disposition flowered into an intense devotion to Catholicism. After two years of her tutelage, Will announced to Camille that he intended to become a priest. Camille considered religion an essential ingredient of the good life, but she did not think the priesthood a suitable career for her son. She informed Will that he was not, in fact, going to become a priest, and began looking for a new teacher for him.[1]

LeRoy shared Camille's misgivings about the education of this outlandish young Percy who preferred praying to hunting. He tried to remedy the situation by forbidding Camille's sister Nana to read Will any more of her favorite sentimental romances until he had read *Ivanhoe*. His purpose was thwarted, however, when Will ignored Lancelot's valorous deeds and became fascinated with medieval monks.

Will's next teacher, accordingly, was Judge Griffin, an aristocratic casualty of the Civil War who spent his days tinkering with models of experimental cotton gins, writing poetry, and wondering aloud in deist fashion about the existence of God. Judge Griffin and Will roamed happily through the classics of English literature until they came to *Othello*. Will informed his teacher that the play was immoral, and seeing that argument would be futile, the Judge switched to *The Merchant of Venice*. Despite such moral concerns, Will found in literature another medium for his artistic impulses. When he was twelve, he wrote his first poem, "Night." It described the passing of night into day and adhered strictly to a simple, regular form of three quatrains set in iambic tetrameter. There was nothing remarkable about the poem, but its regularity of form suggests that Will's attraction to poetry was closely akin to his musical sensibility.[2]

Camille was no more eager for Will to become a poet than a priest. She decided that Judge Griffin was neglecting practical subjects like French and Latin, and transferred Will to the tutelage of Father Koestenbrock, the parish priest. Will's afternoons were spent with Mr. Bass, superintendent of Greenville's public schools, studying mathematics and science. All of this practical instruction did nothing to blunt Will's artistic interests, but it did prepare him for college. When Will was fifteen, LeRoy and Camille sent him to enroll at the preparatory school at Sewanee. When he saw the military uniforms of the school, he decided to enroll in the college instead. He passed the entrance examinations and began taking courses in literature and ethics. Will was incorrigible, and his parents' efforts to educate the poetry out of him were doomed to failure.[3]

LeRoy and Camille's younger son, LeRoy, Jr., fit more naturally into the Percy mold than Will. While his shy older brother sat home writing poetry and playing the piano, little LeRoy could be seen riding horseback wildly down Greenville's sleepy streets on his way to visit his friends in the black section of town. LeRoy once took Camille to Arkansas to watch his son play baseball, and he treated both teams to ice cream after the game. He gave the boy a rifle and showed him how to use it, and together they hunted the fields and woods of the delta. LeRoy saw his own reflection in his younger son and developed a relaxed relationship with him that he lacked with Will.[4]

When little LeRoy was ten, his parents took him with them to Hot Springs for a vacation. While showing a playmate how to shoot his .22, LeRoy was accidentally shot by his friend. He walked to the hotel and demanded that his father be sent for. When the elder LeRoy arrived, his son greeted him with "Hello pop, I am all right." But he was not all right. His bowel was punctured, and his brave facade soon turned to screams of pain. In less than a week he was dead. All of Greenville shared the Percys' loss, including the blacks, who lined the street outside the Percy home in silent grief when they heard of young LeRoy's death.[5]

Will's natural grief over his brother's death was compounded by his realization that it left him squarely in line to inherit his father's public responsibilities. He would have preferred to leave these responsibilities to his outgoing younger brother, as Colonel Percy's older brothers had left them to him. At Sewanee Will had found a congenial environment where he could excel. He was a charter member of Sopherim, a bohemian literary club; an editor of the school magazine; and winner of an annual prize in English. He had discovered a comfortable, satisfying life devoted to literature, and he had little desire to give it up in order to assume his father's role as a champion of the delta's interests.

His frail health and literary interests also made him fear that he was not fit to do so. Will's grief and anxiety spilled over into a poem he wrote about a young hunter who had been slain, in which he asked God to return the youth to the world for a full life and offered to ransom him by spending his own life in purgatory. But Will knew that his prayer would not be answered and that he must now try to live the life that would have been his brother's.[6]

The apparent injustice of his brother's death may also have contributed to Will's loss of his intense faith in Catholicism. Will attributed his loss of faith to intellectual curiosity. "I had been thinking," he wrote. "I had never stopped thinking. I was determined to be honest if it killed me." His ethics teacher at Sewanee, William Porcher DuBose, raised questions about all established religions, and Will could not answer some of them. These unanswered questions, combined with Will's grief over his brother's death, raised doubts about the truth of his faith, while his need to prepare himself to assume his father's responsibilities caused him to doubt its usefulness. Will realized that Catholicism was in part attractive as a refuge from the world, and he could no longer afford such a refuge. One quiet afternoon the simple faith of his childhood slipped away from him, and his search for a philosophy that would help him reconcile his inner, poetic life with the outer world began.[7]

Will graduated from Sewanee in 1904. LeRoy blamed his son's frail health on his bookishness and advised him to take a year off to recover and decide on a profession. Will leaped at the chance to put off such practical considerations for another year and suggested his long-harbored plan for a trip to Paris. LeRoy was thinking of someplace more robust, like Wyoming, but he finally agreed that Will could go to Paris if he would take fencing lessons there. Will agreed, albeit unenthusiastically, and somehow avoided impalement. Most of his days in Paris were occupied with trips to the Louvre, French and piano lessons, and writing poetry. Overcoming his shyness he passed his evenings charming the young ladies whom he escorted to the theater and sharing bohemian suppers with a group of Sewanee friends who were also enjoying the traditional postgraduate year on the Continent.

Will's happy life in Paris was haunted by his realization that soon he must choose a career. Hoping that the necessity of supporting a wife might inspire him, as it had his father, to a career, he tried to fall in love, but even in Paris he was unable to. Only poetry and music enraptured him, and he had no illusions about earning a living at either. Will expressed his anxiety in his poem "To Chatterton," written in Paris, in which he wondered what accomplishments he could show if death came to claim him. He was certain that as a Percy he should be doing something, but he was not sure what to do.[8]

Restless, Will left Paris for Italy in January. In Rome he borrowed a pass and masqueraded as a German baron in order to be introduced to the pope, and then complained in a letter to Camille of the corruption of the Italian Church. Later in the month several of his friends joined him, including two young ladies chaperoned by their mother, who tried in vain to interest Will in her younger daughter. In February he continued south to Naples, then on to Egypt. In April he returned to Italy, then went on to Berlin, where he and two friends spent their evenings making the rounds of the beer gardens and chasing girls. Will enjoyed these escapades but found that "these flaxen-haired beauties seem to lack that something—temperament, Chaucer would say—which rouses one to make sacrifices, do great deeds." Will wound up his summer in Zurich, no closer to knowing what to do with his life than when he arrived in Europe.[9]

Lacking a practicable ambition of his own, Will allowed his family's tradition to persuade him to become a lawyer. His choice of a law school, however, was determined by reasons of his own. Will chose Harvard because living in Boston would give him a chance to enjoy the symphonies, the theaters, and the annual visit of the Metropolitan Opera that he would miss later in Mississippi. He studied diligently by day and did fairly well, keeping his nights free for these amusements. Quieter evenings were spent at dinner parties in the homes of Cambridge's leading families, or with friends who gathered in his room at Winthrop Hall to talk philosophy and politics or listen to him play the piano he had installed there. Summers were spent in Europe or visiting the families of his Harvard compatriots. LeRoy, who had hurried through law school, wondered "how this European business is going to fit, or unfit, him for the prosaic work of digging a living out of law," but he was so relieved that Will was not going to become a priest or poet that he gave him free rein.[10]

Will knew that he could not support himself in the Percy style by writing poetry, but he continued to write for himself. In his last year at Harvard *McClure's* magazine accepted his poem "A Winter's Night." Will requested that the poem appear anonymously, probably hoping to keep separate his public and private vocations. Other poems that he wrote at Harvard suggest the same distinction between Will's inner and outer lives. They celebrate the night, the time when, as Will wrote in "Longing,"

> I may forget
> The fretful work-a-day and midgy round of things . . .
> A smothered pain the long, long day.

Cramped by his studies during the day, Will's imagination took flight at night, as he described in his poem "Soaring."

> My heart is a bird to-night
> That streams on the washed, icy air.
> My heart is a bird tonight
> Twixt the stars and branches bare.

This sharp distinction between day and night, between the everydayness of law school and the occasional splendid raptures of poetry, was the predictable result of Will's effort to fit himself into the Percy mold.[11]

This dichotomy between the inner and outer life baffled another of Will's efforts to follow his father's example—his search for a woman to fall in love with and marry. Will's search for a woman involved more than the normal urges of a young man. One Percy quality that he had in ample supply was gentlemanliness, and a lady companion would have allowed him to express this quality and bridge the gap between his inner and outer life. Furthermore, he hoped that having a wife to support might justify sacrificing his poetic interests to the business of earning a living. Will dated several attractive, charming young ladies and was especially taken with Elsie Singmaster, a Radcliffe student who shared his interest in literature. But try as he might, he was still unable to fall in love.[12]

Will's poem "To Lucrezia," written at Harvard, suggests an explanation of his dilemma. In this poem a young man confesses to Lucrezia that his earlier professions of love, though uttered sincerely, were lies, and he realizes now that he does not truly love her. He has mistaken his "pagan" appreciation of her beauty for love and now realizes that his soul has remained untouched. He admits that "Mayhaps, thy soul twines deep with God's," but he is unable to measure her inner qualities, the qualities that true love is built on, because "Betwixt thy soul and mine ariseth alway / This barrier—thy loveliness!" The strict and apparently irreconcilable distinction between physical lust and spiritual love that Will described in "To Lucrezia" hampered his attempts to develop a spiritual relationship with women he found attractive. His dichotomous view of women as either ladies or whores was aggravated by his desire to fit himself into the Percy mold. When Will thought of ladies, he thought first of Camille, to whom he was very close; however, he invested her with a purity that her own husband would have found hard to live with. Will's young lady friends could match this idealized vision of pure Southern Womanhood only by being completely unattractive to him. Unable to find a middle ground between homely ladies and beautiful whores, Will remained alone.[13]

Another offshoot of Will's effort to fit himself into the Percy mold was the pride he developed in his southern origins while at Harvard. He became interested in Sidney Lanier and wrote his mother that he was especially proud that the South's landscape could inspire such poetry. Will thought that the major difference between southerners and Yankees was that southerners had better manners. This view was hardly uncommon in the South, as Will discovered when he told an amazed and disbelieving aunt that he had, in fact, discovered northerners who were gentlemen. It was, however, a significant departure for the young man who had chosen Massachusetts over Virginia—a departure leading back, albeit circuitously, to Greenville.[14]

Will was in no hurry to get back, however. After he graduated in the spring of 1908 with a B average—which, he assured his mother, was what "nice people" made—he left with LeRoy for Europe. They returned in late September, and Will passed his bar exam in November. Perilously close to becoming a lawyer, he received a reprieve at the last minute, when Sewanee's professor of English, John Bell Henneman, died unexpectedly, and Will's alma mater asked him to fill in for a semester. Carrie Stern, the Greenville schoolteacher who served as

Will's critic in his early poetic efforts, warned him that teaching would not leave him time to write, but Will took the job anyway. He found that she was right; his teaching duties occupied most of his time, and though he enjoyed them, he did not find them interesting enough to make teaching a career. He resigned at the end of the semester and left for Spain with LeRoy.[15]

LeRoy had tried to avoid influencing Will's choice between a career as a lawyer or as a professor. Both he and his brother Willie wrote Will that either choice was all right. LeRoy did influence Will indirectly, however, when he entered the Senate race shortly after Will became a junior member of his law firm late in 1909. Since LeRoy's partner, Judge Moody, was in bad health, Will was responsible for most of the firm's business over the next two years. Handling cases more important than those normally assigned to inexperienced lawyers, Will found the work more interesting and rewarding. He defended the black Knights of Pythias Lodge in a controversial harassment suit filed by the white Knights of Pythias, who resented blacks using the same name. He helped local authorities enforce prohibition, which Will was more enthusiastic about than his father, and committed the firm to represent a new drainage district without a fee, another move that LeRoy might not have made. Will also helped organize relief efforts for the victims of the flood of 1912, and in his father's absence he supervised the Sunnyside and Trail Lake plantations. Even while handling routine legal matters such as claims against the railroads for dead mules and broken crockery, Will admitted to Judge Moody, "I am learning some law and a considerable amount of human nature." Will was seduced through his moral sense by these opportunities for community service. Unenthusiastically, yet inexorably, he became involved in the issues of the delta—agriculture, flood control, race, railroads—all the issues that had concerned his father and grandfather.[16]

Will's role in LeRoy's Senate campaign intensified the air of excitement and purpose surrounding his first years as a lawyer. He helped coordinate the campaign while LeRoy was in Washington, and served as companion and bodyguard on his father's campaign swings through Mississippi. Will shared his father's view of the Senate race as a conflict between a gentleman and a theatrical demagogue. At Harvard he had pondered the importance of manners; the Senate race gave him a chance to fight for them, and in the heat of battle, manners and morals were welded together in Will's mind. His father's defeat did nothing to loosen this connection. In fact, it made the values that LeRoy embodied all the more attractive to the idealistic young poet by making them tragic.[17]

Despite Will's maturing commitment to his family's values, his efforts to conform to them kept him divided within himself. At times he was too miserable to concentrate on his work and complained that practicing law prevented him from writing poetry, yet he wrote more poetry than he ever had before. He complained that his writing was interrupted by visits from his friends, yet he regularly sought their company at the informal meetings of Greenville's young writers at Carrie Stern's. He escorted young ladies to dances and on long moonlight strolls along the levee, yet he feared that "perhaps I shall never marry and more terrible that I shall never love." He confessed that "I seem to be happy only when writing what seems to me beautiful." The everyday world of practical affairs remained for Will a cheap imitation of the inner life, and as his involvement in the life of the delta increased, so did his need for the consolations of poetry.[18]

As Will wrote more, he began to publish more. In 1911 *McClure's* published the poem it had accepted three years before; then in 1914 and 1915 Will's work appeared in *Ainslee's*, the *Colonnade*, the *International*, and the *Yale Review*. These poems attracted the attention of the poet Witter Bynner and others, and in 1915 the Yale University Press recognized the young poet by bringing out a volume of his verse. *Sappho in Levkas and Other Poems* contained some of Will's early poems, including those already discussed, and several newer poems dealing with the same themes.[19]

The title poem, "Sappho in Levkas," is an extended analysis of the conflict Will saw between pagan beauty and spiritual love. Sappho, poetess of the ancient island of Lesbos, confesses to her father, Zeus, that she has betrayed her divine heritage by basely lusting for the shepherd boy, Phaon. Her passion remains unfulfilled because Phaon, disappointed by her impurity, has rebuked her, but she has decided to kill herself rather than remain prey to physical lusts. By using the daughter of a god for a narrator, Will was able to analyze the conflict between love and lust more thoroughly than in his earlier poems, such as "To

Lucrezia." When Phaon rebukes Sappho for not measuring up to his standards of purity, Will sympathizes with her pain and recognizes the injustice of Phaon denying her the affection he reserves for the peasant girls of his village. Sappho's parentage also suggests that such strict standards of purity are unfair, for even her father has violated them in seducing her mother, a mortal. Sappho finally wonders if even the gods laugh at her concern for her own purity, just as Will wondered if his search for a spiritual love would prevent him from ever loving at all.[20]

In his poem "St. Francis to the Birds" Will describes what the inner life of the spirit meant to him after he lost his faith in Catholicism. He casts Saint Francis as a pagan lover of beauty and nature who would rather admire a dawn than say his prayers. Aesthetic inspiration has replaced the inspiration of faith, and the moral code previously fixed and enforced by doctrine has similarly been refocused to deal more directly with Will's isolation from the world. Thus, fearing that his sermon on the traditional Christian virtues will soon be forgotten, Saint Francis adds:

> this last word
> Too simple to be long remembered; but forgot,
> Taking the shining and the wings
> And all seraphic meaning from the life we know—
> And you that glisten through the lovely blue,
> Not singly, but in shoals and multitudes,
> Bear witness to the truth that I would tell:
> That child of God, man-child or bird child
> Or single-winged star-child of the night,
> That lives apart, unto himself,
> Unsharing, unsolicitous, and free,
> Hath vainly lived; for life, this present life,
> Is but the throe to brotherhood!

This simple remnant of Will's Christianity, the idea of brotherhood and concern for others, became the focal point of his efforts to fit himself into the Percy mold and to integrate his inner and outer lives. Concern for others was the point at which manners and morals touched, and it neatly reflected the Percy tradition of service to the community. The idea of brotherhood also offered Will the hope of investing his outer, social life with the meaning he enjoyed in his inner, poetic life.[21]

Intellectually, the idea of brotherhood offered a solution to Will's estrangement from the world, but he could not simply decide to care for others. He needed a catalyst to spark the reaction between his inner and outer lives. Some of the shorter poems in *Sappho in Levkas* sounded a new theme in his work that might serve as such a catalyst— the theme of noble defeat in the battle for a just cause. In "Failure," Will has no pity for those slain in battle, because

> the hand
> Impelling them thus blindly to lay bare
> Their hearts to that unequal contest, grants
> Solace divine for their divine attempt.

This new theme was probably suggested by LeRoy's defeat in the Senate race, but soon after it took on a new meaning for Will. Vacationing in Sicily during the summer of 1914, he saw the approach of war in Europe. In his poem "Girgenti," written that summer, he praised the countless unknown warriors of the past and asked:

> My brothers, proud, tho' unworthy, let me stand with you
>   In stubborn rank against the wall of doom,
>   Opposing meek acceptance of the world;
> Scornful of scorn and vileness and black sloth:
>   Battling, we know not why; dying, we care not how;
>   Glimpsing our kinship with the farther stars;
>   Defeated always—but how splendidly.

Many times war offers a solution to problems that have nothing to do with politics, economics, or any of the other causes used by politicians to justify it. In Will's case the war in Europe offered him a chance to identify with a cause outside himself, to fight for, and thus make a part of the outer world, the values he found within himself. In the epilogue of *Sappho in Levkas*, the poet asks God to "Take back thy gift of song" and make him a warrior. Only by leaving behind the "aerial rapture" of poetry and taking up the "living of the life" of war can he reach his highest potential and fashion his life in the divine image. Will likewise saw the war as an opportunity to reach his highest potential by reconciling his inner and outer lives.[22]

Sappho in Levkas appeared at a crossroads in Will's life. Looking back to his youth, the title poem described the conflict Will saw between the spiritual and material. "St. Francis to the Birds" described what remained of his early Christianity and suggested how this remnant might fit into a new philosophy. In later poems in the collection Will looked forward to a new, active faith that would leave no time for questioning, no time for anything but heroic deeds, and thus would weld his inner and outer lives together in the heat of battle.

Sappho in Levkas was also a crossroads in Will's career as a poet, though it was unclear where the new road led. His first book of verse attracted some attention, mostly favorable, from the critics, but the meager financial returns proved to Will that he was right about the futility of trying to make a living as a poet. At the time, however, it mattered little, for the war in Europe that was supposed to be over by Christmas turned into the Great War. For a time Will would be neither poet nor lawyer.[23]

Chapter 5

LeRoy and Will Percy

The Great War

From every county comes the call made with the earnestness of men who know that their all is at stake, upon every good and true man to be up and doing in behalf of right.
Colonel Percy, calling for the overthrow of
Radical Reconstruction

We could with honor have avoided the present peril, but unless Germany does the unexpected, I do not see how we are going to with honor avoid travelling the rough road that lies ahead of us.
LeRoy Percy, to Captain J. S. McNeilly, May 17, 1915

Physically I was not made for a soldier, nor spiritually, for that matter. . . . Probably I had always wanted to escape a life that seemed to me filled with nothing and less noble than a human life need be. Probably, although I had no liking for hardships, a soldier's hardships and his likely end seemed to me a better poem than I could ever hope to write.
Will Percy
Lanterns on the Levee

My uncle fought in the Argonne. He said it was too horrible. But he also said he never again felt real for the next forty years.
Walker Percy
Lancelot

When Will returned home in the summer of 1914, he found Greenville untouched by the war in Europe. LeRoy was home from the Senate and immersed in his perennial concerns—political scrapping, working for better levees, practicing law, and planting. His new duties as director of the Saint Louis Federal Reserve District also occupied his time. LeRoy took advantage of Will's return and set out to hunt moose in Alaska, leaving his son to handle the daily routine. Even Will was seduced by the tranquillity that enveloped Greenville like the hot August sun. He wrote his cousin Janet Dana, "I really love the life here—it is so unrushing, so natural, even when drab so human."[1]

By the time LeRoy returned in October, the chill of war had reached Greenville. The British embargo of cotton shipments to Germany and Austria sent the price of the delta's commodity plummeting. LeRoy wrote the delta's congressman, B. G. Humphreys, that he wished he were still living in a tent eating moose meat, and predicted that delta planters would be especially hard pressed by the embargo because they had to pay their laborers even in years when cotton was not worth raising. LeRoy's initial concern with the war sprang from his fear that it would wreck the delta's economy. When Blue Cross asked him to raise funds in the delta to save Europe's starving livestock, he wrote back that people in the delta were more likely to spend their money feeding destitute blacks, because while a dead Negro was utterly useless, a dead horse could be made into an excellent soup or hash.[2]

LeRoy's sarcasm sprang from his fear that President Wilson's convoluted idealism would eventually lead America into the war. When Wilson announced that Germany would be held strictly accountable for the lives of Americans traveling on British ships, LeRoy wrote to Captain McNeilly: "I am profoundly convinced that the peace welfare and prosperity of this country is incalculably of greater importance than the right of American citizens to travel on belligerent ships in time of war. If they are being deprived of this right, and this I question, and we are thereby given the right to go to war, I do not believe that the right violated is of sufficient importance to justify the maintenance of it by war." LeRoy had grown up in the defeated South; he knew the cost of war, both in dollars and lives. He was willing to pay the price, if necessary—if, for example, Wilson had declared that "Germany is a mad nation, running amok among the other nations of the world and that her ultimate success would subvert the civilization of the world and therefore we are going to join in the effort to render that success impossible." But to go to war for Wilson's picayune, legalistic reasons struck LeRoy as irrational and beneath the nation's dignity.[3]

Will was more receptive than LeRoy to the allurements of war, and his enthusiasm was fueled by his correspondence with his cousin Janet, who lived in New York. Like Will, Janet Dana was the child of a well-to-do family, was interested in the arts, and was unsure of what to do with her life. Will wrote Janet that "to miss this war is to miss the opportunity of living in this century," and asked if it would be possible for them to serve as Red Cross nurses at the front. Red Cross service appealed to Will because "to live in a trench (particularly if filled with *cold* water) and shoot a fat kindly blonde German doesn't inspire me and I couldn't drive a machine or fly an aeroplane."[4] In December, Janet wrote Will that she was taking a course in nursing at Bellevue Hospital which would prepare her for service in France, and invited him to join her. Will longed to go, but the demands of his family kept him in Greenville. His mother was suffering from a nervous disorder, and LeRoy needed his help guiding the family's finances through the depressed cotton market. Unable to leave under such circumstances, Will contented himself organizing local meetings to raise funds for the Committee for the Relief of Belgium.[5]

While Janet went to France, Will spent the first months of 1915 putting the finishing touches on *Sappho in Levkas*. His attitude toward his poetry remained ambiguous. He wrote Janet that "to write poetry makes me happy and that aside from all else is gift enough from the gods," but in another letter he confessed, "my poor family regards it as a poor way of spoiling a perfectly good career (tho this I learned merely from divination) and I suppose they are right." He worried that he had disappointed Camille, writing Janet that "it's an awful pity I have such a wild queer streak in me—she would have enjoyed so a lot of normal children." Will's old conflict remained. Going to war offered a way out, but his parents' disapproval blocked it.[6]

Meanwhile, Janet's letters depicting life at the front made Will doubt the value of both his daily life and his poetic accomplishments. After one particularly vivid letter Will replied to her: "I shall always regret that in spite of everything I did not go to the front in some serviceable capacity. Since the war began I've done nothing worth while. I seem to be waiting for something to happen. It makes so much we loved seem of little worth." Janet's return from Europe only made the prospect of going more tantalizing. She wrote Will that all her life she had lived "with a queer feeling that some day I could feel overwhelmingly—I think my most intense longing was for that day to come—I always thought it would come when some one loved me that I could love back—For the past two or three years I must say that I've never been more alive—happier—than ever before." Will had also fretted over whether he would ever fall in love, and the possibility that the war might awaken his emotions made it more attractive to him. The likelihood that this might happen seemed to increase in October, when Janet wrote that she had fallen in love with Warfield Longcope, a professor of medicine at Columbia, and then again in December when she married him.[7]

Janet's blossoming happiness presented a stark contrast to Will's feelings of uselessness and boredom. Poetry remained his chief consolation. In December he began a poem, never finished or published, called "The Meeting," in which the poets Shelley and Byron meet at the gates of the kingdom of the dead and discuss the need for poets to live fully and bravely. As the war grew more alluring with each letter from Janet, Will's frustration and need for the consolations of poetry grew also. Early in 1916 he decided to find out whether the publication of *Sappho in Levkas* augured a career as a poet. He moved to New York, rented a garret, and devoted himself entirely to writing poetry. Will regarded this move as a gamble that offered a chance for a fuller life; LeRoy probably regarded it as a way to get his son's mind off of the war. Both were disappointed. Will began a long, dramatic poem called "In April Once," but was too distracted by the war to finish it. In August he volunteered for the Belgium Relief and returned to Greenville, convinced that his application would be rejected, and unsure whether he wanted to be accepted. He wrote Janet that he felt guilty because "it seems as if I were sacrificing nothing except the feelings of mother and father. . . . Isn't it fearful how one attains freedom only at the expense of the blood and tears of others?"[8]

Fortunately, Will did not have to make the decision to go to Belgium; the relief committee decided it needed him and accepted his application. In November, full of trepidation and excitement, Will sailed for London, and in December, across the North Sea to Rotterdam. While waiting there to cross the border into German-occupied Belgium, he steeled himself to his adventure by writing two poems. In "The Dice Throwers?" he wrote that all who complacently enjoy the benefits of civilization while others are fighting to preserve it should be struck down by the gods. In "Grandfather," originally entitled "Grandpere" after Camille's father, the war appears less a duty than an ordeal or test that will lead to personal salvation. The grandfather tells a young man on his twenty-first birthday that "Nobility at last we gain / When whipped and scourged to it by pain." In spite of his parents' opposition, Will saw the war as a chance to align his inner life with his family's traditions, and his choice of his Grandfather Bourges as a symbol of this tradition was probably an attempt to overcome Camille's doubts, and perhaps his own.[9]

Will's duties in Belgium satisfied neither his need to serve nor his desire to test himself by suffering heroically. By the time he arrived, the dangers and hardships faced by earlier volunteers had changed into a daily administrative routine, and evenings were spent at dinners and parties hosted by Belgium's social elite. Will felt right at home and, for the most part, bored. The danger in Belgium was the routine danger of living constantly under the guns of the Germans without ever facing them in battle. The anxiety Will felt was aggravated by his frustration at having to watch and do nothing as Belgium's men were herded off to labor camps in Germany and starved to death when they refused to work. Will performed his duties with a routine courage and competence that later won him the praise of the Belgian government and Herbert Hoover, but his anxiety, frustration, and growing hatred of Germany only increased his desire to be valorous in the old Percy style.[10]

LeRoy suffered from no such need to act heroically, and continued to doubt the wisdom of America's entering the war. As the pressure for American entry mounted, LeRoy kidded John Sharp Williams about his and Wilson's habit of "issuing war fulminations against the Mexicans, Germans, and the balance of the world." He praised former senator Joseph Bailey for "enunciating good old Democratic doctrines as in the days of yore" when Bailey opposed Wilson's plan to purchase private merchant vessels to use as naval auxiliaries. What LeRoy objected to most was "the scholarly idiocy of the present administration," which seemed to be backing America into the war for all of the wrong reasons. He preferred the straightforward belligerence of Theodore Roosevelt and endorsed Roosevelt's call for compulsory military service. LeRoy supported this plan in part as a defense against an invasion of the United States, and he also hoped that military service would stop "the fatty degeneration of the people of this country from lack of high ideals." LeRoy shared Will's belief that ordeal and sacrifice restored values, but he was more aware than Will of the costs of war, and doubted that Wilson was the man to lead such an awakening of the spirit.[11]

LeRoy was especially concerned that the military appropriations that Wilson requested might cut into the funding for levee construction in the delta, and he worked with Congressman B. G. Humphries and the engineers in charge of the levees to prevent this from happening. Wilson's foreign policy did have one effect that LeRoy considered beneficial to Mississippi; Senator Vardaman publicly opposed it. LeRoy joined with John Sharp Williams and some of Mississippi's congressmen to make sure that Vardaman paid the full political price for finally taking an unpopular stand. As it turned out, Vardaman did not need their help in destroying his own popularity. When he voted against President Wilson's request for a declaration of war, he effectively ended his political career. [12]

Once war was declared, LeRoy set aside his doubts and supported his country, just as his father had done when Mississippi seceded. He even supported Wilson publicly, though he continued privately to criticize the President's handling of the war. LeRoy was especially angered by Wilson's refusal to allow Roosevelt to lead a division into battle. He urged John Sharp Williams and other southern congressmen to support Roosevelt's proposal, and commiserated with his friend when Wilson announced his decision. LeRoy had hoped that Roosevelt's volunteer force would boost American morale. He also feared that the war might create a military caste dangerous to the democracy America was fighting for, and thought Roosevelt's division might prevent this by making the professional soldiers share the glory. "West Point," LeRoy wrote Roosevelt, "has always seemed to me to breed that kind of spirit." He urged Roosevelt and Williams to warn Americans that "snobbery is absolutely abhorrent to the ideal of a democracy and unnecessary to military efficiency." LeRoy feared that the war might awaken repressive, militaristic values best left dormant.[13]

Will lacked LeRoy's misgivings, and despite his father's urging him to remain in Belgium, he decided to return home and enlist in the American army. Will and a half-dozen other committee volunteers bade a sad farewell to their Belgian friends and boarded a train for Switzerland. They traveled anxiously across Germany, fearing that at any time they might be taken prisoners and held for the duration of the war. Finally, they reached Berne without incident. Will waited there a month for a ship to America, writing poetry to pass the time. In May he sailed for home.[14]

Will returned to Greenville a war hero "and felt of course the worst of imposters," as he wrote Janet. He spent the summer speaking at Red Cross and YMCA fund raisers in Mississippi, Arkansas, and Memphis. His story of the internment of a Belgian girl who had rebuffed the advances of a German officer, told with the matter-of-factness of one for whom such incidents had become a part of the daily routine, made Will an excellent fund raiser, as did his warning that the YMCA would be virtually the only moral influence on the American army should it be sent to France. Will also received special thanks from the *Delta Lighthouse*, Greenville's black newspaper, for describing his experiences to local blacks even though they could not afford to contribute to the fund drive. Will was flattered by all of this attention, but he was more concerned with gaining ten pounds so that he could get into the next officers' training camp. From his vantage point in Belgium Will had decided that "the old world has blown to bits and dawn hasn't arisen on the new." Given such an enormous crisis, Will believed it his duty to go to the front.[15]

The sense of crisis generated by the war stimulated Will's spirit and his poetic impulse. He wrote a friend that "writing verse these days seems somewhat on a par with Nero's fiddling while Rome burned. But even now ideas have a curious way of popping up and insisting on getting themselves into shape." Two of the poems that Will wrote after seeing the war suggest a reconciliation of ideas he had previously considered distinct. In "In our Yard," Will compared Moses' vision of God in a burning bush with his own experience of seeing and hearing a mockingbird in a myrtle bush, suggesting that the beauty of nature and the beauty of poetry are manifestations of God. In "Overtones" Will made the same point, again using a bird's song as a symbol for both the beauties of nature and poetry.

> I heard a bird at break of day
> > Sing from the autumn trees
> A song so mystical and calm,

So full of certainties,
No man, I think, could listen long
     Except upon his knees.
Yet this was but a simple bird
     Alone, among dead trees.

In many of Will's earlier poems, most notably in "Sappho in Levkas" and "St. Francis to the Birds," aesthetic values appeared as an attractive but pagan alternative to religious values. In these poems aesthetic values become the grounds for religious faith and a means for reconciling the physical world of nature with the spiritual kingdom of God. This reconciliation, in turn, improved the aesthetic quality of Will's verse. Samuel McCoy of *Contemporary Verse* called "Overtones" the best poem in the magazine's April issue, and H. A. Bellour of the *Bellman*, where the poem also appeared, wrote that it was "one of the best things that has been published in this country in a long time." William Stanley Braithwaite reprinted it in his annual anthology of magazine verse, and most critics have agreed in calling "Overtones" Will's best short poem. The greatest charm of the poem is its simplicity, which came from the unambiguous idealism and capacity for faith that the war gave Will.[16]

Because LeRoy lacked Will's enthusiasm for the war, his own fundraising speeches for the Red Cross were less dramatic than his son's. Rather than trying to turn the war into a crusade, he told his audiences that it would be a long war with many casualties who would have to be cared for. He was quite content to let Will make the colorful speeches while he worked quietly behind the scenes to insure that the delta's interests were not lost in the confusion of preparing for war. He tried to get the levee appropriation increased by describing it as a war measure, and fought what he considered a disproportionate draft quota assigned to Mississippi. LeRoy also looked after his own interests. He asked Congressman Humphreys to block the selection of George Creel, author of a slanderous article on LeRoy's election to the Senate, as chairman of the Committee on Public Information. Creel was appointed anyway, and his fantastic press releases worked Americans into the militaristic hysteria that LeRoy abhorred. LeRoy completed his personal preparedness program when Mississippi passed a new bone-dry prohibition act as a war measure, by having a barrel of whiskey shipped from Kentucky a few days before the law went into effect. His preparations complete, he spent August vacationing in Honolulu.[17]

When LeRoy returned, Will left for the Camp Stanley officers' training camp at Leon Springs, Texas. Because of his slight build, Will and his family doubted that he would get through the camp, but after three weeks LeRoy wrote a cousin that Will "thinks he has detected a symptom of a little muscle in his right arm. I think there is an even chance of his getting through." Will did survive the training camp, mostly on grit and determination. He saw the camp as an ordeal, a chance to prove that despite his size he could be as good an officer as the "six-footers, flashy and incompetent," who surrounded him. His experience in Belgium also helped when he was invited to address the camp at a Liberty Loan rally and upstaged the senior officers who preceded him on the platform. In November, Will received his commission as a first lieutenant and returned to Greenville with orders to report to Camp Pike, Arkansas, by December 15.[18]

When Will returned, he was surprised to find that LeRoy had accepted the chairmanship of Mississippi's YMCA fund-raising campaign, even though with Will gone this would interfere drastically with his legal practice. LeRoy still kept the war in perspective; he puzzled his friends by delaying the opening of the fund-raising speeches without explanation, confiding to Will that "it is really due to the fact that the bird season opens on the first and it is up to me to get in three days shooting next week before I am swamped in this work—a perfectly rational explanation but probably it might not be fully appreciated." Once he began, however, LeRoy proved a capable fund raiser. His speeches were so compelling and idealistic that a friend who heard him speak in Jackson wrote that "the tone and tenor thereof compel me to believe that your convictions have nearly persuaded you to be a Christian." LeRoy denied that any change had occurred, replying, "I had religion all of the time but naturally was a little shy in trotting it out in the presence of the ungodly, and therefore you never suspected it." Despite his protestations, LeRoy's war work increased. He accepted an appointment to the War Department's Legal Advisory Board for Washington County and began making plans to go to Europe with the YMCA.[19]

In December LeRoy attended a YMCA war work council in New

York, and in February, he sailed for France. LeRoy knew from listening to Will's speeches that such experience would help him raise funds back home, but his main reason for going was that "this looks to me about the next best job to 'sho nuff' scrapping and it gives me an opportunity to get a close look at the great world drama." In May he returned from France and resumed his fund raising, now spicing his speeches with firsthand observations. LeRoy offended some YMCA workers by criticizing the procedures that led American soldiers to believe the abbreviation stood for "your money cheerfully accepted." Nevertheless, the YMCA asked him to head their war fund drive again in 1919. LeRoy also received an invitation to serve on the War Industries Board but had to decline when he was unable to sell his plantations. Once America entered the war, he supported Senator Henry Cabot Lodge's argument that America should seek a total victory that would allow her to dictate the final peace in Europe. LeRoy thought that such a victory would take at least two years to win, and only then by a concentrated effort of all Americans. Once he decided that the war was inevitable, LeRoy could not resist a good fight.[20]

In the ever-building crisis atmosphere of the war, Will continued reconciling previously dichotomous ideas in his poetry. As his train for Leon Springs pulled out of the Greenville station, he had composed a short poem called "To C.P." in which he used his mother as a vehicle for reconciling spiritual and physical beauty. "Her spirit's loveliness was such / Her body's loveliness I could not see." This joining of physical and spiritual beauty was also apparent in his poem "Poppy Fields," written at Camp Pike. The last stanza asks:

> And would it not be proud romance
> Falling in some obscure advance
> To rise, a poppy field in France?

In "Our Generation," also written at Camp Pike and later published as "The Soldier Generation," Will described the grim faith that had replaced the alienation and uncertainty of his youth.

> Behold, without faith we were fashioned,
> Bereft the assuaging of lies;
> Thirsty for dreams we have passioned,
> Yet more for truth that denies;

. . . .
Accepting the great abnegation
We are fathers, not children, of light.

. . . .
Yet this is our hope—that to-morrow
Will yield of our strivings, God.

By ascribing his own uncertainty to his entire generation, Will suggests that the anticipation of shared suffering in battle helped him reconcile yet another dichotomy—his sense of estrangement between his personal life and the life of the community.[21]

Will's desire to share the suffering of his fellow soldiers set him apart from the other officers at Camp Pike. He preferred fraternizing with enlisted men instead of officers; and when enlisted men were forbidden to drink while officers were allowed to, Will decided that this was undemocratic and vowed to refrain from drinking himself. LeRoy, of course, was amazed by this decision. He cautioned Will to "think rather carefully over the idea of making an iron-clad resolution not to take a drink." He also advised Will to cultivate his fellow officers and, if he could find a country club in Arkansas, to join it.[22]

Will went to France in January. He found his first assignment to billeting and other administrative work too comfortable to be heroic, and he applied for the line officers' training school. He was accepted, but upon graduation he was assigned to train black troops rather than lead a platoon at the front. When his parents suggested that he might be better suited for work behind the lines, he replied testily that "my own special qualifications are those of a poet and they are equally worthless in this business, front or rear." In August Will got his chance to go to the front when one of the colonels in his training unit, William P. Jackson, was promoted to general and given command of the Ninety-fourth Brigade. General Jackson offered Will an appointment to his staff. Will declined, explaining that he wanted to be a platoon leader, but he changed his mind when the general told him he was going to the front. "Still," Will wrote a friend, "I'll never cease regretting not being a platoon leader."[23]

Will's first impression of the front was disappointing. He could see German observation balloons rising on the horizon and hear shells bursting at any time, but somehow the danger did not seem authentic.

"We carry our gas masks about," he lamented, "but it's only to give us a serious air. . . . I've resigned myself to losing all chances of glory, and what's more, of the deep human satisfaction of suffering and fighting with the men." After a few days, however, Will began to enjoy the carnival-like atmosphere of his new post. He wrote his mother, "The last few days have been great fun: we have gas alarms and bombardments on a small scale and patrols and Bosche planes overhead, and still it isn't serious enough to dampen one's spirits or to seem more real than a good movie."[24]

The most dangerous of Will's duties was accompanying General Jackson on his nocturnal inspections of the trenches. The inspections were done at night to avoid enemy sniper fire, but wandering around in the dark proved almost as perilous for the General and his aide. On their first patrol General Jackson caught the seat of his trousers in the barbed wire that protected the trenches. While Will was trying to rescue him from his predicament, a shell burst directly ahead of them. General Jackson disentangled himself "with great promptness and judgement" and leaped into a trench, but Will was so excited at actually being under fire that he stood up to get a better view of what was going on. "The general," he wrote later, "was highly irritated at this performance." Other nocturnal patrols proved equally hazardous. A few nights after his run-in with the barbed wire fence, General Jackson crawled headfirst into an unfinished trench and dislocated his shoulder. Less than a month later, Will collided with a ration wagon while inspecting the trenches in the sidecar of a motorcycle. He escaped unharmed, though his driver suffered a broken collarbone. The accidental and at times absurd quality of these injuries contributed to Will's feeling that the danger of the war was somehow inauthentic.[25]

The authentic danger of battle was closer at hand than Will knew. By September, Allied Command was planning the largest American offensive of the war, the Meuse-Argonne operation, and when it got under way on the twenty-sixth, Will's division was squarely in the middle of it. Like most battles in World War I, Meuse-Argonne was actually a combination of battles. Three American corps were involved, or about 1,200,000 men. The V Corps, to which the Thirty-seventh Division belonged, was placed in the center of the line and given the assignment of capturing Mountfaucon, the Germans' towering mountain stronghold that dominated the center of the battlefield. French army officers warned their American allies that they would be fortunate to capture Mountfaucon in three months; the American plan called for its capture in one day.[26]

V Corps captured Mountfaucon in two days. On the first day Will's division, the Thirty-seventh, encountered only light opposition from German machine guns, and it reached Mountfaucon that afternoon. Their sister division, the Seventy-ninth, was delayed by heavier opposition. The Thirty-seventh was unable to take Mountfaucon on its own, so the men had to spend the night huddling in the mud beneath the enemy's guns. The Seventy-ninth arrived the next day and the fortress fell, allowing V Corps to continue its push north.[27]

Or so the battle appeared to those who had planned it. But for Will and the hundreds of thousands of others charged with carrying it out, the Meuse-Argonne operation seemed destitute of order or purpose. The sensations of battle were too intense, too real to assimilate into anything as purposeful as an "operation." There was only slogging along through the mud and the fog and the smoke, in darkness cut only by the blinding glare of bursting shells. The darkness thundered at times, then became so quiet that Will could hear wild canaries singing in terror. The smells of burning powder, gas, and rotting cadavers rose from the mud as the men slogged on. Will was assigned to make sure that the troops kept going. Stationed at a crossroads, he turned the stragglers and deserters seeking a way out of the madness back into its midst. The next day Will went to the front himself to search for his general. Wandering around lost, he was caught in an artillery barrage that sent a nearby infantry company into headlong retreat. Will helped rally them, then spent the night in a mud trench, fending off mustard gas and trying to keep in touch with headquarters. He returned to the rear the next day, and a few days after the fall of Mountfaucon, the Thirty-seventh Division was relieved by reserves.

The men of the Thirty-seventh hoped for a breather when they were pulled out of the line, but instead they were sent to Belgium to reinforce the hard-pressed French troops there. The arrival of relatively fresh troops tipped the balance between the exhausted Allies and Germans, and the Americans soon found themselves leading a rapid sweep through Belgium. On their way, the Thirty-seventh passed through country scarred by three years of battle. Landscapes often touched the poet in Will; this landscape hammered him. He described it in a letter to LeRoy.

> The roads, mere channels of mud, lose themselves in the craters made by mines or pursue a haunted course through spots shown on the maps as towns where no stone is left to show the passerby men once lived. In the mad welter of shell holes and filth and mud emerge, like prehistoric animals from the slime of creation, the wrecks of battles lost and won—shelters of elephant iron, for in the waterlogged land trenches could not be dug; concrete pill-boxes torn apart till the iron ribs shattered in gigantic explosions, tanks fantastic and terrible, that had crawled to the roadside or into a shell hole to die (you could not believe they belonged to men till you looked inside and saw the skeletons still by the wheel and the guns); planes that crashed down doubtless into the midst of hurley-burley; shells of all sizes; exploded; duds, used and unused, helmets, coats, equipment, belts of ammunition, these were down broadcast over the loblolly and in and around and across the inextricable confusion, pattern without plan, ran the barbed-wire, a crown of thorns on the mangled landscape. Even more horrible were the trees; they appeared everywhere, singly and in clumps, in long lines, but always branchless, leafless, their bark torn away, rising white and distorted and twisted out of the mud, like the skeleton fingers of creatures drawn into the slough, raking and tearing at the dismal sky.[28]

Two elements of this letter's style indicate the havoc actual battle experience wreaked on Will's idealism. The rambling, run-together sentences suggest the impossibility of fitting the flux of battle sensations into the orderly framework of prewar syntax. By loosening his sentence structure, Will tried to create a conciousness capable of assimilating battle sensations without assuming the cause-and-effect relationships that governed ordinary life. Will abandoned this experiment after the war, but other American writers, most notably William Faulkner, used a similar elongated syntax in developing their stream-of-conciousness techniques.

The other notable element of this letter's style is its shift from abstract to concrete nouns. Words like *honor* and *hero* have been replaced by *slime, helmets,* and *pill-box.* Ernest Hemingway's character

Frederic Henry best explained the reason for this shift in *A Farewell to Arms*. "I had seen nothing sacred, and the things that were glorious had no glory and the sacrifices were like the stockyards at Chicago if nothing was done with the meat except to bury it. There were many words that you could not bear to hear and finally only the names of places had dignity." The individual heroics that Will came to the war to perform were swallowed up by casualty lists that ran into the thousands even on days when there were no battles. Ideals and abstractions became meaningless in the trenches, and they faded from Will's vocabulary. Will did not continue this experiment with concrete language after the war either, but he shared the experience of other writers who did.[29]

Will's reaction to the war also paralleled that of the British poets Paul Fussell describes in *The Great War and Modern Memory*. Fussell argues that the shared literary heritage of these poets shaped their reaction to the war into common patterns. Will was as familiar with the English classics as most Englishmen; like Fussell's soldier-poets, he carried the *The Oxford Book of English Verse* into battle with him, using this anthology as a portable container of the English literary heritage. The effects of this shared heritage showed up in Will's letters and poetry.[30]

One such similarity is Will's reticence about describing what he had seen in his letters home. Fussell argues that most British soldiers refused to describe fully the horrors of the front, in part because they believed it was impossible, and in part out of concern for those at home who might be worried about them. Significantly, the one letter in which Will varied from this pattern, the letter describing his trip to the Belgian front, was sent to LeRoy, who had been to the front, rather than Camille, who had weak nerves. Fussell found that many British soldiers at the front believed that they had taken part in an experience so profoundly unique that only those who had shared the experience could understand what it was like. Veterans of the trenches developed a bitter contempt for soldiers who stayed well behind the lines, especially for officers. Will shared this contempt. After the Belgian campaign, he wrote LeRoy that the combat soldiers were "the only portion of the army of which I approve." Will also scribbled a couple of doggerel poems in his field message book that made the same point. One of these commemorated the Services of Supply outfits behind the lines.[31]

> Mother, take down your service flag
> Your son's in the S.O.S.
> He's not so well
> But what the hell
> He couldn't have suffered less!
> He's a little pale
> From too much tale [sic]
> As near as I can guess.
> So mother take down your service flag
> Your son's in the S.O.S.

Unwilling or unable to graphically describe what they had seen to the folks back home, many British soldiers attempted to convey the horror of the war indirectly, through a variety of ironic contrasts. Two of the most common of these came from the English literary tradition, and Will used both. Many Englishmen, Fussell finds, contrasted the battlefields with the peaceful, carefree beauty of the birds flying over them. Will used this device in his poem "Waiting the Offensive," writing that if the birds flying over the besieged Paris were aware of the apprehension below them, they would not fly again. Will's letter to LeRoy after the Meuse-Argonne offensive uses the same device to describe the indescribable. "My only sensation as the sun came up was listening to the wild canaries which were suddenly and strangely moved to music that could be heard above the thunder of the guns."

The other device that Will shared with English soldiers was to contrast the war with the peaceful countrysides that were as ubiquitous as birds in the pastoral tradition. Will gave this device an American twist in "The Farm Again," which begins:

> The dreamy rain comes down,
> And cotton's in the grass.
> The farmers all complain—
> But I watch armies pass.

After the war, Will predicted that this poem would appeal only to veterans of the trenches. He used a similar contrast in one of his letters home, describing the local peasants who carried gas masks while gathering their crops. "The crops," he added, "are quite ripe—Barbed wire doesn't seem to interfere with them and the trees along the roadsides and the curving hills look peaceful as a Perugino landscape." Before the war, Will had contrasted birds and the beauty of nature with the boredom of everyday life. Now they became symbols in the more vivid dichotomy between life in the trenches and life anywhere else.[32]

In his study of American involvement in World War I, *Over Here*, David Kennedy has argued that "those developments [described by Fussell] on British battlefields and in British literature had no American analogues," but Will Percy's experience was the exception that proved the rule. Kennedy argues that because American soldiers were involved in the war for a shorter time than their European counterparts, they did not become as disillusioned, and thus they continued to describe the war in terms borrowed from Walter Scott's medieval romances rather than *The Oxford Book of English Verse*. Will, however, arrived in Europe before most of his countrymen, giving the acidic reality of modern war longer to burn into his romanticism. Furthermore, only a few years before the war, Will had seen his father, whom he often thought of as a character from one of Scott's romances, defeated in the Senate election, and this experience had already increased his appreciation of later, less heroic literary modes.[33]

In November, the Belgian offensive was halted by the armistice. The abrupt, almost overnight ending of the war took from Will the last vestige of his idealism—his sense of an important purpose. He passed the winter in a castle on the Yser River, waiting for his discharge and pondering his future. Now that the war was over, he wrote LeRoy, "Everybody wants so much to get back to the old easy way of things, and that way I suppose will never return." In April he was shipped back to New York. On his way home to Greenville he stopped off at Sewanee to visit friends, and discussed a teaching position in the English Department there. Once home he resumed his law practice but found the old routine boring and meaningless in comparison with the war. He considered quitting the law and taking up planting, but LeRoy convinced him that this would be even more stultifying. Finally, perhaps recalling the four happy years he had spent there as a student, Will decided to accept the teaching post at Sewanee. After one semester there, however, some of the Episcopalian alumni objected to Will's Catholic affiliations, and he was replaced. Will had been right; it was impossible after experiencing war to "get back to the old easy way of things."[34]

Actually, there was nothing new about Will's inability to fit himself into the world. What was new was his determination to overcome the dichotomy between his private and public lives; to preserve the harmony between values and action that he had felt as a soldier, now that the war was over. This determination was most apparent in his poetry. Will had begun collecting his manuscripts and preparing them for publication as soon as he returned from Europe. The result was *In April Once, and Other Poems*, Will's second volume of verse, published early in 1920 by the Yale Press.[35]

Will had begun the long, dramatic poem "In April Once" while he was living in New York; he carried the manuscript with him to the war and completed it only after he returned home. The poem bears the mark of its prolonged origins. Its major theme, Will wrote, was "the conflict, frequently poignant in youth, between the pagan joy of life and the increasing sense of duty." The setting of the poem in thirteenth-century Italy reflected Will's youthful concern with religion. He chose this setting because "it was the great age of faith and somehow in this conflict between beauty and duty religion seemed to me to play an important part." Because it was completed after the war, "In April Once" is also a record of how the war affected Will's youthful concerns.[36]

The life of beauty is represented by Guido, an imprisoned courtier who amuses his jailer, David, with tales of adventure and romance. David is beguiled by these ribald tales until one day Guido persuades him to allow another prisoner, Serle De Lanlarazon, to join them on the parapet and tell his story. Serle was imprisoned for heresy; he had contradicted church doctrine by preaching that evil, like good, was eternal, and the struggle between them the fate of man. David, who has lost his faith because of the evil in the world around him, asks Serle how he can still believe in God after all the punishments he has suffered for his beliefs. Serle replies that he still believes himself correct in his doctrinal differences with the church, but because they live in troubled, war-torn times, he no longer regards these differences as important as he once did. In a passage that sums up the effect of the war on Will's youthful philosophical concerns, Serle tells them:

It is a truth, but one forgetting which
Need not vary one whit the lives of men.
All know that good and evil are at war,
And in that war all lordly souls enlist,
Roman or heretic or infidel.
What matter the first cause? For battle-cry
To all the gallantry beneath the stars,
Two words suffice: "He is!"

Serle convinces David that in times of crisis philosophical questions of doctrine are secondary to action, and they leave the prison together to begin a life of doing good. Guido is killed by prison guards whom he holds off while David and Serle escape. His death is heroic, for Will still loved the aesthetic values he represents, but it is a death nonetheless—the death of the youthful Will Percy who worshiped beauty above all else.[37]

The major ambiguity of "In April Once" is what David and Serle's new life will be like. The poem's primary emphasis is on fusing the dichotomies of Will's youth; what form this fusion of values and action would take for Will was not yet clear. However, some of the lyrical pieces that appeared in the same volume suggested that Will would make his new life in the delta. In "In New York," probably written while Will was doing research for "In April Once," he contrasts the noisy, active life of the city with the peacefulness of the delta. The last stanza is entitled "Home."

I have a need of silence and of stars;
Too much is said too loudly; I am dazed.
The silken sound of whirled infinity
Is lost in voices shouting to be heard.
I once knew men as earnest and less shrill.
An undermeaning that I caught I miss
Among those ears that hear all sounds save silence,
These eyes that see so much but not the sky,
These minds that gain all knowledge but not calm.

In "The Wanderer," Will repeated his desire for "some haven that no tempest mars," and confessed:

I have grown weary of the open sea,
The chartless ways, the storms, the loneliness,

The coast that topples, tall and shelterless—
Weary of faring where all things are free!

Both of these poems point back to the delta, toward the smaller world of home and family, where duty, tradition, and the quiet routine of daily life provided a certainty that Will had not found in the wider world of Europe and New York. The war had challenged Will to act on his values, and in the pinch he had performed as well and bravely as any Percy. Now he faced the even greater challenge of fusing his values into the everyday life of a Percy.

Chapter 6

LeRoy Percy

The Klan

Any Southern man standing out and proclaiming himself as a champion of Southern womanhood and white supremacy should do it in the broad light of day, in the noonday sun, thanking his God that he can stand on his feet and battle for the right. You don't need a masked face for that kind of a declaration. . . . I do not care anything about this war on Catholics and war on Jews. It would not have brought me out here tonight. They can take care of themselves, but I know the terror this organization embodies for our negro population and I am here to plead against it. There is no need of it.

LeRoy Percy, speaking to the
people of Greenville, March 18, 1922

Unbeknownst, strangers had drifted in since the war—from the hills, from the North, from all sorts of odd places where they hadn't succeeded or hadn't been wanted. . . . The town was changing, but so insidiously that the old-timers could feel but not analyze the change. The new-comers weren't foreigners or Jews, they were an alien breed of Anglo-Saxon.

Will Percy
Lanterns on the Levee

Father, I heard them on the phone. They said you loved niggers and helped the Jews and Catholics and betrayed your own people.
I haven't betrayed anyone, son. And I don't have much use for any of them, Negroes, Jews, Catholics, or Protestants.
They said if you spoke last night, you would be a dead man.
I spoke last night and I am not a dead man.

Walker Percy
The Last Gentleman

Will knew that he had been changed by the war and that it would be difficult to fit himself back into Greenville's easygoing way of life. What he failed to anticipate was that the town itself had changed in

ways that would make his readjustment even more difficult. LeRoy
noticed Greenville's changing character even before the war. After devoting much of his career to bringing concrete roads, electric lights,
new industries, and better levees to Greenville, he wondered whether
the town had really progressed. He wrote to a former townsman that
"our town has grown some in population and improved much in comfort and attractiveness, but there were more men and women possessing individuality, personality and charm in the dear dead days when
you knew it, than there are today."[1]

Despite such occasional doubts about whether prosperity meant
progress, LeRoy continued to promote the delta's economic development. In 1920 overproduction of cotton caused prices to drop so
sharply that LeRoy predicted the coming winter would be the worst
for the South since Appomattox. He helped establish a cotton pro-
ducer's association in Greenville to deal with the crisis on the local
front and then headed north to Saint Louis, Kansas City, and Chicago
to line up credit for delta planters. The trip also included a stop in
Memphis, where he supported his friend Governor John M. Parker of
Louisiana, who was leading the movement to establish the Staple Cotton Cooperative Association, an organization designed to limit cotton
production throughout the South. LeRoy also supported the movement to lower freight rates on cotton in Mississippi, even though he
was an attorney for the railroads at the time. An outbreak of boll weevils reduced the surplus in 1921, but even after public interest flagged,
LeRoy continued to support the movement for acreage reduction.
Similarly, even in years when the Mississippi flowed quietly within its
banks, he kept a close eye on the local levee boards, the state legislature, and the levee appropriations committees in Congress.[2]

After the turbulent war years, LeRoy enjoyed returning to his quiet
routine of looking after the delta's interests. Most Americans shared
LeRoy's desire to return to the old ways of the prewar era, and ironically, it was this desire that forced him back into public life. Sapped
dry of crusading zeal by the war, Americans lost interest in the great
social and economic reforms of progressivism and turned to a number
of causes and organizations devoted to restoring an idealized prewar
purity. The religious impulses that were directed by the social gospel
into demand for the regulation of corporations and progressive taxa-

tion turned into a sour, cranky Protestant fundamentalism. Moral issues like prohibition and the control of prostitution gained new support; so, too, did immigration restriction policies designed to keep Catholics from southern and eastern Europe out of Protestant America. Such movements operated on a national level, but the major concern of their adherents was often to restore the moral order they believed characterized their communities in the prewar years. Most associated this moral order with Protestantism, but they did not always agree on how it was most directly threatened. Californians worried about Orientals, Chicagoans were frightened by Irish Catholics and southern blacks who came north after the war, and southerners were surprised to find that the blacks who returned to the South after fighting for liberty and equality in Europe now expected some for themselves. Many social movements succeeded on a national level during the twenties by identifying some threat to the old order broad enough to be feared in a wide variety of communities.

One such organization was the Ku Klux Klan, which grew to between three and eight million members during the twenties. Colonel William Joseph Camp, a former Methodist minister, had revived the Klan shortly before the war, hoping to make a fortune selling insurance to his knights. In 1920 he signed a contract with Edward Clark Young and Mrs. Elizabeth Tyler of the Southern Publicity Association which gave Young and Tyler eight dollars of every ten-dollar membership fee. They launched a public relations campaign that emphasized the Klan's devotion to Anglo-Saxon supremacy, fundamentalist morality, and 100 percent Americanism. Catholics became the favorite foe of the Klan because of their ubiquity, but Young and Tyler were careful to keep the structure of the Klan loose and to use recruiters familiar with local conditions, thus leaving plenty of room to accommodate a variety of local concerns. In their first year, Young and Tyler enrolled 100,000 knights in the Invisible Empire. They reinvested part of their profits in new recruiters who traveled from town to town expanding the Empire and collecting new membership fees.[3]

By early 1922 there was already a small klavern in Greenville, though only its members knew of its existence. Late in February rumors spread that Joseph G. Camp, a Klan organizer, was coming to town. When LeRoy heard that Camp had been given permission to speak at the courthouse, he considered trying to have the decision revoked, but he was unable to find out who had made it. This runaround made him suspect that the Klan had already infected Greenville, so he decided to confront Camp publicly and discredit him before his admirers. A few days before Camp's March 1 speech, LeRoy began encouraging all of Greenville's citizens—Protestant, Catholic, and Jewish—to attend, and lined up speakers to help him answer Camp.[4]

Supporters and opponents of the Klan turned out in force for the speeches. Many were armed, and the normally serene county courthouse vibrated with tension. The crowd had packed the courthouse long before the scheduled 7:30 starting time, and by the time the hour arrived, tempers were short. Sensing this, LeRoy opened the meeting by asking that Sheriff L. M. Nicholson be appointed chairman. With order established, Camp began a set speech designed to appeal to a hodgepodge of fears and prejudices. Claiming that the Klan represented 100 percent Americanism, he warned of the threats posed by Catholics, Jews, and blacks. This part of the speech was so ludicrous that LeRoy was merely amused, but when Camp described how Klansmen enforced their moral standards on the community by spying on their neighbors, LeRoy grew angry. When Camp confirmed that there was already a klavern secretly watching Greenville, his anger turned to cold fury.[5]

As soon as Camp finished his speech, the crowd began to chant for "Percy! Percy! Percy!" LeRoy called the Klan "a menace to the prosperity and welfare of my people"—a menace that arose from the effect that the Klan would have on black laborers in the delta. The labor shortage in the South had grown acute during the war as blacks moved north to take jobs in factories, and LeRoy warned that the Klan would aggravate the shortage. He scoffed at Camp's claim that the Klan was the Negro's friend, and told his neighbors, "You can make three parades in the county of Washington of your Ku Klux Klan and never say an unkind word and you can start the grass growing in the streets of Greenville." Reassuring blacks that the Klan meant them no harm, he said, would be like going into a field with a pack of dogs and reassuring the rabbits you were only looking for foxes. "The best thing for this rabbit to do is to start running now." LeRoy also doubted Camp's claim that the Klan would promote law and order. "Can't you see sheriff

Nicholson," he asked, "if he wanted to arrest a negro for robbing a hen roost wiring to Nashville for a posse of klansmen, and going down the road with a gang of white robed men behind him to arrest the negro; you would have to advertise to find the negro after that parade."

LeRoy paid little attention to Camp's attacks on Jews and Catholics, who had been an established part of the community since its founding. Facetiously he confessed, "I have a partner, a Jew, and at times I think he needs straightening out," but for the most part, he said, Greenville's Catholics and Jews "can take care of themselves."

LeRoy's humor vanished when he described the effect that the Klan would have on the community as a whole. Greenville was a river town, an easygoing place where people liked their neighbors and minded their own business. Klansmen sneaking around spying on their neighbors would destroy this sense of community, he warned. "Instead of finding the latchkey on the outside of each door you will probably find the doors are locked and that it is safer to hail from a distance and explain who you are."

LeRoy had turned the tables on Camp by showing that it was the Klan that threatened the values that Greenville held dear. His audience exploded in applause, frightening Camp so badly that he begged a deputy to escort him back to his hotel. Deputy Denny Shanahan, a kindly Irish Catholic, ostentatiously complied, while the meeting adopted resolutions condemning the Klan.[6]

Even though LeRoy had concentrated on the specific danger of the Klan to Greenville, his speech was reprinted and quoted approvingly in newspapers across the country. Scores of letters poured into his office thanking him for standing up to the Klan and praising his courage. Several black leaders, mostly educators and preachers, wrote to thank him and to discuss the black migration to the north, which undermined their position as much as it did the planters'. Of these the most satisfying to LeRoy was probably the letter he received from Greenville's Reverend William Bell, telling him that many of his parishioners had indeed been frightened by the Klan but that their fears had been alleviated by LeRoy's speech.[7]

Members of other groups threatened by the Klan also wrote to praise LeRoy's speech. Leaders of three Mississippi Knights of Columbus chapters thanked LeRoy for defending Catholics even though he had devoted little attention to them, and William J. McGinley, Supreme Secretary of the Knights of Columbus, asked and received permission to reprint thousands of copies of the speech for national distribution. LeRoy also received letters of praise from Jews in Mississippi, Tennessee, Louisiana, and New York, and from Mexican Americans in Texas.[8]

Several white, presumably Protestant, southerners wrote that they, too, considered the Klan a threat to their way of life. Many of these letters praised the Ku Klux Klan of Reconstruction while condemning the Klan of the 1920s. Many shared LeRoy's fear that the Klan would scare away blacks. Others saw the Klan's efforts to enforce their moral standards on the community as a threat to individual liberty and constitutional government. One writer used a standard rhetorical weapon of southerners by calling the Klan "trash," and another compared the Klan with the populism of Tom Watson. Ralph McGee of nearby Leland wrote LeRoy that his speech was the ultimate expression of the Percy family's tradition of service and leadership in Washington County, adding that the speech would "lead the people of this Country out of the dark back into the same peaceful and harmonious community that it has always been." McGee shared LeRoy's love of Washington County's way of life and his fear that the Klan threatened a radical change.[9]

The Klan's arrival in Greenville was as much a product as a harbinger of change. Will Percy would later recall that during the war Greenville had been inundated by "an alien breed of Anglo-Saxon" unsympathetic with the town's "laxity in church matters." Census figures for Washington County show that this change had actually begun before the war. Membership in churches of all kinds rose dramatically before the war, with Baptists making by far the largest gains. They had rolled into Greenville from the hill country looking for a new start, first in rusted, rotting wagons, later in jalopies converted into pickup trucks. Along with their churns and skillets and children they carried a family Bible that they assumed everyone else read with the fear and awe that they did. Amazed at first by Greenville's electric lights, they soon stumbled into the darker shadows of the evening—the riverfront brothels and gambling houses, which LeRoy had insisted be confined to one part of town.[10]

Shocked by the sinfulness of the easygoing river town, some fundamentalist hill farmers looked to the Klan to protect the values they had cherished in the hills—values that had never taken hold in Greenville. LeRoy's speech did not stop the tiny Klan chapter—which, he discovered later, had originated in the local Masonic temple—from spreading to these eager recruits. Shortly after Camp's speech the Leland *Enterprise* carried a letter from the Klan renewing its pledge to clean up the county. Bootleggers and gamblers were warned, "We have our eyes on you, and we are many; we are everywhere, and you will not escape." Adulterers were told to change their ways, and young men who were discovering the romantic possibilities of parked cars were asked, "Had you ever thought that what you do, some other boy is entitled to do with your sister?" Blacks were told, "We are your best friend, but we wish you to do right." A cancerous fear and distrust spread with the Klan through the county, even reaching into the Percy home. For the first time in her life, and over LeRoy's objections, Camille began to draw the blinds at night.[11]

The Klan was creating similar disturbances in other communities. Judge Hiram Garwood of Houston, an old friend of the Percys, wrote describing parades and murders perpetrated by the Texas Klan. Marcellus Foster, president of the Houston *Chronicle*, corroborated Garwood's story and invited LeRoy to address a law and order club that he proposed organizing to fight the Klan. LeRoy declined the invitation, arguing that organizing to oppose the Klan was a serious step that should be taken only by the people who would have to live with the consequences. As an outsider, he did not believe he had the right to influence such a decision. LeRoy also refused to speak at an anti-Klan rally in Alexandria, Louisiana, for the same reason. LeRoy opposed the Klan because he did not want it dictating its values to Greenville; he had no intention of dictating his own values to other communities.[12]

LeRoy was willing to denounce the Klan and warn other communities of the harm it had done in Greenville. He sent copies of his speech to several friends, including C. P. Mooney, editor of the Memphis *Commercial Appeal*, and Ellery Sedgwick, editor of the *Atlantic Monthly*. Sedgwick was so impressed that he asked LeRoy to broaden the speech into an article. LeRoy agreed and with Will's help rewrote the speech for a national audience. The article, "The Modern Ku Klux

Klan," discussed the threat to Negro labor only briefly. In order to convince northerners of the seriousness of the situation, it concentrated on the Klan's destruction of community spirit. "The most malign effect of the organization," LeRoy wrote, "is the destruction of the spirit of helpfulness, cooperation, and love in the community where it intrudes itself. . . . Whatever may be its aspirations, it can breed only suspicion and distrust among the members of a community."[13]

LeRoy's thoughts on community spirit came from his immediate experience. While he wrote the article, the Mississippi River was threatening another overflow. When the waters rose, the people of the delta banded together out of necessity to reinforce the levees against a flood. Leroy considered their success further proof that the delta's social structure and values, particularly its subordination of blacks, needed no protection from the Klan. He wrote Sedgwick that "nothing could be more interesting, so far as racial study goes, than to see five or six thousand free negroes working on a weak point under ten or twelve white men, without the slightest friction and of course without any legal right to call upon them for work, and yet the work is done not out of any feeling of patriotism but out of a traditional obedience to the white man." Concerned over the migration of blacks out of the South, LeRoy underestimated the community spirit of those who remained, but he was right in thinking that the delta did not need the Klan's scare tactics to keep blacks subordinated.[14]

The Mississippi floodwaters cooled Greenville's feverish divisions but could not wash away the stain of the Klan. Unknown members of the community continued to spy on their neighbors, creating suspicion and distrust. Meanwhile, across the river in Louisiana, the Klan was growing bolder. Morehouse Parish contained the same two groups that were at war in Washington County, only there they were separated geographically as well as culturally. The parish seat of Bastrop was, in one historian's words, "a grimy town of about 3,000 people, dominated by the Baptist church and fiercely proud of the pulpmill and carbon plant located nearby." Down the road was the village of Mer Rouge, the more relaxed, genteel home of such planters and aristocrats as the parish could muster.[15]

When the Klan moved into Bastrop, it simply took over the Law and Order League that the leading citizens had established to protect the

town's morality. After breaking into the homes of some alleged bootleggers and driving a dangerous teenage girl out of town, the Klan
threatened to go into Mer Rouge to clean up the moonshiners and
prostitution there. Mer Rouge's citizens dared it to try.

The Klan would not go into Mer Rouge, but on August 24 five men
from the village were ambushed and abducted by a score of armed,
black-robed men while returning home from Bastrop. Later that night
Exalted Cyclops J. K. Skipwith, head of the Bastop Klan, ordered the
telephone operator to disconnect service to Mer Rouge. When she refused, the lines were cut. Three of the abducted men were released.
The other two, Watt Daniels and Thomas Richards, were among those
who had dared the Klan to come into Mer Rouge. Shortly after their
abduction Skipwith announced that they would never return. They
never did.

When the Morehouse Parish Grand Jury tried to whitewash the murders, Governor Parker was outraged. He and Attorney General Adolph
Coco traveled to Washington and persuaded the Justice Department to
enter the case. In December federal agents arrested Jeff Burnett, a Bastrop Klansman, and Dr. B. M. McKoin, head of the Klan's whipping
squad, for kidnapping and murder. The agents presented a strong case,
but the grand jury still refused to indict anyone.[16]

Parker's bold action in the Mer Rouge case earned him a national
reputation equal to LeRoy's as an opponent of the Klan. In February
Parker received an invitation to speak at an anti-Klan rally in Chicago
sponsored by the American Unity League, a predominantly Irish Catholic organization that had been courting LeRoy's support for months.
Chicago had twenty Klan chapters and the largest Klan membership of
any city during the twenties. The American Unity League had successfully opposed the Invisible Empire by publishing the names of its
knights. But LeRoy was reluctant to endorse the league because it was
too conspicuously Catholic. He thought that Protestants should lead
the fight against the Klan in order to avoid lending credence to its
charges of a Catholic conspiracy. He declined an invitation to speak at
the rally, but apparently Parker changed his mind. The day before the
rally the league's newspaper, *Tolerance*, announced in headlines "Ex-
Senator Percy of Mississippi comes to Join Fight on Klan."[17]

The turnout for the All Nation's Rally was disappointingly small, perhaps mercifully so, for the aristocratic Parker and Percy really had very little to say to the urban, working-class Irishmen who were the Klan's major target in Chicago. For Parker, who was a better politician than LeRoy, this was not a problem. He praised the American Unity League, quoted some presidents, endorsed government aid to parochial schools, and entertained the crowd with the details of the Mer Rouge murder case.[18]

Unlike Parker, LeRoy had never had to troll the bayous of south Louisiana for Catholic votes, and his lack of such experience showed in his speech. Ironically proving his own point that the Klan should be fought on a local level, he outlined a strategy that made a great deal of sense in Washington County, but virtually none in Chicago. LeRoy told his audience that because the Klan's appeal was to Protestants, "whether there shall be a Klan does not depend upon what Jew, Catholic, nor negro thinks." Protestantism must lead the fight to destroy the Klan by refusing to "enter as its champion in the lists a simpleton astride a hobby-horse, clothed not in shining armor, but in a sheet, with a mask for a vizer [sic] and armed not with a flaming sword, but with a bucket of tar and feathers." The crowd's reaction to this chivalric imagery was not sufficient to warrant recording; it would have brought down the roof at Greenville's Opera House.[19]

The high point of LeRoy's trip to Chicago was his stopover in Vicksburg to tour the model hog farm. Back in Greenville he found an invitation from Patrick H. O'Donnell, chairman of the American Unity League, to a follow-up conference to be held in April or May. LeRoy declined, arguing that the Klan was too decentralized to be resisted effectively by the kind of national organization O'Donnell had in mind.[20]

On the other hand, LeRoy believed that the need to fight the Klan locally was more acute than ever. During 1922 more blacks left the delta than ever before, a trend that the Klan could only aggravate. LeRoy had hoped that the Mer Rouge murders had revealed the Klan's true character; instead, he now estimated that it had 150 members in Greenville. The town was spared the torchlight parades, whippings, and atrocities that other communities suffered, but nevertheless, LeRoy wrote, "They have already done what I anticipated and predicted they would do—absolutely destroy the feeling of community harmony which had always prevailed in this county more than in any place I have ever known."[21]

To counter the Klan's growing power, LeRoy helped organize the Protestant Organization Opposed to the Ku Klux Klan. The Protestant Organization conformed exactly to LeRoy's strategy for fighting the Klan. It was a local organization, and membership was limited to Protestants to forestall charges that it was a Catholic conspiracy. Unlike the Klan, it disdained secrecy and published a list of its officers and members. On March 21 the Protestant Organization took out a large advertisement in the Greenville *Daily Democrat* to announce its goals and to refute various rumors circulated by the Klan. Future rumors, the ad promised, would also be answered publicly.[22]

The most ominous threat facing LeRoy and the Protestant Organization was the Klan's attempt to take over Washington County's government and law enforcement machinery, as it had done in Morehouse Parish. Political subterfuge was the favorite strategy of the Klan's new leader, Hiram Wesley Evans, a Dallas dentist who described himself as "the most average man in America." Evans hoped to rid the Klan of its violent image even as it retained its power by supporting candidates who would surreptitiously join the secret order or agree to abide by its dictates. The implications of such an arrangement for democratic government were frightening indeed; the potential for violence in a county with a Klansman for a sheriff was even more alarming.[23]

The Washington County Klan played upon already existing political differences by centering their attack on LeRoy. As the leading political figure in the county for twenty years, LeRoy had made several enemies. Hoping to draw these disgruntled and generally disappointed politicians to its cause, the Klan charged that LeRoy was a political boss and was using his influence to force others to oppose the Klan. In a speech at Leland, District Attorney Ray Toombs, the Exalted Cyclops of Washington County's Klan, referred to LeRoy as "the Big Cheese." The Reverend Mr. Walker, a local Baptist preacher who publicly supported the Klan, echoed the charge of bossism from his pulpit. The Klan apparently hoped to shift public attention from its members to LeRoy, and by joining their votes with those of LeRoy's local opponents, take over the county government.[24]

In a letter to the *Daily Democrat* Dr. J. D. Smythe, chairman of the

Protestant Organization, responded to the charge that LeRoy was using the anti-Klan movement to perpetuate his own influence. Smythe,
a former Vardaman supporter, pointed out that he and other members
of the Protestant Organization had differed with LeRoy on other issues
and that many of the men now rumored to be leaders of the Klan, including Ray Toombs, were formerly LeRoy's allies.[25]

Part of the difficulty of fighting the Klan lay in not knowing who the
enemy was. By late April LeRoy had discovered the identity of more
politicians affiliated with the Klan, including the superintendent of education, the chancery clerk, and the circuit clerk. Some of these men
were old friends, but with Greenville's welfare at stake LeRoy set personal considerations aside. On the evening of the April 23, 1,500 people gathered at the People's Theatre to hear LeRoy denounce these
men bitterly. Unsure who in the audience was friend or foe, LeRoy
called out the names of those that he did know were in the Klan and
gave them one final chance. "Can't you come back and take part with
us in the life of the community?" he asked. "Come back," he repeated,
"to your father's house." Granting that many had joined the Klan for
noble purposes, he promised forgiveness to any who would admit that
they had made a mistake. But for those who would not, he warned,
"We are going to clean you up from top to bottom." Angrily LeRoy
described the Klan's increased spying, warning that "a spy in time of
war is shot like a dog." He ridiculed the Klan's absurd assortment of
kleagles, kluds, cyclopses, and other officers, comparing it to a Negro
fraternal order. He flatly declared that no members of the Klan were fit
to hold public office and predicted that if they carried the coming elections, they would kill him and go unpunished. LeRoy also answered
the Klan's charges against him, saying, "If I had been a boss, I would be
proud of the job." He pointed out that the Klan had not accused him of
the corruption the term *boss* normally implied, and he challenged the
audience to name anything he had ever done that had hurt the county.
The audience answered with applause.[26]

LeRoy's speech was also praised by many southerners who read
about it in their newspapers. He had given the Klan just the kind of
publicity it was trying to avoid as it moved into politics. But when J. K.
Skipwith, head of the Bastrop Klan, read the speech, he decided that
LeRoy had given the Klan the ammunition it needed to silence its op-

ponent for good. LeRoy had said that the Klan had become less violent because of the bad publicity it received from Mer Rouge. He sarcastically thanked Skipwith for restraining the Klan, declaring that a monument should be built to him "of white marble and smeared with blood." Hoping to trap LeRoy, Skipwith wrote him a letter in which he quoted the parts of the newspaper account of the speech dealing with himself and the Mer Rouge murders and asked whether this report was correct. But subtlety was not Skipwith's forte, and he tipped his hand by adding that he hoped LeRoy had been misquoted so that he would "not be branded before the public as a wilful malicious character assassin of your fellow man." The Morehouse Parish Grand Jury had cleared Skipwith of the Mer Rouge murders, and his letter was a clumsy attempt to ensnare LeRoy in a libel suit.[27]

LeRoy saw through Skipwith's plan and decided to catch the Cyclops in his own snare. He wrote back admitting that since no one had been convicted in the Mer Rouge murders and since he had not been a witness to them, he could not have charged the Klan with murder as a matter of fact. Rather, he had expressed his own personal conviction that the Klan was behind the murders and that Skipwith, as the head of the Bastrop Klan, was morally responsible. As for Skipwith's insinuation that LeRoy had slandered him, he wrote, "I had no intention of slandering you: I did not know that it could be done." LeRoy had Skipwith's letter and his reply published in the local newspaper, giving the Klan more unwanted publicity and reinforcing its connection with the Mer Rouge murders, while at the same time sidestepping a lawsuit.[28]

A few days later the Klan tried again to trap LeRoy. He received another letter, this time on the stationery of a Louisiana attorney, asking what he would charge to deliver six speeches attacking the Klan. The Klan had been spreading rumors that the Catholic church paid LeRoy for his speeches; the Klan may have believed the charge, since it compensated its own speakers with a cut of the Klectoken. LeRoy was suspicious because the letter was semiliterate. He replied honestly that he had never been paid for speaking against the Klan. Outflanked again, the Klan attacked LeRoy a few days later in their newspaper, the *Tri-State American*. The headline of the article, "Percy's Puny Propaganda Plays Political Pranks Pervertly," probably reinforced LeRoy's doubts about the literacy of Klansmen.[29]

Undaunted by the Klan's attempts to trap him, LeRoy continued to fight back by unmasking its knights. By May 9 he had somehow discovered the names of several more local officials affiliated with the Klan, including a county supervisor who was running for sheriff. LeRoy knew that once the Klan candidates were publicly identified, they could only lose votes, for their supporters already knew who they were.[30]

Unable to silence LeRoy by outwitting him, the Klan reverted to more familiar tactics. One Sunday evening LeRoy was sitting in his parlor listening to the heavy rain outside while he waited for Sheriff Nicholson and some other friends to drop by for a game of bridge. With Camille sick in bed, Will answered the knock at the door, expecting to greet his father's guests. Instead he found a dark, grizzly, heavyset man who asked to speak to LeRoy. Will called him and lingered in an adjoining room, his suspicions aroused. The rain-drenched stranger told LeRoy that his car had broken down and he had been forced to leave his two sisters in it while he walked to town to get help. LeRoy was always an easy mark for anyone with a tale of woe, especially when it involved a damsel in distress, so he offered to go with the man to bring his sisters back to town. Just as they were preparing to leave, LeRoy's guests arrived. Seeing Sheriff Nicholson among them, the stranger slipped out the door and disappeared into the night. Later LeRoy's neighbors confirmed what he had come to suspect; his visitor had not arrived on foot, as he claimed, but in a car driven by another man who remained parked across the street. The stranger was not seen again until two years later, when Will ran across him in jail, charged with several counts of robbery. Recognizing Will, he said tersely, "Old Skip nearly put that one over." LeRoy had almost walked into a trap that would have silenced him for good.[31]

More angered than alarmed, LeRoy turned the Klan's attempt on his life to his own advantage. The next day he wrote Ray Toombs, charging that the Klan had tried to kill him. As he anticipated, Toombs denied the Klan's involvement. LeRoy then had Toombs's denial published along with his letter to Toombs in the *Daily Democrat* and the Memphis *Commercial Appeal*. Once again, the shadow of Mer Rouge fell over the Klan.[32]

Will was no more convinced by Toombs's denial than LeRoy was.

He marched into the Cyclops' office and told him, "If anything happens to my father or to any of our friends you will be killed. We won't hunt for the guilty party. So far as we are concerned the guilty party will be you." Had a gunfight broken out, the Percys would not have stood alone. J. B. Hebron wrote, "When-ever you need me you know where I am." From LeRoy's Panther Burn plantation, manager W. C. Winter wrote, "If I can be of any service to you at anytime, I am ready." Several others also pledged to stand by the Percys in a fight. Will kept them posted and ready in case they were needed. After learning of the attempt on his uncle's life, LeRoy Pratt Percy of Birmingham wrote, correctly, that "if they should kill you nothing could stop the wholesale massacre of the Ku Klux's."[33]

While tension mounted in Greenville and men went about their business armed with pistols, LeRoy concentrated on winning the upcoming elections. He sent letters and pamphlet copies of his speech to supporters across the county and the country, and when the Klan tampered with his mail, he sent more pamphlets. The Klan's attempt on his life had reminded Greenville of Mer Rouge. LeRoy sensed his advantage and pressed it. Candidates were found to oppose incumbent Klansmen, and where more than two candidates were running, LeRoy stressed the overwhelming importance of the Klan issue to avoid splitting the anti-Klan vote. LeRoy believed that if this line could be firmly drawn, the Klan would be defeated.[34]

The first primary proved indecisive. The anti-Klan forces elected a majority on the board of supervisors, but the Klan won three offices. LeRoy blamed these narrow losses on the plethora of candidates and the inevitable confusion over who was for the Klan and who against it. Ray Toombs's personal popularity and competence also helped him win reelection as county attorney. In three weeks there would be a runoff between the Klan's candidate, George Archer, and George Alexander for the all-important sheriff's office. LeRoy looked forward to the runoff as an opportunity to prove decisively that Washington County did not want the Klan; for the Klan, it was a chance to seize control of the county's law enforcement machinery and take the law into its own hands.[35]

The race was close, as everyone knew it would be. Finally the results were announced: Alexander had won; the Klan was defeated. The crowd that gathered outside the polls marched triumphantly to the Percy house, where LeRoy sat playing bridge. He made a short speech and sent out for four kegs of whiskey. There is no record of any of the whiskey being left over. Feeding on the tremendous sense of relief, the party turned into the greatest celebration Greenville had ever seen. All through the night and far into the morning the guests danced and sang and cheered each other's courage. Outside in the night the Kluxers looked on, feeling justified by the heathenish doings inside, yet impotent, for they knew their spying would do them no good now.[36]

The election of Sheriff Alexander marked the beginning of the end for Greenville's Klan. Once it became obvious that the Klan would cost a candidate more votes than it could deliver, politicians began drifting out of the Invisible Empire. Two years later Greenville repudiated the Klan again by electing a Catholic mayor, but by that time most local politicians had already deserted the local klavern.[37]

The impact of LeRoy's victory was not confined to Washington County. He had become a symbol of resistance to men and women in Klan-plagued communities across the country, and the election gave them new hope. Among those who shared LeRoy's triumph was the former President, Chief Justice William Howard Taft, who wrote LeRoy: "I cannot speak too strongly of the comfort and pleasure it gives me to know that our civilization is not to be sacrificed and our institutions are not to be destroyed without every sacrifice made by those who appreciate their value in support of them. I have a feeling that the period of flagrant and vociferous assault upon all that makes life worth living in the family, home, community, state and nation is nearing an end." Taft regretted that LeRoy was no longer in the Senate but added, "The work you are doing at the place where it is to be done is perhaps more important."[38]

Taft's latter point must have pleased LeRoy, for the fact that his greatest accomplishment had taken place almost entirely within Washington County was thoroughly consistent with his philosophy of government and public service. LeRoy believed passionately in democracy; he also believed that democracy worked only when the community recognized and elected its natural leaders. In his bid for the Senate this attitude had made LeRoy appear aristocratic and removed from the people; in Greenville, his friends deferred to his leadership because he had earned their respect. The natural aristocracy that LeRoy envisioned could be tested and selected only through close and prolonged contact with those who were expected to defer. When LeRoy had tried to extend his authority by running for the Senate, he appeared haughty, presumptuous, and ironically, corrupt.

In the Klan fight, LeRoy was on his home ground. Delta folks listened to LeRoy because they thought he was the smartest man in the county. LeRoy told them what they should do, because he thought he was the smartest man in the county and considered it his duty to lead. He blamed the rise of the Klan on the waning of the old southern aristocracy and more particularly on the Protestant clergy's abdication of leadership. He wrote Taft: "No class of American citizenship can escape responsibility for the rise of the Klan, but no class seems to me to have been as recreant to its duty as the protestant ministry. . . . In their hatred of catholicism they have been led into a betrayal of trust of the people who had a right to look to them for guidance."[39] LeRoy's fight against the Klan fit his conception of duty exactly. Advising and leading people who trusted him because of his long record of service to the delta, he had saved them from a threat to their distinctive way of life—a way of life that he had shared with them for sixty-three years.

After the sheriff's race LeRoy took a smaller part in the fight against the Klan. In 1924 he led an anti-Klan delegation from the delta to the state Democratic convention, but he was defeated when the credentials committee refused to seat it. He continued sending out pamphlets of his speeches to all who requested them, and corresponded with Professor John Moffat Mecklin, who was writing a book on the Klan, and Judge Ben Lindsay, the juvenile-court reformer who was fighting the Klan in Denver. For the most part, however, LeRoy left the fight to others, in part because he was growing old and his health was failing, but mostly because he knew that Greenville was safe.[40]

Chapter 7

First page of Chapter XVIII in Will's manuscript of Lanterns on the Levee

Reconstruction

I have done what you have not, passed the time of life when there is a danger of becoming foolish, always a real danger to a book lover until he is in the midst of the battle of life, when the real crowds out the ideal. Whether one becomes "foolish" is only slightly dependent upon the number of books read, more upon the absorption in what is read, it is in the living in and thinking of the books you read rather than taking part in the life you are living . . . while men of duller brain forge to the front by doing not dreaming. The antidote to the disease is in mixing with people and things even though it takes an effort to do so. The real things and people of life are interesting tho not so easy to read: we pass by the comedies and tragedies of life without notice saving our laughter and tears for the characters of fiction, because some writer by clever phrases portrays those, while we must take the trouble to find the others for ourselves. But on this stage of life we are all actors and the angels lookers-on, and we must not only or chiefly read what others do, but do our own parts well.

LeRoy Percy, to My Dear Son

Compassionate and wise in pain,
Most faithful in defeat,
The holy Marys I have watched and loved
Live on our street

Will Percy
"The Holy Women"

The search is what anyone would undertake if he were not sunk in the everydayness of his own life.

Walker Percy
The Moviegoer

Shortly after the war, Will wrote, "I have a need of silence and of stars." He sought silence in the routine of practicing law in Greenville. Gradually he took on the civic duties appropriate to a Percy—raising funds for charities and alumni associations, attending meetings of the bar association, commanding the local American Legion post, and serving as president of the local Rotary. With the thunder of war still echoing through his mind, Will welcomed the relative silence of everyday life.[1]

Will found his stars in poetry. He continued to lead a double life; a lawyer by day, he became a poet when the sun set. Before the war Will had used poetry to escape boredom and frustration and to express ideals that he was unable to incorporate into his everyday life. The war inured Will to the ambiguity of the active life his heritage demanded. War had been horrible, but he knew that he would never again experience the immediacy of life and sense of common suffering that were his in battle. The Treaty of Versailles failed to realize his idealistic expectations, but at least the Germans had been stopped. As he came to expect less of life, the tension between his active and reflective lives slackened. He drew more satisfaction from performing his community and family duties, and he increasingly incorporated the world around him into his poetry. His landscapes gradually became more recognizably southern, his ideas more clearly those of a planter's son.[2]

Will's first two volumes had already established him as one of the South's leading poets. The reviews of *Sappho in Levkas* had been mixed. William Stanley Braithwaite of the Boston *Evening Transcript* had praised its "restrained beauty"; Llewellyn Jones said it showed "restraint as well as beauty, dignity as well as passion." Modernist critics were less kind. *Poetry* magazine objected to the frequent classical allusions and said *Sappho* "represents certain tendencies which the modern poet should avoid with every fibre of his being and every effort of his art." The classical forms and subjects that divided Will's critics had a definite purpose: by setting his poems in distant times and places, he excluded traces of his daily life from his work and maintained its purity as an expression of his youthful passions.[3]

The appearance of *In April Once* shortly after the war brought Will more critical attention. Published just as the imagists and other new experimental schools of poetry were becoming prominent, *In April Once* again divided the critics according to their taste for classical references. The *Nation*'s Mark Van Doren blasted its traditionalism. Llewellyn Jones defended Will from his modernist detractors, arguing that the title poem "expresses in terms of thirteenth-century religion and life the same sort of dilemma in which youth finds itself today." Jones argued that despite the poem's historical setting, its theme of disillusioned idealism was quite appropriate for a generation disillusioned by the Great War, and that this theme made the poem modern.[4]

Will continued to hope that using historical settings would separate his poetry and personal life, and voiced his disapproval when critics mixed the two. He objected to C. P. Mooney's favorable review in the Memphis *Commercial Appeal*, because like many other newspaper reviews, it described him as a soldier-poet and praised his war record rather than analyzing the poems. He was even more exasperated by Stirling Bowen's review in the Detroit *News*, which commended Will's maturing sensuality. "To be described as sensual is the last straw," Will lamented. He wanted his poetry judged on its beauty and content, and regarded any but the most perfunctory personal references as irrelevant obfuscations.[5]

Will put his historical setting to a new use in *In April Once*. By describing the disillusionment of thirteenth-century idealists, he denied that the disillusionment of his generation was unique and restored continuity between the past and present. This continuity suggested that the tragedies, the comedies, and the nobility that Will found in classical literature might also be found in the world around him, and thus he opened a door between his life and poetry.

Will's use of classical and historical imagery, his adherence to established forms, and his belief that poetry should be judged on its merits rather than as the product of a particular life placed him in the humanist movement, which emerged during the twenties as the major opponent of modernist, experimental movements. Stuart Pratt Sherman, one of the leading humanist critics, recognized a kindred spirit in the author of *In April Once* and wrote a mutual friend that Will "has an authentic poetic gusto; and I hope Mr. Percy will not devote himself too assiduously to the law." Sherman brushed aside objections to Will's use of classical imagery, arguing that there was nothing wrong with this, provided the poet realizes that "the gods of Greece have steel sinews beneath their silken surfaces" and emulates their discipline. Will received a copy of Sherman's letter and was delighted "because he is one of the critics in the country from whom praise is really worth while."[6]

Sherman's praise and Will's appreciation of it indicate the direction

Will's poetry took after the war. Many American poets came out of the Great War disillusioned and searching for values. Although there were innumerable variations, most took one of two broad courses. The imagists and other experimental schools sought new forms of expression capable of bearing new values and restoring man's ability to communicate meaningfully with his fellow man. The humanists and other conservatives objected to this rejection of the past. They attempted to fit contemporary experience into traditional forms and language in order to fill the spiritual void of the twenties with the values of the past. Like Sherman, Will chose the latter path. He expressed his conservative philosophy himself in a letter to another critic. "If only our poor old world would hang on to the eternal verities which we have been building up in the last few hundred years, I believe there is a chance for a great literary and artistic revival."[7]

Despite the assumptions that he shared with Sherman, Will was not a doctrinaire follower of any school of poetry. "In art," he wrote, "there can be no real leader but the fight is always a solitary one." Will granted that "it is worthwhile trying the newer forms and the various individuals experimenting in them are doing valiant and valuable pioneer work." But he judged most such experiments unsuccessful. "Their results, I must confess, leave me cold, seeming as far as I am concerned, to fail in the sense of perfection which is surely a necessary attribute of any great work of art."[8]

Will experimented with the newer forms in a series of poems called "Greenville Trees," written in 1920. Four of the five poems in the series were traditional in form, but one, "The China-berries," used the free-verse technique popular among the modernists. Will also borrowed another technique used in "Greenville Trees" from the modernists. In four of the poems a tree indigenous to Greenville is described first in a historical setting and then in its contemporary surroundings. Lombardy poplars see King Richard and his knights leaving on a Crusade, then Greenville boys marching off to the Great War. The chinaberries grace an Oriental garden and then supply young Greenville boys with small, hard berries that they load into their pop-guns and fire at sparrows and "ancient negroes." This technique is similar to that used by the imagists, who attempted to produce new metaphors by combining seemingly disparate images. Will's contrasts were not as abrupt as the imagists', and his aim was conservative. By setting the apparently different past and present next to each other, he hoped to suggest that the values of the past held meaning for the present.[9]

"Greenville Trees" also demonstrates Will's increasingly conscious effort to incorporate his southern surroundings into his poetry. Will did not want to be a peculiarly southern poet; his primary concern remained the representation of universal themes in a beautiful form. If, in the process, he could find and portray the beauty of the South, that was all the better. When a correspondent praised another of his southern poems, "In the Delta," Will replied: "There is so much unexploited, unappreciated beauty down here, as there is everywhere I suppose, that people miss just because they have not been told about it. If I can do anything toward making our own people appreciate our own best qualities, what I have written is worthwhile."[10] Will's increasing use of southern landscapes invigorated his work with a directness sometimes missing in his earlier works set in distant times and places.

Will was not entirely comfortable with some of the compliments he received from his fellow southerners. When the poet DuBose Heyward called him the "dean" of southern poetry, Will confessed that "it makes me feel rather bald-headed and whiskery." Nevertheless, he took more than the usual satisfaction from Heyward's compliment and the praise of other fellow southerners. He was also frankly surprised by their appreciation. As a young man he had identified poetry with Harvard and other intellectual centers in the North; now he was discovering that as long as he demanded no significant revenue from his art, there was nothing in the South to prevent him from being a poet, perhaps even a poet with an audience.[11]

Will knew that the increasing interest in his work was part of a general awakening of interest in poetry taking place across the South. He was encouraged by the success of several southern literary magazines such as the *Double Dealer* in New Orleans, the *Lyric* in Norfolk, Virginia, and the *Review* in Richmond, and by the emergence of promising young southern writers like Heyward, Stark Young, and Allen Tate. Will encouraged these young writers by praising them and, more important, by publishing poems in their magazines, thus lending them his established name.[12]

The most remarkable of the new southern poetry magazines to receive Will's help was the *Fugitive*. The group that published it included many young writers, among them John Crowe Ransom, Donald Davidson, Allen Tate, and Robert Penn Warren, who would go on to illustrious literary careers. Will had no way of knowing that these young men would soon help turn the awakening of literary interest he had noticed in the South into a full-scale renaissance; he was not even particularly fond of much of their work, which was often experimental. Will cared only that they were fellow southerners and fellow poets. When the fugitives decided to open their December, 1922, issue to poets outside their group, Will was among the first to receive a request for a contribution. He responded with the only finished poem he had on hand at the time, "Safe Secrets." Will also sent along his encouragement, writing Tate that the fugitives, the *Double Dealer*, the *Lyric*, and the Poetry Society of South Carolina "have about succeeded in putting the South on the map, as far as poetry is concerned." Tate was pleased with the poem and the encouragement, and John Crowe Ransom called "Safe Secrets" the "great poem of the number." Will published another poem, "Hymn to the Sun," in the August-September issue, and served as a judge in a poetry contest sponsored by the magazine. He confessed to Tate that he did not like all of the poetry in the *Fugitive* but told him, "You are pioneering and that is worthwhile."[13]

Will hoped that the artistic spirit of the fugitives would spread through the South, but he realized that there were still many obstacles to be overcome. He wrote J. R. Moreland, editor of the *Lyric*, "So far our people have been so occupied with making a living, obtaining a decent local government and fighting for justice to the negro, that no leisure was left for more beautiful and lasting things." And he wrote another friend, "If we could get rid of the boll weevil and Ku Klux and pressing poverty and religious bigotry and a few other things, we would be in a fair way to make things hum artistically down here." Will hoped that the South was nearing a point where southerners could devote more of their time to art, and less to the problems of daily existence.[14]

Will's belief that the South must solve its social and economic problems before it could expect a literary renaissance reflected the conflict he felt between his lives as a Percy and a poet. Projecting this conflict onto his society also helped Will overcome it, by changing the conflict into a progressive, evolutionary succession. Colonel Percy and LeRoy had devoted their lives to improving the delta's economy because economic problems were the delta's most pressing concern. Social problems persisted, particularly in the area of race relations, but Will hoped that the delta's increasing prosperity would create more leisure for literature and art. By viewing artistic achievement as the next evolutionary step after economic prosperity, Will could see his own interest in poetry as an evolutionary change in his family's tradition of leadership, which paralleled the developing needs of the delta.

Will's hope that poets and other artists would be the leaders of the developing South prompted him to write two poems that dealt explicitly with contemporary matters. In "Mencken," which Will submitted to the *Double Dealer* though it was never published, he blasted H. L. Mencken for dismissing the values of the past precipitately. "In Black and White," which appeared in the *Double Dealer*, expressed Will's reaction to the growing laxness in sexual mores that the South and the entire nation experienced during the 1920s. The poem is about a young woman who cheats on her husband. She escapes the social opprobrium formerly attached to adultery but pays the price for her unfaithfulness when she discovers that her lover's glib show of affection means no more to him than her marriage vows have meant to her. Will's message is plain: the moral values of the past are more than arbitrary rules, and whether society continues to uphold them or not, violating such rules carries with it a punishment of its own. Both of these poems took a predictably conservative stance. What was surprising about them was that they dealt with contemporary issues so explicitly.[15]

Will's use of sexual promiscuity to represent the rejection of the values of the past suggests that he was still bedeviled by his distinction between spiritual love and physical lust. Thirty-six years old, charming, handsome, youthful in appearance in spite of prematurely greying hair, Will remained one of Greenville's most eligible bachelors. He led an active social life, but none of the women he met satisfied his apparently mutually contradictory standards. Maturity did not solve his dilemma, but it did bring a certain reconciliation to his fate, which Will described in his poem "A letter from John Keats to Fanny Brawne." Will wrote Ellery Sedgwick, editor of the *Atlantic Monthly*, that "it was not only a study of Keats, but also a study of the influence of love or passion on any artist, for that matter on any real man." The poem takes the form of a letter from the dying Keats to his lover, Fanny. Keats thanks Fanny for her love, even though it has turned to ashes. Keats blames himself for his dissatisfaction.

> At last I dare to recognize the cause
> Of why I found love like a bloody sweat;
> You could not love me but in your own way,
> And that—that was a way that was not mine.

Nevertheless, Keats acknowledges his great debt to Fanny:

> out of this
> Impossible, precipitous, starved love
> Came all that I may claim of worth and beauty.

By turning Keats's "starved love" into the inspiration for his poetry, Will found a reason for affirming it. Will also discussed the relationship between love and art in his letter to Sedgwick. "The situation is fundamental and eternal. Much of our greatest art is directly traceable to the sex instinct and all of it is influenced by that instinct. I possibly care as little as you for the present vogue of sex filth, but I do very deeply believe in facing the facts, and I know of no love in which the overtones of beauty and nobility are not discernible." Will's acceptance of an imperfect, unfulfilled love, like his acquiescence in everydayness, was accomplished by recognizing the dependence of the ideal world of poetry on its inevitably imperfect models—the beauty and nobility found in everyday life.[16]

Will was more comfortable with his life in Greenville after the war, in part because of the security and sense of being accepted he experienced there. He had returned to Greenville a hero, and his election to offices in the American Legion, the Rotary Club, and other community organizations confirmed his status and sense of belonging. The praise his poetry received from fellow southerners reinforced his feeling that the community had accepted him for what he was. But Will's increasing involvement with the community also made him more vulnerable to its tensions and the hostility of his neighbors.

Because of his growing attachment to Greenville, the arrival of the Klan had an unsettling effect on Will. His always frail health deteriorated; he began having trouble with his heart, and he was unsure whether his bad temper was caused by his physical ailments or the stress and irritation of suspecting that he was being spied upon. The pistol that he carried with him when he left the house mocked his sense of being among friends. He recalled later that the Klan fight had been more disillusioning and bitter than the war and that it was then that he learned what it was like to hate and be hated. His hate was compounded by his disappointment. He had hoped that the South would look to its poets for leadership; now it appeared that at least a part of it preferred kleagles and kluds. What LeRoy considered the Klan's stupidity Will saw as anti-intellectualism; and Will's lingering affection for Catholicism may also have made him worry more about the Klan's religious bigotry than LeRoy did. Because of these vulnerabilities and because his attachment to the delta was not as firmly and deeply rooted as his father's, Will felt keenly the loss of community spirit that LeRoy had predicted the Klan would bring to Greenville.[17]

Will's attachment to the South was dealt another blow two months after the Klan announced its presence in Greenville. In May, Will was elected to the board of trustees at Sewanee. Since his days as a student there, Will had regarded the mountain campus as a sanctuary for artists and intellectuals. He visited friends there frequently, had taught classes in English on two occasions, and raised funds for the alumni association. His election acknowledged his contributions to Sewanee, but the day after he was elected, the board passed a resolution requiring that all of its members belong to the Episcopal church. Will had "a very tender feeling for the Episcopal church and a very great sympathy for the difficult role it is now called upon to play in a world where idealism and intellectualism are held in low esteem," but he was not a member and had no desire to become one. The board's resolution was understandable in view of the church's role in supporting the university, but coming as it did on the heels of the Klan's arrival in Greenville, Will took it as yet another instance of religious intolerance. The fact that it came from what Will considered a refuge for free thinkers made it even more painful. He resigned from the board, calling the resolution foolish and predicting that it would alienate many alumni.[18]

The Klan's arrival in Greenville and the Sewanee board's resolution challenged Will's hope that the South would evolve into a culture led by poets and other artists. His doubts affected the direction of his poetic interests, which turned inward again, away from the world around him. Shortly after the Klan arrived, Will decided to edit a volume of Arthur O'Shaughnessy's work. The obscure English poet's equally obscure yet haunting lyrics had first won Will's allegiance when he was a student at Sewanee, and the legitimate scholarly need for a volume of his best poems offered Will a chance to return to the more purely aesthetic concerns of his student days. He asked his publishers at the Yale Press if they would publish such a volume, and they agreed to do so if Will would write an introduction. Their acceptance arrived a few days after the Sewanee board's resolution passed. Will threw himself into the work and had the volume ready in three months.[19]

Will's introduction explained his interest in O'Shaughnessy's poetry. O'Shaughnessy was, Will proclaimed, "a poet who had no range, no profundity or originality of thought, no interest, so far as his art reveals, in everyday life, or simple joys and sorrows, or heroic deeds, no ability to construct or invent a tale because facts in themselves meant nothing to him." Despite his lack of interest in the world around him, O'Shaughnessy was "authentically of the sacred band, blessed with the divine gusto." Will endorsed O'Shaughnessy's lack of interest in the world by paying no attention to the details of his subject's life. He wrote the introduction before reading O'Shaughnessy's biography, and at the suggestion of the editor he grudgingly added a single paragraph sketching his life. To the sketch he defiantly added, "If further I am pressed to explain what were those inward facts of his life that so evidently colored his art, I shall have to answer I do not know. But if I did, let me add, I should not tell." Indeed, Will's introduction reveals more about his own life and approach to poetry than about O'Shaughnessy's. After rereading O'Shaughnessy's poems Will speculated that "All that is wistful and baleful and hopeless in love he seems to have experienced. Perhaps the Freudians would say he suffered from an unsatisfied sex complex. My care, however, is to give thanks for hearing his rapturous outcry, no matter what the pain or the delight from which it sprang." Will recognized in O'Shaughnessy a kindred soul who had shared his romantic disappointments. His refusal to delve into O'Shaughnessy's biography was an attempt to prevent the flow of aesthetic value from the spiritual to the physical from backing up, reversing direction, and devaluing the poetry by making it a mere by-product of unsatisfied lust.[20]

After completing the O'Shaughnessy volume Will escaped Greenville's intense summer heat by going to Europe. He wandered around France and Italy for a couple of weeks, then settled down for the rest of the summer on the island of Capri. Capri was something of an artists' colony; writers from all over Europe and America came for the summer or longer to concentrate on their work and enjoy the cool Mediterranean breeze. Everyone knew each other and left each other alone. Will soon began to feel like a regular citizen of the town. Like many of the expatriate Americans who went to Europe during the twenties, he was better able to write about his home from a distance. He settled down to work on a long poem that he had sketched while touring France. The poem, "Enzio's Kingdom," was also set at a considerable distance from Greenville, in thirteenth-century Italy, in the court of Emperor Frederick II. The two major related themes of the poem, however, deal with Will's effort to fit himself into the world: the failure of Wilsonian idealism during the war, and the failure of his father's aristocratic leadership to produce a society that would accept the leadership of planter-poets.[21]

The parallel between Frederick II's attempt to unify the world under an enlightened, peaceful administration and Wilson's attempt to do the same thing with the League of Nations is so obvious that there is a danger of reading too much into it. Will's publisher noticed the parallel immediately and suggested that he dedicate "Enzio's Kingdom" to Wilson. Will declined, explaining, "I, of course, had the failure of the League in mind when I was writing the poem. But I am not an unqualified admirer of Mr. Wilson and do not feel strongly inclined to dedicate the poem to him." Will had read extensively of the Emperor's life, and could have pointed to several historical similarities between Frederick II and Wilson. Both men, for example, were stricken ill during their crucial battles. Will, however, said of Frederick II that "his mind was steady to the end." He considered Frederick a greater man than Wilson, and he had no desire to make a hero out of the latter. His concern was to describe "some of the dissolutions of war," but even this phrase is deceptive, for Will was more concerned with dissolution than with the evil of war itself. There are bloody battle scenes in "Enzio's Kingdom," but they are romanticized, heroic, more in the style of literature before the Great War than after. War was a symbol of dissolution, not a cause.[22]

Furthermore, the dissolving values in the poem are not those of Wilsonian idealism. Rather, they are the aristocratic values of the Percys. Will's Frederick II is more like LeRoy Percy than Woodrow Wilson. The poem is narrated by Frederick's son Enzio, allowing Will to accentuate the Emperor's fatherly traits. Will reiterated the father-son relationship by introducing into the poem the ancient myth of Helios and his son Phaethon, who perished trying to drive his father's chariot, the sun, across the sky. In the myth and in the main story line, the son is decidedly inferior to the father. Enzio is not the leader and warrior that his father was, and the poem ends with him a prisoner of the papacy. Enzio's imprisonment and Phaethon's demise suggest a dimming of Will's hope that he might after all prove fit to succeed his father as a leader.

Will's hopes of assuming his father's role had grown from the encouraging evidence of an artistic revival in the South. He hoped that the social and economic progress brought about by men like his father would be accompanied by cultural progress and that southerners would become more tolerant and appreciative of art and the world of ideas. If this happened, then Will's poetic temperament would no longer appear to be an aberration in the family pattern, but would become an evolution in that pattern mirroring the evolution of southern culture.

Enzio also hopes for a kingdom where poets would be honored, for like Will, he is less a man of the world than his father. Frederick II shares his son's dream. At the height of his powers he describes the kind of society he hopes to build.

> Protect the masses in their breeding moil;
> Feed them; and sweeten them by fear's remove;
> But do not build for them, for they are doomed to everyday
>   contents
> and grievances—
> Unspeculative, level, themselves their study.
> But, oh, the flashing eyed minority,
> The Enzios of the world, the sons of light—
> These I would turn free-pinioned on an earth
> That they would make august and radiant!

This dream of a kingdom ruled by poets and philosophers eventually proves to be Frederick's undoing. His followers are stirred by his brave

pledges to conquer all who oppose him, but they lose their nerve when
Frederick's desire for intellectual freedom leads him to oppose the
Catholic church, which serves throughout the poem as a symbol of
opposition to free thought. Will's description of Frederick's demise
neatly parallels his interpretation of LeRoy's defeat by Vardaman,
which he attributed to the resentment of the masses when confronted
by a candidate who openly violated their superstitions by drinking,
playing cards, and hunting on Sunday. Will's choice of the Catholic
church as a symbol of opposition to intellectual freedom was dictated
by the poem's historical setting. He meant to attack religious dogma of
any kind, whether it be the theological doctrines that he lost faith in at
Sewanee or the decision of the Sewanee board to limit its membership
to Episcopalians.

Frederick is finally defeated, and Enzio is taken prisoner by the
papacy. Enzio remembers the days when his father's dream seemed
possible.

> He called me the Aldebaran, the prince
> Of stars, and was as proud as I, but not
> As far as very far, from doubting tears.

Frederick, this passage suggests, had always been skeptical of his
chances of success, and Enzio is now embarrassed by his own belief in
such a dream.

In the epilogue, Enzio locates whatever remains of hope beyond the
world of the "evanescent actual," and in the realm of "the never-heard,
the never seen, / The just beyond my hands." Even beauty and wisdom were no longer enough to "make credible this hard decree of living." Life now appeared too worthless for even poetry to justify. Despairing of making life worthwhile, he places hope beyond it.

> Oh, I have heard a golden trumpet blowing
> Under the night. Another warmth than blood
> Has coursed, though briefly, through my intricate veins.
> Some sky is in my breast where swings a hawk
> Intemperate for immortalities
> And unpersuaded by the show of death.
> I am content with that I cannot prove.

Will ended "Enzio's Kingdom" with a renunciation of his hopes for
this life, but he did not renounce the values that he had hoped would

make life worthwhile. Frederick, like LeRoy, remained a hero to Will despite his defeat. Will continued to live by the standards he identified with his family, raising funds for charities and schools, encouraging young poets, representing aggrieved blacks and feeding indigent ones, and filling his father's role as the delta's advocate. The difference between Will and LeRoy was that Will lacked his father's faith that adhering to the values they shared would lead to a better society. LeRoy saw progress in the increasing population and cotton production of the delta, while Will searched in vain for a corresponding improvement in the nature and character of mankind.

In this sense "Enzio's Kingdom" was a response to the breakdown of progressivism during the twenties. Will was familiar with one of the most influential challenges to progressivism that appeared after the war, *The Education of Henry Adams*. His cousin Janet Longcope had visited Adams frequently during the winter before his death in 1918, and finding "the taste of ashes in his philosophy" appealing, she introduced Will to his work. Will apparently found Adams appealing, too, for the cyclical view of history in "Enzio's Kingdom" is similar to Adams', as are Will's aristocratic doubts about democracy.[23]

Will's sympathy for Adams' views is not surprising, for both men faced a similar predicament. The Adams family was far more illustrious than the Percys, but they shared a tradition of public service and leadership, and both faced the problem of maintaining that tradition in a democratic system that ignored familial ties in choosing leaders. James Truslow Adams described Henry Adams' predicament in words that apply equally to Will's. "The members of each generation would have to stand or fall by their own abilities and, quite as much, by the particular relation that those abilities and qualities might bear at any given moment to the national life, temper, ideals and aims about them." This was why it was so important to Will that the South develop a respect for the arts, for only then would he be in a position to live up to his family heritage. Like Henry Adams, however, Will found that his family had evolved in a different direction from the society around it. Again, James Truslow Adams described in words applicable to Will why this disjointed evolution led Henry Adams inevitably to despair. "Having always had their hands on the lever of power, success, however distinguished in science, the arts or other careers, could scarcely fail to spell comparative failure."[24]

Success in the arts was better than no success at all. Encouraged by LeRoy's promptings, his publisher's praise, and perhaps by the stunning success of Adams' autobiography, Will tested his stature as a poet by submitting the manuscript of *Enzio's Kingdom and Other Poems* to a commercial press, Charles Scribner's Sons. When it was rejected, he seemed relieved and immediately sent the manuscript to the Yale Press. Will explained to Yale's editor, Wilson Follett, that LeRoy thought a commercial press would do a better job of advertising his books, but he added, "On the whole I do very little worrying about publicity." Follett, who shared LeRoy's desire to increase Will's audience, passed along Vachel Lindsay's suggestion that Will add a preface explaining the relevance of *Enzio's Kingdom* to the failure of the Treaty of Versailles, but Will decided against doing so, explaining, "After all, my interest is almost exclusively in doing the best work I am capable of. Whether people read it or not does not seem exactly my business."[25]

Will's indifference to public acclaim proved fortunate, for *Enzio's Kingdom* won little favor with the critics. Even those critics who detected sincere inspiration in the poem argued that it was not properly finished and its form and selection of words showed carelessness. Will probably paid less attention to the aesthetic considerations so evident in his earlier, simpler poems, because he was preoccupied with describing a set of values disintegrating in the face of history. He was best inspired by silence and stars; "Enzio's Kingdom" was his most ambitious attempt to describe his world view in a poem, and its beauty suffered from his didactic intentions. Furthermore, the similarities between Frederick II and Woodrow Wilson obscured his message, leading readers to believe they were reading a poem about the Great War, when in reality Will's theme was more personal. The ideas in "Enzio's Kingdom" would have been more clearly understood had Will expressed them in some form other than a poem.[26]

One indication that a poem was not the best form was that Will had to rewrite "Enzio's Kingdom" several times. Normally he wrote quickly when inspired, and his first drafts needed little polishing. One other poem that appeared in *Enzio's Kingdom* also required a great deal of reworking, and its theme is similar to the longer poem's. In "Holy Women" Will compared the selfless suffering of Mary with that of women he knew, and concluded:

Compassionate and wise in pain,
Most faithful in defeat,
The holy Marys I have watched and loved
Live on our street

"The Holy Women," in much simpler form than "Enzio's Kingdom,"
conveys the idea that nobility, though doomed to pain and defeat, oc-
curs throughout history. No longer hoping that society would progress
to a level capable of honoring such nobility, Will tried in both poems
to let those who suffered nobly share the timeless consolation he
found in poetry. Placing the people and values and causes he admired
in poems became a way of separating them from time so that they
could be properly appreciated in spite of their ephemeral nature.[27]

Will persisted in his search for nobility in the world around him, because given his view of the situation, there was little else to be done.
The Klan's appearance in Greenville had convinced him that the community and the South were not ready to accept poets as leaders. He
was a historical dead end who had failed to evolve in step with his
times. His task, therefore, became to remove his family's values from
the stream of time and place them in a setting where they could be
esteemed in themselves. Lost and out of place in his own time, Will
became a chronicler of a lost cause.

Chapter 8

Percy home during the 1927 flood

The Last Flood

*It was here that I first saw the light of day, here that I found the
great love of my life, here my little children were begotten. All
that I have of worldly goods is here invested. In this soil rest the
bones of my fathers, and when I have ceased to labor I ask but
this, that it may be said: "He rests among his friends."*
                                                    LeRoy Percy, on the delta

*So during every high-water scare Delta citizens walk the levee
all night with pistol and lantern. . . . Each guard walks alone,
and the tiny halo of his lantern makes our fearful hearts stouter.*
                                                    Will Percy
                                                    Lanterns on the Levee

LeRoy Percy's idea of leadership required that he assert himself publicly only in times of crisis. Most of government, he believed, was a
matter of dealing quietly and efficiently with practical concerns like
building roads and levees and bringing labor to the delta. LeRoy stepped
into the limelight only when Greenville was threatened, be it by Var-
damanism, floods, or most recently, the Klan. Once the Klan was defeated, he slipped back behind the scenes.

LeRoy had originally opposed the Klan because he predicted that it
would aggravate the labor shortage in the delta by frightening blacks
away. His prediction proved correct; blacks left the delta in large numbers during the early twenties. LeRoy realized that the Klan had only
aggravated a long-term trend and that as long as northern industries
offered blacks relatively high wages, they would continue to migrate
North. Accordingly, he continued his two-point strategy of dealing
with the labor shortage. To slow the migration of blacks he cooperated
with the efforts of fellow planters like L. C. Hayes of Hollendale and
W. W. Stone of Greenville to provide their tenants with decent food
and housing, educational opportunities, and entertainments, and to insure that tenants received an honest annual settlement of their ac-

counts. LeRoy hoped that this would buy enough time to bring in settlers to replace the departing blacks. Despite his frustrating experience with Sunnyside Plantation, LeRoy continued to hope that America's immigration laws could be reformed and that European immigrants might fill the void left by departing blacks. In a letter to the Memphis *Commercial Appeal*, he attacked restrictive immigration laws and the labor unions that supported them. He also denied the claim made by the Klan and other nativist groups that immigrants were a threat to social order, arguing that "no more lawless people come to our shores than the native born American citizens." The Klan's lawlessness proved LeRoy's point, but the widespread nativism that fed the Klan and similar groups made any loosening of America's immigration laws unlikely. The Johnson-Reed Act of 1924 made immigration even more difficult, again closing the door on LeRoy's hopes of peopling the delta with European farmers.[1]

In LeRoy's mind only levees were more important to the delta than labor, and as the Klan menace faded, his attention returned to this perennial concern. The members of the local levee board were appointed by the governor and were therefore immune to LeRoy's influence on local elections. LeRoy continued trying to return the levee boards to local control, but he knew that no governor was likely to surrender such a valuable source of patronage. He concentrated on keeping the board honest by backing legislation that would open all levee board sessions to the public. He also influenced levee policy through the army engineers who supervised federal projects on the Mississippi River. They respected LeRoy's understanding of their technical engineering problems and valued his ability to explain their needs to politicians, while politicians like the delta's new congressman, W. M. Whittington, valued LeRoy's advice because they knew that it was technically sound.[2]

Another perennial concern of the delta, the cotton market, also continued to occupy LeRoy. He made good crops at Trail Lake and at Panther Burn Plantation, in which he had recently become a partner; and like most successful planters he kept up with the latest innovations, such as the use of crop dusting airplanes to control weevils and hoppers. The problem facing the delta was not supply, however, but lack of demand caused by overproduction. In 1926 Panther Burn yielded a bale an acre, and the entire delta made its best crop ever, but the price the cotton brought barely covered the expense of producing it. LeRoy believed that the only solution was to force an acreage reduction on southern planters. He did not think that the government could constitutionally enforce such a reduction, and he opposed the McNary-Haugen farm bill, the forerunner of the New Deal's price stabilization programs. Instead he urged bankers who dealt with planters to force them to limit their production by threatening to cut off their credit. He also supported state legislation that would allow Mississippians to enter the cotton futures market, which he saw as the most reliable method of stabilizing cotton prices without government intervention.[3]

LeRoy's concern for the delta shaped even his participation in organizations with a national or international scope. He became a trustee of the Carnegie Foundation for the Promotion of Peace but treated the office more as an honor than a vocation. On the other hand, his position as a director on the regional Federal Reserve Board at Saint Louis gave him an opportunity to represent the credit needs of planters, and he served three active terms on the board. The same local focus characterized LeRoy's professional activities. He declined an appointment to the American Bar Association's Committee on International Law, but took an active interest in legal practices closer to home. He spoke out for chancery-practice reform in Mississippi and, later, against a bill that would have placed judges from other parts of the state on the delta's benches. Explaining to Judge C. C. Moody his opposition to the bill, LeRoy wrote, "We are entirely a separate people in the delta from the people in the hills." LeRoy never forgot which part of Mississippi he came from.[4]

With no crisis threatening the delta, LeRoy was able to spend more time traveling with Camille. He knew they were growing old, and though he remained active, his own health was failing almost as rapidly as his wife's. Their last years, he decided, should be spent enjoying the world and each other. In 1924 they cruised the Mediterranean, with a side trip along the Nile. They spent the next summer in the South Seas, and the following spring leisurely toured Italy and the Riviera. LeRoy loved Camille as deeply as always, and even canceled hunting trips to spend more time with her. When Camille returned from Italy with Venetian linen bearing a 90-percent duty, he grumbled that "her disregard of the value of figures is something which is a constant source of surprise," but he paid the duty so that she could have the "real Venetian stuff" and "laud [sic] it over the inferior women who have been content with domestic purchases." Camille also bought a pantry table in Europe but upon its arrival decided it was too nice for such a utilitarian purpose. LeRoy wrote a friend that he expected Camille would want to build a new room to put the table in, but he was resolved to oppose this because of low cotton prices. Since the room was never built, we may assume Camille never asked.[5]

Will also took advantage of the quiet times to travel, arranging his vacations around LeRoy's so that one of them was usually in Greenville to look after their law firm and planting interests. As often as possible Will visited New York, where he called on other writers, including William Faulkner and Sherwood Anderson, and old friends like his cousin Janet Longcope and Huger Jervey, a Columbia professor. Summers he spent at Sewanee, where he and Jervey bought a summer home. Once he resigned from the school's officialdom, he found plenty of tolerance for his religious differences. He described Sewanee as "a prime abode for lost souls and nobody pays much attention to anybody else, fighting out their own particular problems. The top of the mountain is littered up with various religious organizations, nuns, monks, and things, mostly of the Episcopal persuasion, but there is plenty of room for anchorites." Will was content now to avoid the "top of the mountain" and spend his time at Sewanee quietly entertaining friends and writing poetry. He expressed his contentment with private life in a short poem. "Some, a few, must be mere incense burning / On a lonely mountain to the unknown god."[6]

Will had finally accepted his irrelevance to the times and his inability to lead in the way his father had, and he turned Sewanee into a symbol of his reconciliation with irrelevance. In an article in the *Sewanee Review*, Will described the campus as an "Arcadia" peopled by happy, charming young gentlemen who were quite out of place in the modern world. The education they received, Will wrote, was designed not to make them successful in their careers, but to improve their inner lives. This embracing of the irrelevance of the liberal arts curriculum was quite common among conservative intellectuals in the twenties; the humanist movement of Stuart Sherman and Irving Babbitt was closely identified with the universities, and Albert Jay Nock made the same connection between irrelevant education and inner worth in his *Memoirs of a Superfluous Man*. For many of these conservatives, withdrawal from the seats of power was a positive act based on the premise that the inner life was more important than the sound and fury of public events. Temperamentally Will sympathized with this view, but his family's tradition of public leadership imposed a sense of responsibility on him, so that even after he had given up living up to it, his guilt prevented him from embracing his superfluousness with the same joy and enthusiasm as Nock.[7]

Many conservative intellectuals shared Will's sense of irrelevance to his times. In a review of *Enzio's Kingdom* fellow Mississippian William Faulkner lamented that Will had been born in the wrong age, "like alas! how many of us—." Estranged from his own time, Will explored the past for some age in which he might have felt comfortable, and this accounts in part for the historical settings he gave his poems. Like the conservative literary critic Joseph Wood Krutch, Will was particularly attracted to the Roman Emperor Marcus Aurelius, who ruled at a time when barbarian hordes threatened to overrun the civilized world. Will, too, thought that his civilization, the civilization carved out of the delta's swamps by his family and other planters, was threatened by barbarians like Vardaman and the Klan. He admired the stoic philosophy of endurance and adherence to public duties in the face of overwhelming odds that Marcus Aurelius developed. Many of the poems that Will wrote after *Enzio's Kingdom* stress this theme of endurance in the face of suffering that holds no promise of abatement. In "At Sea" Will wrote, "Endure, my heart, endure: that is the ultimate courage"; and in "Stirrup Cup" he reminded himself, "We come not of weaklings and weepers." In addition to writing poems with a stoic theme, Will also studied the works of Marcus Aurelius and his modern interpreters, Gilbert Murray and Matthew Arnold.[8]

Will's stoic endurance was tested beginning in 1925 when he became the editor of the Yale Series of Younger Poets. Will warned the Yale Press when he took the job that he had little critical ability and that "I loathe reading bad verse and I am not always quick at detecting good new verse." His job was to select one manuscript each year from those submitted by young, previously unpublished poets, for publication in the series. Most of the manuscripts submitted were undistinguished, but Will plowed through them like a true stoic. Helping young poets appealed to his sense of duty, and whenever a contestant showed promise, he tried to offer constructive criticism. Will's advice was simple: write with sincerity and passion; discipline the passion into a beautiful form; and don't pay too much attention to critics, including himself. Will also used his editorship to encourage interest in poetry outside the traditional literary centers. One of his first acts as editor was to solicit a manuscript from the young black poet Countee Cullen, who later played a major role in the Harlem renaissance. Will also took a special interest in southern poets. The next year he was so delighted with "the first really excellent manuscript I have received from the South" that he invited its author, Henri Faust of nearby Monticello, Arkansas, to come to Greenville and discuss poetry. Although much of the work as editor of the series was tedious, the opportunity to help young poets allowed Will to salvage a bit of his hope of reconciling his public duty as a Percy with his literary interests.[9]

Ironically, while Will worried over his inability to fill his father's shoes, he found himself assuming more and more of LeRoy's duties, especially during LeRoy's trips with Camille. Like his father, Will used his influence to defeat unscrupulous candidates in local elections, to prevent the appointment of corrupt men to the levee boards, and to protect blacks from lynchings and other abuses. Will inherited some of his influence, such as that over local post office appointments, from his father, but he had also made contacts of his own. For example, he wrote to Secretary of Commerce Herbert Hoover, whom he had met while serving in the Belgium Relief, asking him to consider a plan for marketing cotton proposed by the Staple Cotton Cooperative Association that LeRoy had helped found. In 1926 Will showed that the community could count on him, as it had on his father, in times of disaster. When a cyclone hit the delta that year, Will served as chairman of the Red Cross relief efforts. He took special satisfaction in dispensing relief supplies in a way that satisfied both the blacks who received it and the planters on whose land they lived and worked. Will's sense of inadequacy came from comparing himself with his father. He was actually an influential and respected local figure, and for a self-confessed poet living in Mississippi, a remarkably effective leader.[10]

Greenville was fortunate to have two Percys who could be counted on in a crisis, for in 1927 the town faced perhaps the greatest crisis in its disaster-plagued history. In April the best levees that the delta had ever boasted proved inadequate when the greatest flood in memory poured down the Mississippi River valley. Disdaining the frail barriers erected to restrain them, the murky brown waters of the Mississippi spread over 12.5 million acres of adjacent land, submerging homes, farms, livestock, and crops beneath a sheet of water three to twelve feet deep. Hundreds of people were killed by the flood, and countless others were left owning nothing but mud.[11]

When the levees protecting Greenville gave way north of town, Mayor John Cannon appointed Will chairman of the flood relief committee. Laying aside the poem he was working on, Will waded to the Knights of Columbus building and set up headquarters in the rooms normally reserved for poker games. Perhaps inspired by their surroundings, Will and his committeemen said a short prayer and then began bluffing. With no authority save his title, Will confiscated every boat, wagon, and truck he could find. All of the food and livestock feed in Greenville's stores also passed quickly under the committee's control. It was fortunate that no one challenged Will's commands, for thousands of wet, hungry backcountry planters and tenants were soon crowded into Greenville's remaining unflooded buildings and along the high ground of the levee. Some straggled in on their own, arriving in anything that would float; others were brought in by a band of bootleggers from White River, who searched the backcountry in their motorboats, rescuing old customers and prohibitionist Klansmen alike from atop barns and trees. The local food supply was quickly exhausted, but fortunately Will was able to open a road to the outside so that supplies could be brought in by truck. From Greenville these supplies were carried in boats to the patches of high ground around the county where people had congregated.[12]

While Will worked day and night to keep his ramshackle transportation system functioning, LeRoy acted as a troubleshooter. He found an old river rat named Dulaney and persuaded him and his two black helpers to round up the carcasses that bobbed up and down Greenville's flooded streets. Will remembered that Dulaney's "odor proved conclusively that he had not left the dirty work to his assistants," but

LeRoy was less easily offended than his son. He roamed the country-side in Dulaney's small boat, conferring with committeemen, straight-ening out differences between the various relief organizations, and do-ing whatever else needed doing. One night the unlikely pair traveled down the flooding river to Vicksburg so that LeRoy could confer with Herbert Hoover, director of the relief efforts.[13]

Roaming the countryside in Dulaney's boat, LeRoy discovered that not all of Will's decisions were popular among the local planters. When getting relief to those who needed it became impossible, Will decided to evacuate as much of the local population as he could. White women, children, and the elderly were taken first, although there were a few exceptions. Camille and her sister treated Will's order to depart with unconcealed contempt. Camille told the chairman, "I should like to know how you and LeRoy and Charlie could manage without us!" Fortunately, most of the white population was more cooperative.[14]

Will's authority received a more serious challenge when he decided to evacuate the 7,500 blacks who had poured into Greenville from the surrounding plantations. Will would have been a far more absolute dictator had he not had to deal with so many Percys, for this time the opposition was led by his father. Like most planters in the area, LeRoy feared that if the blacks were evacuated, they might never return, and the delta would be stripped of its already scarce labor supply. Replying to a suggestion that Greenville's blacks be taken to the unflooded Roundaway Plantation, LeRoy wrote, "The trouble is I appreciate the fact that if I were a negro living in a tent on Trail Lake, looking over thousands of acres with not an acre of cotton, and would go for a visit to the fertile lands of Coahoma County and reside in a well equipped cabin on prosperous land for a few weeks, those few weeks would be indefinitely prolonged." LeRoy also realized that blacks would be en-couraged to make their departure from the delta permanent by labor-hungry planters in areas unaffected by the flood, and by the swarm of agents who had descended on the prostrate delta to seek labor for northern industries.[15]

When LeRoy told him that the planters were opposed to evacuating the blacks, Will was furious that they would put their own economic welfare above the health and safety of their tenants. Seeing that Will's mind was made up and that direct opposition was hopeless, LeRoy per-

suaded him to repoll the relief committee, which had already approved
evacuating the blacks. Before the committee met that night, LeRoy
met with each of its members and persuaded them to change their
minds. Unaware of what his father was doing, Will was shocked that
evening when he discovered that the committee no longer favored
evacuation. Disgusted, Will bowed to the majority.[16]

The difference between LeRoy and Will on this matter arose from
their different priorities. Both were anxious to preserve the delta's way
of life. LeRoy, however, had grown up in the impoverished postwar
South and never forgot that that way of life depended on economic
prosperity, which in turn depended on the vagaries of the weather, the
cotton market, and the labor of a race of people he never claimed to
understand. LeRoy's loyalty was to the delta as a whole, and he refused
to allow it to be destroyed by the loss of one of its necessary parts.
Will, on the other hand, emphasized the element of noblesse oblige in
his family's aristocratic code. "Enzio's Kingdom" had revealed his rejection of the notion that economic development led ineluctably to
cultural progress, and he came to consider it his special duty to protect
blacks from the manipulations of their economic superiors. Delta
blacks, more than anyone else, seemed to need Will's benevolent paternalism and therefore provided the most satisfying outlet for his
concern for others.

Neither Will nor LeRoy considered the wishes of the blacks huddled
along the levee in deciding whether they should be evacuated. Will believed that "they had no capacity to plan for their own welfare; planning for them was another of our burdens." LeRoy saw them as one
segment of the delta whose welfare must be considered in relation to
the good of the whole. LeRoy and Will have both been criticized for
making this decision for Greenville's blacks and for jeopardizing their
health by leaving them on the levee. No one, however, has established
that the blacks wanted to leave, or disputed Will's claim that the contrary was the case. It is unlikely that Will would have falsely claimed
that the blacks wanted to stay, for this would have weakened his credentials as their guardian and also required that he credit them with
the same ability to form regional and familial attachments that inspired Camille and other older whites to refuse evacuation. In fact,
Will played down the blacks' objections to leaving in the final version

of his autobiography. In an earlier typescript of the same chapter he described an unsuccessful attempt to persuade them to board a train to Greenwood. The train overturned on the way, probably increasing the blacks' reluctance to venture off their high ground. They may also have read in their newspapers that black refugee camps were, in the words of one historian who criticized LeRoy's decision, similar to "policed concentration camps." The blacks should have been given the opportunity to decide for themselves whether to leave or stay, but to imply that they would have left is to again deny them the right to choose for themselves.[17]

Unable to evacuate the blacks, Will did everything he could to take care of them. When the river dropped temporarily in June, he urged planters not to return their labor to the plantations until it was certain that the river would not rise again. If it did, he warned, it would be impossible to get food to the stranded blacks. His warning proved fortuitous, for the river did rise again briefly. Will knew that many blacks feared they would be cheated out of their proper share of rehabilitation supplies from the Red Cross if the distribution process were left, in the words of the NAACP's Walter White, "in the hands of these Crackers"; thus he appointed a committee of local blacks to determine who deserved what. When a black man was shot to death by a young policeman, Will forestalled further violence by going alone to a church full of angry black men, expressing the white community's sorrow over the shooting, and, predictably, lecturing his black audience on their civic responsibilities. Not many white men in Mississippi could have gotten away with that, and fewer still would have tried.[18]

As the floodwaters ebbed away, Will and LeRoy bent their efforts toward rebuilding the soggy delta. Will supervised the distribution of furniture and household supplies and the repair of homes, while LeRoy concentrated on salvaging the economy. It was too late in the year to make a cotton crop, but hay crops like alfalfa, peas, and soybeans, even though they would not produce a profit, could be used to choke out weeds and keep the land ready for next year. LeRoy also hoped that planting these crops would hold the delta's laborers, many of whom had already left on their own. He also sought relief for planters facing mortgage payments that they could not meet because of the flood. In a letter to L. A. Downs, president of the Illinois Central Railroad, LeRoy urged that banks and other financial institutions holding mortgages on delta land either scale down the debts by 25 percent, accepting this loss as their fair share of the disaster, or else take over the land themselves and pay off the back taxes owed on much of it, so that the rehabilitation process could start afresh.[19]

LeRoy knew that all of his efforts to revitalize the economy depended on restoring faith in the delta's levee system. In April, 1927, the levees were higher and stronger than they had ever been before, and they were the product of decades of investment and care; yet they had proven inadequate to the challenge of the river. Burdened by debts carried over from bad years, with no crops to sell and short on credit, the people of the delta would need years just to rebuild the levees, and there was no guarantee that another flood would not again wash away their work. LeRoy saw the immensity of the problem, but he had seen other floods, and he knew that such times provided the best opportunity to press for increased federal funding for levee construction. Deciding to act while public sympathy was at its peak, LeRoy joined other leaders throughout the Mississippi River valley in their attempt to persuade the federal government to take over the levee system completely, once and for all.[20]

LeRoy knew that in order to persuade Congress to take over the levee system, the proponents of such a move would have to unite behind a single plan. Early in June he leaped at an opportunity to work for such unity by serving as chairman of the Resolutions Committee of the National Flood Control Convention in Chicago. His work on the Resolutions Committee got him appointed to the permanent Executive Committee of the organization, and in July he traveled north again to attend a meeting of the Executive Committee on a lake in Wisconsin. From there he went on to Washington and then back to Saint Louis for a meeting of the Mississippi River Commission. Late in July he returned to Greenville and entertained Vice-President Charles G. Dawes and other visiting dignitaries. Exhausted by his travels as the delta's ambassador to flood control meetings, LeRoy dreaded these visits. He found his guests uninteresting, though too important to be neglected. He was encouraged, however, by the general support he found for flood control legislation.[21]

Late in August LeRoy was able to get away for a couple of weeks of rest. When he returned, Will left on a trip to Nikko, Japan, where he rested from his previous five months of supervising the local relief program. As was his habit, Will spent part of his travel time writing poetry. Though he produced no major poems on this trip, the two lyrics that he did write displayed the haunting beauty that distinguished his best work.[22]

Meanwhile, LeRoy continued to represent the delta at flood control meetings across the country. In September he attended a levee meeting in Hot Springs, Arkansas, with Herbert Hoover, then went on to Washington to serve on the United States Chamber of Commerce Committee on Flood Control. Toward the end of the month LeRoy returned west to Chicago, where he hoped to see the Dempsey-Tunney fight. He was called back to Greenville before the fight, however, when Camille suffered a heart attack brought on by having a tooth extracted and, probably, the strain of the previous six months. Camille recovered only slowly, forcing LeRoy to remain close to home. He spent his time rebuilding the cabins at Trail Lake that were destroyed by the flood and trying to "inspire the belief in the negroes that living in tents is more salubrious than living in houses."[23]

LeRoy's investment in new cabins at Trail Lake reflected his growing optimism about the prospects of federal flood legislation. In October he wrote a cousin that such legislation stood a good chance, "provided every creek from the Rocky Mountains to the Gulf of Mexico does not want to capitalize our tragedy" by demanding local projects of their own. LeRoy was encouraged by the efforts of Chicago's colorful mayor, William Hale Thompson, who was also chairman of the National Flood Control Executive Committee and the moving force behind the calling of the convention the previous June. While LeRoy preferred working quietly in committees, Thompson planned to have twenty special trains and several automobiles parade through Washington during the congressional hearings on flood control. Anxious for help of any kind, LeRoy wrote Will that "it seems a rather stupid way of getting through legislation, but it may have some effect."[24]

The congressional hearings were crucial to the campaign for federally funded levees. LeRoy's approach to them was less colorful than Big Bill Thompson's but just as important in making them a success. In November LeRoy appeared before the House Committee on Flood

Control, which had opened its hearings before Congress convened in order to expedite the government's response to the disaster. LeRoy thanked the committeemen for their prompt action and assured them that it was warranted by the situation. He had seen many floods, he told them, but none had had the effect of this one. "It shook the people of the valley to their very soul," he told the committee. "It stripped them of courage and hope. It made them realize for the first time how puny and futile their efforts to secure protection had been." Only the federal government could restore their confidence in the levees now, and if it did not do so promptly, he warned, the valley would soon be deserted.

LeRoy framed his testimony to answer what he considered the four crucial questions that Congress must address in dealing with flood control. The first question was whether the river could be controlled, and LeRoy of course insisted that it could. He argued that the problem was one for engineers to solve, but he was also aware that the issue had political implications, for different sections of the valley favored different engineering techniques. Hoping to avoid divisions within the ranks of his allies, LeRoy advocated a system combining the two most popular plans: levees to restrain the river, and reservoirs to carry off overflows.

The second question LeRoy addressed was whether the expense of controlling the river could be justified economically, and again he answered affirmatively. The Mississippi Valley, he pointed out, encompassed twenty million acres of arable land. Although only one fifth of it was presently in cultivation, the valley produced $250 million worth of agricultural products each year. Much of this was cotton, which was vital to America's favorable trade balance. After describing the efforts of foreign countries to develop their cotton-producing resources, LeRoy concluded that "there is not in all Europe a nation with a treasury so depleted that it would not gladly pay the cost of protecting this area if it was the beneficiary of such production."

The third question facing Congress was who should pay for this protection. Disdaining compromise plans that called for local contributions, LeRoy argued that the federal government should assume the entire cost. Calling the Mississippi "the Nation's stream," he argued that the commerce on the river benefited the entire nation, and therefore the entire nation should share in the cost of maintaining it. LeRoy cited two objections to requiring local contributions for levee maintenance. The first was that many areas along the river would simply be unable to afford them, for they were already heavily in debt from previous floods. Furthermore, he argued, if the federal government assumed the entire cost, it would have the centralized control necessary to make the project a success. LeRoy remembered the political considerations that often determined local appointments to the levee board, and he wanted no such considerations to endanger the federal flood control program. A progressive at heart, LeRoy was more comfortable with engineers than politicians.[25]

The last question facing Congress, LeRoy said, was when the work should be done, and he answered that it should be done immediately. "The disaster of 1927," he told the committee, "is not a past disaster. It is hanging like a pall over the entire valley today, and in the shadow of it men go about in fear and misgiving, and no one ventures to build for the future until he knows whether the government is going to do this work." LeRoy had already spent sixty thousand dollars rebuilding the cabins on Trail Lake; repairing his own home would cost another three thousand. He knew that other planters would be reluctant to make similar investments until Congress acted to restore their faith in the levees.[26]

After testifying, LeRoy remained in Washington for two weeks, working with other flood control proponents to come up with a plan that Congress could agree on. He returned to Greenville late in November for five brief days with Camille. Finding that her health was slowly improving, he returned to Washington late in the month, stopping briefly in Chicago and New York to confer with levee supporters. He planned to stay in the capital through the winter, but a few days before Christmas he was called back to Greenville when Camille took a turn for the worse. With Camille holding tenuously to life and the future of the delta reeling and bouncing from committee to committee in Washington, it was a somber holiday for the Percy household.[27]

In January Camille's health improved enough to allow LeRoy to return to Washington. After two weeks of conferences, he testified before the Senate Committee on commerce. Congress had not yet been able to agree on a plan. Hoping to prod them into action, LeRoy described the effects of their delay. The shadow of disaster that he had described to the House committee still hung over the valley, he said. "No farmer turns a furrow, no carpenter drives a nail, but he questions the wisdom of his work and fears the futility of it." Redevelopment, he warned, would not take place until Congress acted, and if they failed to agree on a plan, "in five years 80 per cent of it [the valley] will revert to jungle."[28]

LeRoy also advanced other arguments for prompt action. He had spent his entire life lobbying for levee appropriations, and never during that time had he seen federal levee appropriations increased except in years following a flood. If Congress were ever going to fund a flood control program adequately, it must do it now while public sympathy was aroused. Furthermore, he argued, "the control of the river is an emergency work, it is like fighting fire, because at any time before the completion of the plan your work is liable to be destroyed and swept away and devastation follow it." Although the engineers had testified that the work would take ten years, LeRoy thought that this estimate was based on a fear of seeming to demand too much money from Congress at one time. LeRoy told the committee that with adequate funds, the work could be completed in five years, thus reducing the threat of an intervening flood by half.

LeRoy was more specific than before about what engineering techniques should be incorporated into the flood control program. He discussed several proposals that had been submitted to the committee, pointing out the problems and advantages of each. He concluded this discussion by advocating a combination of strengthened levees, outlets, reservoirs, and spillways. He reiterated his belief that the federal government should pay the entire cost of the project, and asked the committee to "give us a plan that will protect us and do not give us a burden that we can not bear."[29]

LeRoy remained in Washington until late in February, when he was again called home to be with Camille, who had suffered another heart attack. Although he had to leave the capital before Congress passed a flood control bill, when it finally did act in May, it was apparent that LeRoy's combination of engineering expertise and political savvy had influenced Congress. The Flood Control Act of 1928 assigned complete responsibility for the building and maintenance of levees to the federal government. The act required local districts only to provide the right of way, and subsequent legislation waived even this requirement in some cases. Furthermore, the Flood Control Act included both strengthened levees and reservoirs, as LeRoy had advocated. Most important, it worked. The delta has suffered no major floods since the passage of the act. LeRoy's quiet role in the act's passage had helped give the delta what it needed most—security from the mighty river and the promise of future prosperity.[30]

While LeRoy was in Washington, Will remained in Greenville caring for his mother and supervising the Red Cross rehabilitation program. When LeRoy returned, Will took the opportunity to go to New York, where he visited with friends and heard the symphony. Later in the year he traveled west and spent a month motoring through Arizona and New Mexico, where he visited the Grand Canyon and Taos.[31]

Will's literary wanderings at this time also showed a combination of old and new directions. He continued writing poetry and reading it as the editor of the Yale Series of Younger Poets. In April he took a new direction by publishing his first prose fiction, a short piece entitled "Cadenza on a Popular Theme," in the *Southwest Review*. Set in the Italian past, this piece is a dialogue between a lady in her garden and a young man who has wandered in to lie in the sun. What plot there is consists of the young lady's gaily refusing the wanderer's flirtations. Will developed no new ideas concerning the conflict between decorum and sexuality, but perhaps the evocation of a time when such problems did not exist was all that he sought. The significance of "Cadenza on a Popular Theme" was that it marked Will's growing interest in prose as a vehicle for expressing his ideas.[32]

While Will was exploring new directions, LeRoy remained in Greenville attending to his perennial concerns. As a planter he was plagued by the labor shortage he had predicted and by the lack of available credit. He also kept an eye on state legislation such as road bills and utility company regulation that affected the delta. During the summer and early autumn, much of his attention was devoted to the presidential election. LeRoy supported Al Smith, the Catholic, antiprohibitionist governor of New York. He was delighted when the Democrats nominated Smith, and campaigned for him in Greenville. LeRoy considered Smith's candor on issues like prohibition an "intelligence test" to the American people, so he was probably not too surprised when Smith lost.[33]

Camille's health remained precarious through the summer. Hoping to cheer her, LeRoy bought her a new car, but most of the time she was too ill to ride in it. She gradually grew stronger during the autumn, and shortly after the presidential election and Will's return from the Grand Canyon, LeRoy and Camille left to spend the winter in Florida. LeRoy took a couple of dogs along in case he got the chance to do some hunting, and enjoyed playing golf with Al Smith, who was also vacationing in Florida. The winter sun improved Camille's condition, and by the time they returned to Mississippi, it was April again.[34]

April again, and the river was rising. In May the threat of a flood became so serious that Major John C. H. Lee, commanding the government levee builders in the area, called for two hundred workers at the Mounds Landing levee, where the first break had occurred in 1927. In June the weather improved and the threat of another flood passed, but the close call prompted LeRoy to criticize the government's decision to take ten years to build the new levees and thus risk another flood in the interim. This decision, he wrote a friend, was "stimulated by Coolidge's attitude toward economy, making a fetish of it." LeRoy expected few improvements under the new administration, for, he wrote, "I have the impression that Hoover felt that he was the kind of a Republican that probably I, and certainly Will, would support against Smith, and possibly resents the fact that neither of us did so."[35]

LeRoy also saw a danger to the delta from the state government when Governor Bilbo threatened to ask the legislature to rescind the Rehabilitation Act, which granted tax relief to victims of the 1927 flood. LeRoy helped state representative H. C. Hamblen formulate a strategy to oppose this move. By this time LeRoy's primary concern was to defend what the delta had already won. After the federal government's assumption of responsibility for the levees, there was little else for him to do.[36]

As he grew old, LeRoy's thoughts turned increasingly to the young. He continued to raise funds for the YMCA. He took a special interest in young lawyers and opposed a proposal to increase the requirements for entry into the profession to four years of college and three years of law school. Such lengthy schooling, he argued, would have "a tendency to build up snobbishness in the profession and to keep poor men out of it." Furthermore, he argued, it would encourage lawyers to believe "that they are much better qualified to practice than they really are." LeRoy was also very interested in the younger members of his family. Since his brother William Armstrong's death, LeRoy had supervised his estate for his widow, Caroline Percy, and her children, Willie, Walker, and Lady. LeRoy was as concerned for the childrens' character as for their inheritance and occasionally offered them the fatherly advice he had given Will. When Caroline worried over Lady's desire to work for a while before marrying and young Walker's plans to take a summer job, LeRoy reassured her that "many intelligent women today prefer living by their own work and retaining their freedom to sacrificing their freedom for a much easier living. With it somewhat fashionable for boys to work in vacation, I think it is all right for Walker to take a job. If it was absolutely unfashionable, I would probably think it all the more right."[37]

Tragically, that summer LeRoy had to extend his care to other young Percys when his nephew LeRoy Pratt Percy of Birmingham, Alabama, committed suicide. LeRoy Pratt had been very dear to his uncle; they had hunted and played poker together and corresponded regularly. After LeRoy Pratt's death, LeRoy took an interest in the education of his three sons, Walker, LeRoy, and Phinizy. He asked his nephew's widow, Mattie Sue, of whom he was also very fond, to write him often about the boys and to try to get them in the habit of thinking about him and Will.[38]

As autumn followed summer, death tightened its grip on the Percys. Camille passed away on October 15. Hoping to console his heartbroken father, Will took LeRoy to a resort in Indiana. LeRoy dutifully followed Will's prescriptions, but during his golf game his mind would return to Camille, and Will would find him standing, club in hand, with a faraway look in his eyes.[39]

After Camille's death LeRoy's health faded rapidly. While returning to Greenville from Indiana, he suffered an appendicitis attack that forced Will to take him off the train at Memphis. The operation was successful, but LeRoy's old friend and Senate colleague John Sharp Williams understood the real danger facing him. In a warm and elegant letter Williams reminded LeRoy of the good things of life, admitting that his appetites for food and drink had faded but avowing his desire to remain in the world even if only as an onlooker; and he added that he would like LeRoy to stay in it with him.[40]

For a while LeRoy appeared to improve, but in December his strength faded. Recognizing his fate, he had Will send for his secretary and dictated his final argument to the War Department concerning flood control measures in the Third District. General Lytle Brown, the army's chief of engineers, called it the most comprehensive report he had ever seen on the subject. After completing the report, LeRoy died on Christmas Eve.[41]

Of the many tributes paid to LeRoy, Will's was the most appropriate. On his father's grave he placed a bronze statue of a soldier in armor, bearing the inscription PATRIOT. On the back was inscribed LeRoy's favorite poem, Matthew Arnold's "The Last Word."

> They out talked thee, hissed thee, tore thee?
> Better men fared thus before thee;
> Fired their ringing shots and passed,
> Hotly charged—and sank at last.
> Charge once more then and be dumb!
> Let the victors, when they come,
> When the forts of folly fall,
> Find thy body by the wall![42]

Chapter 9

Will Percy

Uncle Will's Garden

Old orders change I know. . . . But new orders change too. Only one thing never changes—the human heart.
                                                    Will Percy
                                        Lanterns on the Levee

For to have lived in Will Percy's house, with "Uncle Will" as we called him, as a raw youth from age fourteen to twenty-six, a youth whose only talent was a knack for looking and listening, for tuning in and soaking up, was nothing less than to be informed in the deepest sense of the word. What was to be listened to, dwelled on, pondered over for the next thirty years was of course the man himself, the unique human being, and when I say unique I mean it in its most literal sense: he was one of a kind; I never met anyone remotely like him. It was to encounter a complete, articulated view of the world as tragic as it was noble.
                                                    Walker Percy

Born Sartoris or born quality of any kind ain't is, *it's* does.
                                        Elnora, in William Faulkner
                                            "There Was a Queen."

After his father's funeral Will left for New York to collect his thoughts. Without his parents, he wrote, "my life seemed superfluous." In January he returned to Greenville to assume his new duties as elder of the Percy family. The ceremony accompanying his ascension was a simple one, administered by Holt Collier, the aged black hunter who had captured a bear cub and offered it to President Roosevelt, and the friend of LeRoy's who had known those things about him that only a hunting companion can know. Holt met Will in the hall of the Percy law office and, motioning toward LeRoy's desk, told him, "Set there where he sot. That's where you belong."[1]

Although he was a bachelor, Will's new responsibilites included looking after several other members of the family. LeRoy had been guardian of the trust left for his brother's widow Caroline Percy, and Will gave her the same kind of hard-nosed, realistic advice that his father had offered—a combination of practical suggestions regarding her financial interests, and admonitions to let her children stand on their own. Will refused to take over the guardianship of the estate, insisting instead that it be administered by Caroline's oldest son, Willie, whom Will thought mature enough to handle such matters.[2]

Will also assumed responsibility for the Alabama branch of the family. After the death of his cousin LeRoy Pratt Percy, Will invited Pratt's widow, Mattie Sue, to bring her three sons to Greenville for a visit. Martha Susan was "a most charming woman," a daughter of the Phinizy family of Athens, Georgia. Like Will, she had recently experienced a great loss, and this common bond made each a great comfort to the other. At such times, manners and charm involve a great deal more than the placement of forks at the dinner table, and the discipline of actively caring for one another kept Will and Mattie Sue from slipping into despondency.[3]

Mattie Sue's three sons also cheered Will. Along with their adolescent energy, they offered a sense of continuation, an assurance that the Percy family had replenished itself. Walker, the oldest at fourteen, had already shown signs of sharing Will's literary interests by writing a short story and submitting it to *Liberty Magazine*. LeRoy Pratt junior, a year younger than Walker, inherited his great-uncle LeRoy's interests in planting and business. The youngest, B. Phinizy, born in 1922, would become a lawyer and law professor. Will was so pleased with their company that he invited Mattie Sue and the boys to stay with him in Greenville.[4]

Two years later Mattie Sue was killed in an automobile accident. Will adopted the boys and set about trying to become a father at the age of forty-six. Will frequently called on his aunts for advice. Even more often, he relied on the English and classical literature that he admired to provide the boys with sound values. Despite Will's natural ability as a teacher, this tactic was not always successful, particularly with Walker, who preferred *The Brothers Karamazov* to Will's recitations of Keats and tales of Marcus Aurelius. Will knew that the boys considered some of his interests old-fashioned. He wrote later, "I had no desire to send these youngsters of mine into life as defenseless as if they wore knight's armor and had memorized the code of chivalry. But what could I teach them other than what I myself had learned?" And thus Will continued, "out of my own darkness," to "try to point out to them the pale streak I see which may be a trail," punctuating his disquisitions with performances of Brahms and Wagner at his enormous Capehart piano.[5]

His three new sons could not wholly fill the void left in Will's life by the death of his parents. His sorrow and his increased responsibilities ended his career as a poet. "I can see no more writing," he told an interviewer in 1931. "I sincerely wish I could." Will's loss of poetic inspiration may have been aggravated by his continuing failure to win the attention of critics. In 1929 he had written a preface for a book by Norman Douglas; in 1930 he had gathered his favorite poems from his three earlier volumes, added some of the poems that he had written in the late 1920s, and published them under the title *Selected Poems*. A few conservative critics praised *Selected Poems*, but most critics ignored it. Will did find one review in a Sherman, Texas, newspaper amusing, and he quoted a passage from it in a letter to his publisher, Norman Donaldson. "William Alexander Percy lifts up and bears on the fallen flower of southern gentility and to this he adds universality." Donaldson was also amused and suggested that for Will's next book they commission for the cover a woodcut by Norman Rockwell picturing Will "lifting up and bearing the flower of southern gentility. But," he added ruefully, "I confess I don't see how we could add 'universality' to the illustration."[6]

Will was irritated by the critics' habit of dismissing his work as anachronistic. To fellow conservative Donald Davidson, he complained "I get so damn tired of people assuming that because of our medieval and Greek themes, I am interested only in archaeology or history of literature." Many of the newer poems in Will's *Selected Poems* did present Will's stoic philosophy in a classical setting; but the genesis of his beliefs lay in his daily life, and he resented the critics' failure to recognize this. Will also objected to being dismissed out of hand because of his background. "Another thing that irritates me," he wrote Davidson, "is the expectation that all artists in prose and verse should write about the poor and the illiterate and the ill-bred. I know nothing about the psychology of the negro nor of the poor white. But I do know something of the feelings and problems of the descendants of that class which was once the slave-owner class in the South. Northern critics seem to forgive us anything except following our own best tradition. I never could see any point when you were born a gentleman in trying to act that you are not one." Will believed that his ideas were being dismissed without a hearing because of his style and his background, and this belief contributed to the termination of his poetic career.[7]

Will found an alternative means of expressing his stoicism in the duties he assumed after LeRoy's death. He handled them differently than LeRoy had. To critic John Chapman he wrote, "I am interested in contemporary problems—the conflict between capital and labor, the injustice of the present tariff, etc. etc. etc., but I am much more interested in what seems to me the eternal things of human nature—Man and God, man and love, man in the trap of fate."[8] LeRoy's view of the world had been primarily economic while Will's was humanistic, and this difference altered the way that Will played the Percy roles of planter, lawyer, and public-minded citizen.

Will was less interested in the financial aspects of running his Trail Lake Plantation than LeRoy had been. Initially he entrusted such matters entirely to his managers, but after two years he found the previously unencumbered plantation mortgaged to the hilt. An investigation uncovered embezzlement, and the guilty parties were replaced. New managers Walter Beard and Walter Boland put Trail Lake back on a sound financial basis while Will supplied the funds from his thriving legal practice to keep it afloat, but it took years to pay off all of the mortgages.[9]

Will's primary concern was for the blacks who sharecropped and share-rented at Trail Lake. He believed that most blacks, particularly those living at Trail Lake, were irresponsible and incompetent to look after themselves and that it was his duty to protect them from a hard world and from themselves. He was willing to recognize exceptions and set up trust funds designed to make landowners of enterprising tenants, but it was the blacks who conformed to his belief by remaining at Trail Lake whom Will really cared most about and needed most. They provided him with an object for his stoic concern for others and thus with a justification for his own life. At the same time, their seemingly irresponsible ways provided Will with an image of a life free of the burdensome duties that he could escape only by contemplating those who seemed oblivious to care.[10]

When Will brought Walter Beard in to manage Trail Lake, he told him to treat the tenants honestly, avowing that if a plantation could not be run on that basis it deserved to go broke. Accordingly, prices at the company store remained in line with prices in town, and no interest was charged on furnish accounts. Settlements with tenants were honest. Will also made sure that the tenants' cabins were kept in good repair and that proper sanitary conditions were maintained. Part of Will's interest may have been aesthetic—he also encouraged the tenants to grow flowers, and awarded prizes for the best garden—but his primary concern was for their health. The incidence of malaria and pellagra at Trail Lake was lower than in other parts of the delta. Will also financed a program to detect and treat venereal disease, which afflicted as many as 90 percent of his tenants. At times his efforts were frustrated: when he had screens installed on the doors and windows to keep out disease-bearing mosquitoes, some tenants cut holes in them for their cats to come and go. Will replaced the screens, probably adding a lecture that was more trouble to listen to than getting up and letting the cat out. Will also looked after the spiritual and intellectual interests of his tenants. He supplemented the small state wage paid to black schoolteachers at Trail Lake, and matched all contributions made to the three churches on the plantation.[11]

One aspect of the tenants' lives that Will could not soften was the backbreaking nature of their work as cotton farmers. LeRoy had kept Trail Lake up to date on the latest breakthroughs in agricultural science: crop diversification, chemical fertilizers, and pesticides were all used to good effect. But Will refused to take the final step and completely mechanize the operation. Tractors were used to break the land in the spring, but the planting and cultivation was done by one-mule middlebusters and two-mule cultivators. Tenants also had to hoe their cotton by hand for much of the season. Picking the cotton was the hardest job of all, for it required bending over all day in the hot August sun. Some of these jobs could be done more efficiently by the new agricultural machinery that was beginning to be used in the delta, but Will knew that using such machines would force some of the tenants off the land. Raising cotton was hard work, but during the depression it was better than no work at all.[12]

Will's opposition to mechanization went beyond economic considerations. He told Hodding Carter, "We've got to think of the human side. The tenants have their homes and their roots here, and I'm not going to pull them up." Will shared the fears of his friend Donald Davidson and other Agrarians that southern farmers who left the soil for greater economic opportunities would lose more than they gained. They would leave behind a community where their place, no matter how humble, was assured, and enter a world that treated them as interchangeable parts of a vast economic engine. Will knew that modernization was unstoppable and that the Agrarians' strategies of resistance were futile. He could not and would not stop his tenants from leaving in search of economic opportunity. For those who stayed, however, he could make Trail Lake a sanctuary from the iron rule of economic efficiency that the Agrarians opposed. For Will, Trail Lake was more than a place to grow cotton. It was a garden, like the one at his home in Greenville that was the envy of the town, where life could unfold its natural beauty undisturbed, a garden where the rich brown earth became white at the behest of fabulous black Pan-like creatures who were themselves the garden's greatest marvel.[13]

Will took a more practical approach to his law practice. He and his partner Hazlewood Farish did a thriving business as corporate attorneys. Will never completely adjusted to being a lawyer and sometimes spent the night before he had to argue a major case vomiting from nervousness. Nevertheless, he was a very good lawyer and often took great satisfaction from his work. When a guest asked him how he had fused reality with poetry, and pointed out that Coleridge had done so with opium and Poe with alcohol, Will replied, "And I am a lawyer." The cases Will enjoyed most were those in which he defended a helpless black from injustice. Before becoming the senior member in the firm, Will had been christened "little Jesus" by local blacks for his passionate defense of a black man who claimed that he could cure the lame and blind by baptizing them in a nearby spring. Will argued that since the man gave credit to Christ for doing the actual healing, he was not making excessive claims, and added that if Christ came back to earth, he too would be considered an impostor. Will's client was acquitted, though he was arrested again later for shooting at a planter who came to the spring to fetch his tenants home to tend their crops. In another case a young black prisoner named Jim was injured while being forced to work. Will demanded that the sheriff in charge of the work accept responsibility. When he refused, Will sued for damages and, in spite of threats from the sheriff's friends, pushed the case and won it. Will also hired Jim as a house servant to protect him from the sheriff, but Jim soon grew tired of dusting, robbed Will, and took off for Memphis.[14]

Not all of Will's kindnesses to blacks were as controversial as this one, because most were unknown to the public. One night Will was awakened by a loud knocking at the door. It was a black man who had been shot in a fight and needed help. Will called him a fool, had him patched up, and gave him enough money to flee his pursuers. Frequently Will sent indigent blacks out to Trail Lake, where Walter Beard let them run up supply bills even when it was obvious that they were unlikely prospects as tenants. In his short story "Kansas Brown," Will's friend Roark Bradford described the situation succinctly: "It made the manager's balance sheet look bad, but Mr. Will understood."[15]

Not all of Greenville's whites approved of Will's paternalism. He admitted that because of his concern for blacks, "they call me a Negrophile." Actually, this term was probably confined to Greenville's gentry; those more recently arrived from the hill country preferred the down-home term "nigger lover." Such criticisms had little effect on Will. He considered most hill people incapable of thought, and their threats only encouraged him. Will was concerned about (though undeterred by) the criticism of visitors to the delta. Jonathan Daniels, who was a guest in Will's home, lamented that "nobody knows how many hungry Negroes Will Percy has fed. Nobody knows how many Negroes in trouble have had the benefit of his counsel and his pocket book." Daniels had no objection to helping blacks, but he disapproved of Will's refusal to judge blacks by the same moral standards that he applied to whites. "I had the feeling," Daniels wrote, "that Percy loved Negroes as another gentleman might love dogs and that somehow the fiercer the beast the more he might prefer it."[16]

Daniels was partly correct: Will did apply different moral standards to blacks, but not because he admired their fierceness. Another visitor to the delta, sociologist Hortense Powdermaker, described Will's attitude more accurately as a belief that "Negroes were happy Pan-like beings living only in the present, fundamentally and mysteriously different from white people."[17] Will believed that blacks were fundamentally different from whites, but given his doubts about the course of Anglo-Saxon civilization, this did not mean that he considered blacks inferior.

In fact, Will believed that the Negro's simpler way of life led to a greater spiritual awareness than that found among whites, and he was more than willing to point this out to his neighbors. On Easter morning, 1938, over three thousand people gathered at the river for a sunrise service. Will was among them, and though he was impressed by the spiritual hunger of the crowd, he was disappointed by the service. In a letter to a local newspaper, Will wrote that those who had arisen before dawn and braved uncertain weather had received only "a few perfunctory prayers, uttered apparently to catch the ear of an audience, but not God, some execrable, listless singing and the worst playing ever done by the un-uniformed Greenville Public School Band. The only saving grace was the singing of a song spiritual by the timid negroes—their sole participation in the service—and even their habitual fervor was dampened by the apathy of the white participants." Will urged that in the future blacks be given a larger part in such services, not because they sang better than whites and certainly not because they represented a certain percentage of the population. Rather, Will hoped they could give their white neighbors something they could no longer find within themselves.[18]

Will also admired the simple charm of blacks which allowed them to cut painlessly through the pretensions of whites. He frequently had Lige, his gardener, serve at the formal dinner parties he gave on Saturday nights. Will had a flair for mixing people who would enjoy each other's company, but his talents as a host were put to the test one evening when Hodding Carter's mother-in-law, Mrs. Philip Werlein of New Orleans, was the guest of honor. Mrs. Werlein's full figure, draped magnificently in a low-cut, formal evening gown, combined with her office as mother-in-law, gave her the air of one not to be trifled with, and the dinner conversation remained rather formal through the opening courses. The main course was teal duck, and only twelve had been prepared for the twelve guests. As Lige brought in the platter laden with ducks, he made a quick turn, and the ducks went flying across the room. Perhaps following some migratory instinct, one of the birds lodged in the front of Mrs. Werlein's dress, and she began screaming and trying to remove it. Unruffled, Lige reached down and retrieved the duck, adding politely, "Scuze me, ma'am, we needs that. Ain't got but twelve." Their genteel decorum shattered, Will's guests proceeded to enjoy themselves.[19]

Lige and other blacks were for Will a symbol of innocence—children not yet consumed by the white man's passion for wealth or burdened by a sense of responsibility. He feared, however, that the delta's blacks had lost much of this innocence through their constant contact with whites and their attempts to adopt white standards. The black man, Will wrote, "makes at best a second-rate white man: He could have been something far more precious in the eyes of any god, a first-rate Negro."[20]

Will found a purer symbol of innocence and simplicity in the inhabitants of Samoa. He visited Samoa in 1936 and lived among the villagers of Laulii, who adopted him as one of their own. In an unpublished essay entitled "The White Plague" Will compared Samoan and American morals, devoting most of his attention to the absence of a concept of private property among the Samoans and their Edenic approach to sexual relations. Will used these features of Samoan culture to describe the simplicity and innocence that American blacks were losing because of their contact with white civilization, and he feared that his Samoan friends would soon be likewise corrupted by the "white plague." He was disturbed by attempts to use English in the schools and warned, "Substitute English as the language of the people and their whole culture falls." Will doubted that the Samoans would resist the destruction of their culture.

> They are eager to take our comfortable beds, ice-boxes, radios and victrolas, our varied and devitalized foods, our bicycles and automobiles, never suspecting that taking these they must take too our weariness, our restlessness, our unhappy hearts. We are the nomads of the world, without home fires, wandering by stars not fixed, whose passion is to force the older and younger tribes of the race to join our tumultuous and futile pilgrimage. We bribe

them with our gold and our gods, they arise from their hearths and little fields and join us, receiving from us things, amusing things, miraculous things, but leaving behind them the one thing for the lack of which we sob ourselves to sleep—sweet, sweet, content. We give them the whole world and they fall down and adore us: we take from them only happiness which in our hands vanishes.[21]

Will's admiration for the simplicity and innocence of blacks and Samoans was stimulated by his despair over the direction of modern civilization. He doubted that this direction could be reversed all at once. He told Hodding Carter, "None of us can remake the world, but we can try to be men of good will in the little places in which we live, and that will help." Will held little hope for the great, modern cities; he hoped only that stoics like himself might preserve their Epicurean gardens for a time in the hinterland. The gardens might consist of an entire town or a single individual. To a contestant in the Yale Series of Younger Poets competition Will wrote: "Your problem is saving your soul in a typical mediocre American environment. God knows that is hard enough, but it is easier than saving it either in Greenwich Village or among the so-called intelligentsia of New York. Sometimes when we fight hard enough for our own integrity, beautiful things sprout out of us, maybe deeds or thoughts or poems. What difference does it make . . . whether our leaves make good fertilizer or acorn sprouts; we would have fulfilled the purpose of our own obscure destiny." Will knew that sooner or later the walls of his garden must crumble, but his stoicism steeled him against the ultimate futility of his efforts.[22]

This same sense of duty dictated that Will's garden encompass his community. The gardens at his home suggested a retreat from the world, and Will himself called them "the best sort of Ivory Tower." Water oaks and evergreens shaded the vine-covered brick walls; iron and tile benches invited the visitor to pause and admire the iris, azaleas, blue Spanish scilla, and bleeding heart that bloomed about the splashing fountains. The imposing wrought iron gate at the garden's entrance reinforced the appearance of a retreat, but Will never locked it, and ladies from the garden club dropped by regularly to discuss their petunias.[23]

Will wrote that "the major moral afforded by a garden comes from watching the fight for sunlight waged by those unhappy things rooted against their will in shade. . . . Standing at the post-office corner I recognize my poor sunless plants in the passers-by, sickly, out of shape, ugly with strain, who still search for a sunlight vital to their needs and never found, or found and lost." Will emerged regularly from his shady garden to shine a little light on Greenville's civic affairs. His political connections were not as extensive as LeRoy's, but local politicians shuddered when Will delivered candid comments on their character and ability. Will decided that the local newspaper was too reticent in pointing out violations of the public trust, and he encouraged Hodding Carter to establish his Delta *Star* in Greenville. Carter's willingness to offend anyone later won him a Pulitzer Prize for journalism, and the only time Will criticized his editorial policy was when Carter was a bit slow in getting an editorial condemning a lynching into print. Will also brought a little light into the local Rotary Club by laughing at his fellow members when they spent their meetings singing songs, and cajoling them into discussing serious problems facing the community. Will continued the family's representation on the Delta Cotton Council, and as chairman of the Delta Chamber of Commerce's floods committee, he took over LeRoy's monitoring of levee construction and maintenance to insure that corruption and incompetence did not jeopardize the delta. Will also encouraged others to shine some light into the delta's darker corners. David Cohn lived at the Percy home for a year while he prepared his study of delta blacks, *God Shakes Creation.* When Hortense Powdermaker arrived in nearby Indianola to begin her own study of delta race relations, she received a cool welcome from local whites until Will, who had never met her before, told the mayor of Indianola that she was an old friend of his family. After that, Powdermaker was able to rent the only room in town with a private bath. Will even opened his own plantation to the scrutiny of Raymond McClinton, a graduate student at North Carolina. Will believed that a little sunshine was good for everyone.[24]

Among the most carefully tended flowers in Will's garden were the young people who shared his artistic interests. As editor of the Yale Series of Younger Poets Will encouraged many young writers and made a special effort to help black poets. He relinquished his editorship to Stephen Vincent Benet shortly after he adopted his three nephews, and

thereafter he concentrated his attention on local artists. The most successful of these was Leon Koury, an Assyrian grocer with poetic aspirations. Koury saw one of Will's poems in *Scribner's* and, without knowing that Will lived in Greenville, wrote him at the magazine. Will
invited him over to talk, and though Koury's poems did not impress
him, the drawings on the back of his notebook did. Will encouraged
Koury to concentrate on drawing, and supplied him with art books and
materials. He also showed Koury's drawings to Malvina Hoffman, a
sculptor he knew in New York, and to William Van Dresser, a portrait
painter from New York who was visiting Will in Greenville. Both were
impressed, but Van Dresser thought Koury was working in the wrong
medium and sent him the modeling tools necessary to try sculpture.
Van Dresser was right: clay proved to be Koury's best medium. Will
was especially impressed with the busts he did of delta blacks, and he
helped another Greenville writer, Ben Wasson, set up an exhibition of
Koury's work on the West Coast, where Wasson was living. Koury
thanked Will by sculpting a bronze bust of him.[25]

Will placed the bust and others by Koury in his study where it could
be seen by the stream of artists, some established, some amateurs,
who came to visit. Like his garden, Will's study had the aura of a retreat from the world. The grand piano standing by his desk, the books
and musical scores scattered about the room, the pictures of previous
generations of Percys, suggested the quiet retreat of a gentleman-
scholar. But like his garden, Will's study remained open to visits from
local writers and artists like Hodding Carter, David Cohn, and Roark
Bradford, as well as prominent writers from other parts of the country.
Vachel Lindsay visited Will, and in accordance with his desire to write
poetry that appealed to ordinary people as well as intellectuals, got
roaring drunk one night and shouted one of his poems out to the slum-
bering neighborhood from Will's front porch. William Faulkner came
over to play tennis with Will. Facing each other across the net they
might have played for the bragging rights in Mississippi, with Faulkner, whose grandfather had been a Vardaman man, challenging the corrupt delta's leading aristocrat on behalf of the prohibitionist hill country. Unfortunately the match did not come off: Faulkner showed up
too drunk to play.[26]

Lindsay's nocturnal orations and Faulkner's besotted flailing of his racket probably reinforced Greenville's belief that poets like Will were a bit different from most folks, and the mere appearance of black poet Langston Hughes for a visit must have had a similar effect. Visits from poetic "institutions" like Carl Sandburg, Stephen Vincent Benét, and the aristocratic writer and critic Stark Young probably reassured the townsfolk. Will's Aunt Nina, who lived across the street from him and often acted as hostess at his home, probably summed up Greenville's attitude when she said of some of Will's friends, "They write filthy things about the South, but I sometimes get charming letters from them." Quite a few writers and artists lived in Greenville, and the town had learned to overlook almost anything except bad manners.[27]

Will's health forced him to retire from his law practice in 1937, and when LeRoy Pratt returned from college, Will began turning the Trail Lake operation over to him. Despite his failing health, however, Will continued to offer encouragement to local artists and also to Greenville's WPA workers, who found his knowledge of the delta useful in combating the poverty of the depression. In the summer of 1938 Will found a way to marry these concerns when he read an article in *Time* magazine describing the community arts centers being established around the country by the Federal Arts Project. Will realized that an art center in Greenville would provide jobs for the unemployed and, more important, give the area's artists a place other than his study to meet and display their work. He discussed the idea with several local artists, and in October the Delta Art Association was formed with Will as chairman of the Executive Committee. From October until April of the next year Will's home became the center of the association's activities, as the members put together a prospectus of delta arts and crafts, including paintings, sculpture, quilts, furniture, and other wood crafts that would win them a grant from the Federal Arts Project. They also raised two thousand dollars locally for the project, and the city donated a site for the center. Impressed with this evidence of local support, the Federal Arts Project granted Greenville fifteen thousand dollars for the center. In May the Delta Art Association, featuring the work of Leon Koury, held its first exhibit in its temporary gallery at the Elks Club. Will had sown a new garden.[28]

The Greenville Art Center illustrated Will's strategy for confronting a world that was "without convictions, without morals, without joy in living." Even in the midst of the depression, Will believed that "the present breakdown in the world is far more moral than economic." The art center gave artists, who dealt directly with moral problems, a chance to share their concerns with the community and, Will hoped, to revitalize it. The scale of the center was also characteristic of Will's strategy. A few local artists might go on to win national reputations, but the major role of the center was to provide a forum for artists who lacked the talent to earn such attention. The inclusion of crafts in the scope of the center also indicated that Will hoped to encourage all kinds of people to weave what beauty and meaning they could create into their daily lives.[29]

Will struck a similar note in a letter to his adopted son Walker, who was studying chemistry at the University of North Carolina. Will's letter indicates that Walker was troubled by the belief that "to be anything less than the greatest in your line would be failure." Will advised Walker, "My whole theory about life is that glory and accomplishment are of far less importance than the creation of character and the individual good life." Will admitted that "this may be a poor philosophy and one bred from defeat" and that his own poetry "does not rank with the greatest and may well be forgotten soon." But there was more to Will's commitment to living in Greenville than a desire to be a big fish in a small pond, to be the best poet in Greenville if he couldn't be the best in New York. Will believed that art should infuse life with meaning, and if art proved as mortal as man, it mattered little, for the "individual good life" justified itself.[30]

Will did not believe that the individual good life was a life of isolation. He told the Mississippi Press Association that the good life was unavailable in large cities; individuals had a better chance of living it in small or medium sized towns, where they could know their neighbors and be certain of their place in the community regardless of whether they were the best at what they did. Will was also unconcerned about the individual's choice of vocation. In a speech to the Delta Cotton Council he said, "All of our jobs are petty jobs but how we do them, whether we put loyalty and courage above all, makes the difference between being God-like and beast-like." The individual good life did not require glory, but it flourished best in a close-knit community where its joys and sorrows could be shared with one's neighbors.[31]

The gardener is tender with his plants, yet deals forcibly with any pestilence that threatens his garden from without. In the late thirties Hitler's Luftwaffe spread across Europe like a plague of locusts, and Will was among the first Americans to foresee the German threat to the United States. Will had learned to dislike Germans while working and living under their authority in the Belgium Relief project. He retained his dislike after the war, jotting in one of his poetry notebooks, "I am sure it would make for improved international relations if the Germans didn't clip their hair or wear a roll of fat above the collar." Hitler turned Will's dislike into alarm and rage. "Having listened to the speeches of Hitler," Will wrote, "hysterical, crafty, bullying, and to one speech of Churchill, truthful, quiet, sorrowful, I know that it is better that all Germany be exterminated than that one Englishman die."[32]

Will was disgusted by most Americans' reluctance to enter another war in Europe. He had joined the Belgium Relief when America was too slow in entering World War I to suit him; now again he refused to wait for his countrymen and volunteered his services to the governments of France and Canada. He offered to serve wherever he was needed and in any useful capacity, adding, "Not being married I have nothing special to live for and would esteem it a privilege to be permitted to fight (in any way) for a cause I consider noble." Will was characteristically modest in describing his qualifications, saying, "I am reliable, good-mannered and tolerably intelligent." He was less honest about his health, claiming it was good. Actually, he suffered from chronic high blood pressure and stomach problems, and knew that he had only a short while to live. He wanted more than anything to feel one last time the joy of devoting himself to a noble cause. Both the French and Canadian governments, of course, turned him down because of his age.[33]

Will applied to the Canadian government just two weeks after completing his autobiography, *Lanterns on the Levee.* Perhaps the finality of having summed up his life contributed to his feeling that he had nothing left to live for. He had begun work on *Lanterns on the Levee* a year and a half before, in March of 1939, when Harold Strauss of Alfred A. Knopf publishers wrote to ask if he would be interested in writing the memoirs of a country lawyer for Knopf's Lives of Americans series. Jonathan Daniels had told Strauss that Will would make an excellent representative of the old southern aristocracy. Will objected to writing about the law, but Strauss assured him he could write about whatever he pleased. Will still doubted the wisdom of embarking on a prose career so late in life, but he sent Strauss four chapters that he had already written, and when Strauss replied that they were exactly what he was looking for, Will decided to go ahead with the autobiography.[34]

Will had considered autobiography as a literary mode on and off throughout his career. During LeRoy's Senate campaign he had begun a diary but gave it up after a few weeks of sporadic entries. One of the chapters that he gave Strauss was his essay on Sewanee, which appeared in 1927. Another was written at Jackson Hole, Wyoming, in 1932, and his essay "The White Plague" was written in 1936. The most recent of the chapters he gave Strauss had been written at Sewanee the summer before he received Strauss's letter.[35]

Will was also encouraged to write *Lanterns on the Levee* by the growing threat of Hitler's Germany. He took time off from writing to tell a convention of Mississippi's newspaper editors that "I appreciate your feeling that I have been silent too much. There is still a lot of poetry in the world and a lot that poets need to say, but somehow it does not fit into the old pattern. We need a Peter the Hermit, or a St. Francis. The right person, I believe, could kindle a great religious revival. Something of the kind must happen to the democracies, if they are to be saved."[36] Will did not think that *Lanterns* would make him a Saint Francis, but he did hope that it would help awaken Americans to the threat posed by Hitler. In the early drafts of the chapter published as "1914–1916," he specifically compared the situation facing America then with the situation in 1939, arguing that the Germans were still barbarians, and excoriating Americans who refused to face the current menace. Mindful that the isolationism of many in the thirties had grown out of their disillusionment with the results of the Great War, Will wrote, "I have never been one of those who thought the war was not worth fighting." The early versions of his chapter "At the Front," which were also edited before publication, contained in their original form more of Will's letters home from the battlefields. The letters that Strauss removed suggest that he shared Will's hope of encouraging Americans to enter the war, for they contained Will's most graphic descriptions of the war, while those left in were more heroic and less frightening.[37]

Lanterns on the Levee was much more than a war tract or an appeal to patriotism. The threat of Hitler only helped crystallize ideas that Will had held and lived by for years. Despite its lyrical accounts of the charms of delta life, of the care-free black sharecroppers at Trail Lake and the aristocrats who fought gallantly for dependable levees, the prevailing tone of *Lanterns* is melancholic, because Will saw that the way of life he loved was fading into history. This consideration was more important than events in Europe in determining Will's choice of autobiography as a literary mode. Will knew from his interest in Henry Adams that autobiography is an especially appealing form for conservatives who see values they hold dear slipping away. Writing an autobiography allowed Will to describe these values while they were intact and then to trace their decline, thus preserving them, if not in practice, at least in memory. More important, describing these values in their cultural setting was a way of validating them, of showing that they were a reliable guide to the individual good life.

Many conservatives of Will's generation shared his desire to demonstrate the continuing usefulness of values considered outdated by contemporary society. Appalled by what they considered the degeneration of American culture after the Great War, conservative intellectuals as diverse as Ralph Adams Cram, Joseph Wood Krutch, Donald Davidson, and Albert Jay Nock gave up on preserving the entire nation's values and concentrated their efforts on some more constricted sphere, whether the universities or the rural South, where the good life could still be lived. The individual life was the ultimate constriction of one's sphere of interest. Many conservatives resisted this last step into complete isolation by stressing the individual's need for a compatible, rewarding community, but the further such communities receded into the past, the more isolated the conservatives became. The individual life was their last fortress, and the autobiography was the most natural form in which to describe the struggle of anachronistic individuals to lead their version of the good life.[38]

Will had tried with little success in "Enzio's Kingdom" to describe the values that he feared were being lost. Since that time he had wondered if a memoir of some sort might be a better form for doing so. Despite the warning of his cousin Janet Longcope that embarking on a prose career at his age might be dangerous, once decided, Will took up

Strauss's commission enthusiastically. By July he had completed nine chapters, and though he was physically exhausted, he pressed on. In January he went to Fort Walton, Florida, where he recovered his health temporarily and completed five more chapters. In March he went to New York and met with Alfred Knopf, who, Will discovered, liked four of the chapters Will thought dull, and disliked the final three chapters, of which Will was particularly fond. Will spent May at his summer home at Sewanee, working twelve to fourteen hours a day on *Lanterns*, then suddenly lost interest in the book and volunteered his services to Washington to fight Hitler. He wrote his friend Huger Jervey that he was going to send the manuscript off to the publisher as it was, adding, "It will be rotten and I don't care—nothing seems worthwhile but the war." David Cohn found the manuscript under a sofa cushion and talked Will into finishing it rather than burning it, as he threatened to do.[39]

On June 23 Will received a little encouragement when he listened to the CBS Radio Workshop perform his "In April Once." The next day he sent "The White Plague" to Strauss, and in July he returned to Sewanee to finish up the book. In August he found that he would have to make further revisions, because Strauss objected to "The White Plague." Will suspected that Strauss objected to this chapter, not because of his views on Samoa, but "because of my views on the negro." This may have been true, for in discussing blacks Will made not the slightest gesture of obeisance to liberal opinion. However, his doubts about the abilities of blacks were as apparent in the revised version of the chapter, retitled "A Note on Racial Relations," as they were in the original essay. It was Will's doubts about the course of Western, white culture and his suggestion that nonwhite, primitive cultures might have advantages over their more "advanced" counterpart that were missing from the final version. Perhaps Strauss wanted to avoid publishing anything critical of the civilization the Allies were fighting to protect, or perhaps he simply failed to understand Will's argument. Whatever his reasons, the net result of the revisions Strauss demanded was to simplify Will's argument so that it could easily be labeled paternalism and be dismissed by liberal critics. Strauss's demand for the revision had made Will's belief in racial differences appear to scholars to be a belief in the inferiority of other races, a value judgment that Will would not have endorsed.[40]

Will had become disgusted with the whole project. In early September he left for the Grand Canyon to finish his revisions. His destination was curious even to himself; he wrote his cousin Janet that "it is certainly a very queer place to go and I don't know why I want to go there. I wish there was the old Europe to go to for six months. . . . But our world is definitely gone, and I feel superfluous, if not posthumous." Will finished his revisions and took the completed manuscript to New York in October. Through with *Lanterns* at last, he sent off his application for the Canadian militia.[41]

Will had hoped that his autobiography would preserve the values of his community and inspire his readers to find similar values in theirs, but he never expected *Lanterns* to have very many readers. He called the book "just a tale told with no listeners, a monologue to the autumn air." He had wanted to title it "Jackdaw in the Garden," after the blackbirds who visited his garden, perhaps thinking, too, of the jackdaws in his volumes of English literature, who had a reputation for loitering about old castles and cathedrals and mimicking human voices to no one in particular. Strauss feared such a title might become a self-fulfilling prophecy and asked Will to change it to something more appealing. Charlotte Gailor of Sewanee suggested "Lanterns on the Levee," which Will adopted even though he thought it too "la de dah Old South." He probably added the subtitle "Memoirs of a Planter's Son" himself: planters' sons often become gardeners when they move to town.[42]

Will was amazed by the tremendous popular reception accorded *Lanterns on the Levee* when it appeared in the spring of 1941. The book made the best seller lists and by the end of the year had been reprinted ten times. Unlike many best sellers, *Lanterns* continued to sell even after the initial wave of enthusiasm and publicity. In 1942 Knopf ordered another printing that brought the total to over 33,000 copies, and by 1948 it had been reprinted fourteen times. In 1973 the Louisiana State University Press recognized *Lanterns'* enduring appeal by issuing a new edition. Will's cousin Janet, who had told him that he was a poet and should not publish prose, told him after *Lanterns* was published that she would now have to walk around wearing a sign proclaiming herself a fool, and Will may have enjoyed this confession as much as any other part of his newfound literary success.[43]

Lanterns was also well received by critics writing in the popular

press. Southern newspapers were particularly enthusiastic: Ralph Mc-
Gill, writing for the Atlanta *Constitution*, argued that Will's picture of
the South was far more accurate than that found in recent sociological
studies. Thomas Lomax Hunter struck a similar theme in the Richmond *Times-Dispatch*, praising Will for taking issue with northern reformers who were proposing legislative solutions to the South's problems. The Charlotte (North Carolina) *Observer* located the appeal of
Lanterns in its "beautifully stated defense of the aristocratic ideal," an
ideal the *Observer* believed "still survives in thousands of Southern
men and women—men and women no longer a unified band, but scattered like tiny islets through a culture, or lack of it, which they can
understand intellectually but not spiritually." Similar sentiments were
echoed from Fort Worth to Greensboro, from Nashville to New Orleans. Southerners alarmed by changes within their region and by
northern proposals for reforming it praised *Lanterns* for describing and
defending the better elements of their culture.[44]

Many northern critics also praised *Lanterns*. A few, like Edwin Tribble of the Washington D.C. *Star*, criticized Will's views on blacks and
his defense of sharecropping, but most defended such views by arguing
that they were the product of Will's experiences living among blacks.
Charlotte Becker of the Buffalo *News* wrote that Will's comments on
blacks "put sententious sociologists to shame," and *Time* magazine
described Will's practical experience in managing Trail Lake. Most
northern reviewers praised Will's portrait of the South. Carl Sandburg,
who had read the manuscript, said *Lanterns* was "among the auto-
biographies requisite to understanding America." Lawrence Olsen of
the New York *Herald-Tribune* called it "an indispensable addition to
the record of Southern life and Southern tradition," and praised Will's
use of dialect. While most reviewers focused on Will's description of
the South, Hirschell Brickell of the New York *Times* pointed out the
universality of Will's themes by quoting Jonathan Daniels' comment
that Will was "more nearly a citizen of the solar system" than of
Greenville. Even Brickell, however, admitted that what he liked best
about *Lanterns* was its local color and focus.[45]

Lanterns on the Levee also caught the attention of several literary
and scholarly journals. The reviews in these publications were mixed.
William Jay Gold, editor of the *Virginia Quarterly Review*, wrote in

the *Saturday Review of Literature* that *Lanterns* was beautifully written and "as autobiography it has few equals in recent books." His own journal, however, carried a review by James Orrick that acknowledged the book's charm but added, "It would be easy to write a review that was all appreciation, were it not that on every issue of real importance Mr. Percy is so baldly reactionary, arrogant, and irrational that it is staggering." Orrick was especially appalled by Will's views on race, as were the reviewers for *Nation* and *Commonweal*. Most of these reviewers shared Orrick's assumption that what was "of real importance" were Will's views on particular political and social issues such as race relations and sharecropping. Even more literal-minded was George Osborn's review in the *Journal of Southern History*. Osborn treated his readers to an assortment of statistics on how much cotton Trail Lake produced and how many families lived there.[46]

Conservative essayist Albert Jay Nock defended *Lanterns on the Levee* in the *Atlantic Monthly*. "It is full of authentic information, it reflects a rich experience, and above all it is wholly free from the neurasthenic drivel which afflicts so many of the current outpourings about the Old South." Nock's review was unfortunately short, but it is easy to imagine why he enjoyed *Lanterns*. According to his biographer, the things Nock valued most in life were "a useless liberal education, good breeding and manners, detached analysis, tolerance," all of which received considerable attention from Will. When Nock's own autobiography appeared two years after *Lanterns* was published, he described it in terms applicable to Will's as "a purely literary and philosophical autobiography with only enough collateral odds and ends thrown in to hold the narrative together . . . the autobiography of a mind in relation to the society in which it found itself." *Lanterns on the Levee* contained more "collateral odds and ends" than Nock's *Memoirs* because Will had inherited a tradition of involvement in community affairs, but the focus in both books is the same. Both record the images and events that made an impression on the author's mind in order to describe the ideas and beliefs that the events generated. Will's tale of his adventures in the war, for example, was an essay on the rewards of fighting for a noble cause; his description of the fight against the Klan was a plea for tolerance; and his essay "The White Plague," before it was edited, was a discussion of the price of technological progress, or, as Will would more likely have put it, an essay on greed. Will shared with Nock an idealism, a belief that enduring truths were more important than ephemeral events, which made them both feel superfluous in modern America.[47]

Curiously, the reviewer who best described the idealism underlying *Lanterns* was W. J. Cash, who had only recently published his *The Mind of the South*, a history generally unsympathetic to the southern aristocracy. Cash wrote, "Percy is that exceedingly rare thing, a surviving authentic Southern aristocrat. . . . And his book is a fine one, the merits of which ought not to be obscured by any ideological disputes. The passages which concern his childhood and the struggles of a sensitive young man to adjust himself to the world are as good as any American novelist has produced." Cash's willingness to see *Lanterns* as literature rather than sociology was all the more surprising because he was himself usually preoccupied with social and economic issues.[48]

Will was pleasantly surprised by the success of *Lanterns on the Levee*, but he refused to take himself too seriously as a prose writer. He wrote to an admirer of his poetry that "although people generally seem to like my recent prose attempt better, I still like best my poems, so I am happy you like them too." Prose had brought him success; poetry, satisfaction.[49]

In August, Will visited Knopf in New York to talk about the collection of his poetry that his publisher had proposed when *Lanterns* hit the best seller list. Will was not interested in the project; he didn't think his poems would sell, and he dreaded the effort of putting together another book. He left New York for his cousin Janet's summer home at Lee, Massachusetts, and attended the Berkshire Music Festival with her. During his visit his chronic high blood pressure became acute, forcing him to check into Johns Hopkins Hospital. The doctors there told him that he had the oldest body for a man his age that they had ever seen, and advised rest.[50]

Will returned home to relax, stopping briefly at Sewanee to visit some old friends. When he reached Greenville, he found his old friend Tommy Shields dying. During his last days Shields cried out for Will in his lucid moments. Will had suffered a cerebral hemorrhage that impaired his speech, but despite his own failing health he moved in with Shields so that he could be there when he was needed. When Shields died, Will had him buried in the Percy plot.[51]

On December 7 Will was lounging around the house in his black kimono when he heard the news of the Japanese attack on Pearl Harbor. Despite his love of Japanese culture, he was delighted by the news, for now the United States was in the war. But Will would not live to see the great drama unfold. He was in great pain throughout the Christmas holidays, and in January checked into a Greenville hospital with an intestinal hemorrhage. He betrayed no fear of the death he knew to be upon him. He received visitors for a week; on January 21 he died.[52]

Although Will had not asked for the last sacraments, his funeral the next afternoon was presided over by Father Igoe of Saint Joseph's Catholic Church. The *Mississippiana*, a black newspaper, paid tribute to Will for helping blacks win justice; the lower house of the state legislature adjourned for the funeral. Will's death also brought tributes from the literary world. The Poetry Society of America honored him that year with a reading of his poems, and Will finished third in the voting for the Pulitzer Prize for biography. The remembrances that Will would have enjoyed most came later. In 1943 Knopf issued *The Collected Poems of William Alexander Percy*, and ten years later Hodding Carter's Levee Press issued a small collection called *Of Silence and Stars*.[53]

The appearance of Will's *Collected Poems* caused novelist Caroline Gordon to wonder in a review why he had not become a better poet. Looking back over his poetry she found indications of real talent and decided that his commitment to delta affairs had infringed too much on his poetic meditations. Gordon underestimated the positive impact of Will's daily life on his poetry. However, she was correct in recognizing that Will was never able to completely integrate his life and poetry, or, for that matter, to fully separate them. The poetry within him overflowed into his daily living of the good life, and those who heard the ageless rhythms of his music were comforted.[54]

Chapter 10

Walker Percy

Planters, Gardeners, and Such

During my day I have witnessed the disintegration of that moral cohesion of the South which had given it its strength and its sons their singleness of purpose and simplicity. Today there is fretting and fuming on the part of young people over what they should do, how they should act, what is worthwhile. Standards are in flux: there is no commonly accepted good way of life—and the hospitals can't hold the neurotics, the mental cripples, the moral anemics, the blasted who strove to build a pattern because none existed.

Will Percy
Lanterns on the Levee

In his case, though, it was part of a family pattern. Over the years his family had turned ironical and lost its gift for action. It was an honorable and violent family, but gradually the violence had been deflected and turned inward. The great grandfather knew what was what and said so and acted accordingly and did not care what anyone thought. He even wore a pistol in a holster like a Western hero and once met the Grand Wizard of the Ku Klux Klan in a barbershop and invited him then and there to shoot it out in the street. The next generation, the grandfather, seemed to know what was what but he was not really so sure. He was brave but he gave much thought to the business of being brave. He too would have shot it out with the Grand Wizard if only he could have made certain it was the right thing to do. The father was a brave man too and said he didn't care what others thought, but he did care. More than anything else, he wished to act with honor and be thought well of by other men. So living for him was a strain. He became ironical. For him it was not a small thing to walk down the street on an ordinary September morning. In the end he was killed by his own irony and sadness and by the strain of living out an ordinary day in a perfect dance of honor.
As for the present young man, the last of the line, he did not know what to think. So he became a watcher and a listener and a wanderer.

Walker Percy
The Last Gentleman

Lanterns on the Levee was Will Percy's last attempt to apply his family's values to life in modern America. Since his passing, America has changed dramatically, and most of his views on specific political and social issues are valuable now only as reflections of the compassion, the sense of duty, and the pessimism about the course of modern civilization that lay behind them. Which recent changes Will would have applauded is hard to say. As his adopted son Walker wrote, "Will Percy's strong feelings about the shift of power from the virtuous few would hardly be diminished today, but he might recast his villains and redress the battle lines."[1] None of the changes would have shaken Will's conviction that there are villains aplenty and a virtuous few, and that it is the duty and joy of the latter to battle the former, however overwhelming the odds.

Fortunately Walker Percy has taken up his uncle's task of writing about the world and the Percys. In his novels and essays Walker has clearly distinguished himself from Will by rejecting Will's stoic resignation for a more optimistic existential Catholicism. Walker has also avoided the public duties that occupied Will, preferring instead to devote himself to writing and "living a life." Walker has not, however, repudiated his legacy. Rather, he has made a further adjustment of the Percys' values to modern America. When LeRoy Percy was defeated in his Senate race, he decided that shooting at stars was poor marksmanship and that "it is best to draw a bead on something that you have a chance to hit." After the election he focused his attention on the delta. Will assumed many of his father's public duties, but he never equaled LeRoy's political influence, and only his chronic need to help others prevented him from retiring to a quiet life of poetry, music, gardening, and travel. He found it difficult to identify a "commonly accepted good way of life" and never completely reconciled his inner and outer lives. By eschewing public life and concentrating on "living a life," as he puts it, Walker has followed his great-uncle LeRoy's advice and chosen a target within his range. While his brother LeRoy Pratt and LeRoy Pratt's son Billy fought for civil rights in Greenville, Walker sought a cure for the malaise that alienates men from each other and from their own lives. In one sense Walker has withdrawn behind the innermost wall of individuality. By recording the fruits of his search in his novels, however, he has preserved his family's influence and tradition of leadership in an increasingly democratic society that has little use for aristocrats.[2]

Reading Walker Percy's novels without considering him as the heir of his family's values is a perfectly reasonable approach to them; it is, in fact, probably the approach Walker would prefer his readers take. The novels stand on their own as a record of Walker's battle with the malaise that he sees descending on the modern world. Furthermore, looking for references to his family's past or his own life is fraught with perils. Walker has been reluctant to identify such references and has complicated the matter further by using incidents from the lives of his father LeRoy Pratt and his Uncle Will. It is possible, however, to identify in Walker's novels, and in what we know of his life, some of the themes that occupied Will and, in some cases, LeRoy. Walker's treatment of these themes from his existential Catholic viewpoint places them in a new perspective, and examining how he has adapted them to modern conditions may give us some idea of how the Percys' values have weathered the malaise.

Most accounts of Walker's early life focus on his roundabout course to a writing career. He had written a short story even before his father's death. In Greenville, he wrote a gossip column for the school paper and befriended classmates Shelby Foote, who became a novelist and historian, and Charles Bell, who became a poet. Walker once entered some of his poetry anonymously in a contest judged by his Uncle Will, and won, though Will told him later, "You needn't be happy about it because it was the worst bunch of poems I've ever had occasion to judge." Will introduced all of his sons to literature, but he never encouraged Walker to choose writing as a profession, or anything else, for that matter. The boys were left free to choose their own careers, and Walker chose medicine. Walker was genuinely interested in medicine and science, but he was also honoring the Percy tradition of learning a profession whether or not one intended to ever practice it. He recalled recently that "I think what happened was I felt obliged to go into a profession. I didn't want to go into law. It's like a hangover from the old Southern tradition of "what do you do?" Maybe it goes back to the English or the Europeans. Certain vocations are open to you, you know, what is it? Law, medicine, army, priesthood. I got it down to medicine, which is a hell of a bad reason for going into medicine."[3]

Walker prepared for a medical career by majoring in chemistry at the University of North Carolina. During his sophomore year he also wrote two articles and a couple of book reviews for the campus literary publication, the *Carolina Magazine*. In one of the articles, "The Willard Huntington Wright Murder Case," Walker argued that Wright, an art critic and brother of synchromist painter Stanton McDonald-Wright, had murdered his better self by writing lucrative murder mysteries under the pseudonym S. S. Van Dine. Underlying this argument is the Percy assumption that practicing a profession should not be allowed to interfere with living the good life. Furthermore, like Will at about the same age, Walker identified the good life with the creative inner life of the artist, and also like Will, saw the necessity of practicing a profession as a threat to this inner life.

Walker did not let such cares prevent him from enjoying Chapel Hill's version of the good life. He joined the Sigma Alpha Epsilon fraternity and two secret honorary societies, the 13 Club and the Order of the Gimghoul. As a senior he joined the Amphate Rothen and became one of the five rulers of Gimghoul. Upon graduating, he abandoned such collegiate socializing and took up the task of mastering his profession. Following Will's advice, he entered the Columbia University College of Physicians and Surgeons. Will, who had gone to the Harvard Law School because it was near the Boston Symphony, recommended Columbia to Walker because it was near the Metropolitan Opera.[4]

While studying at Columbia, Walker underwent daily sessions with psychoanalyst Janet Rioch. Rioch was recommended to Walker by psychologist Harry Stack Sullivan, whom he had first encountered sitting in Will's kitchen drinking vodka martinis. Walker probably hoped that analysis would help him overcome the conflict between his outer, professional self and his inner artistic promptings. Analysis offered him a chance to approach his inner problems armed with the professional knowledge of his outer life. Furthermore, a career as a psychiatrist, which he probably would have taken up had he remained in medicine, would have offered him the opportunity to pursue his interest in the inner life while practicing a profession. Science failed him, however. After three years of analysis, he was still unsure what troubled him.[5]

Walker spent the autumn of 1941 working at the Gamble Clinic in Greenville and looking after his dying Uncle Will. In January he returned to New York to intern at Bellevue Hospital. Shortly after Will's death Walker discovered that he had contracted tuberculosis while performing autopsies at Bellevue, and had to enter the sanitarium at Lake Saranac, New York. He spent the next two years there, resting, practicing medicine part time, and spending most of his time reading. He began with Dostoyevsky, whom he had read in high school, and worked his way through several modern European novelists and philosophers including Albert Camus, Jean Paul Sartre, Gabriel Marcel, Martin Heidegger, and most important, Sören Kierkegaard. After two years he tried to continue his medical career by returning to Columbia to teach pathology, but a relapse forced him to spend another year at the Gaylord Farms Sanitarium in Connecticut, where he resumed his reading.

Walker has described this period in his life as "the best thing that ever happened to me because it gave me a chance to quit medicine. I had a respectable excuse." He was still not certain exactly what he wanted to do. "I don't know whether I was thinking of being a writer by then, or a bum, or what," he recently told an interviewer. His uncertainty suggests the increasingly existentialist cast of his thought. Existentialist literature is full of "bums," if we take *bum* to mean one who refuses to sacrifice his personal interests and leisure in order to earn a living or make a contribution to society. Walker associated art with the inner life, but art remained only a means to a more personal end. His reading had convinced him that art could make statements about the inner life that were as important and valid as the truths of science. When he set out to live a life, he began using writing as a tool to structure and record his findings.[6]

Walker's new purpose began to crystallize when he left the sanitarium. His health would have permitted him to return to medicine, but he did not do so. He returned to Greenville for a visit and then moved to Santa Fe, New Mexico, with Shelby Foote. Walker stayed only a few months, but he apparently came upon an important truth in the desert. In his second novel, *The Last Gentleman*, Will Barrett calls the desert "the locus of pure possibility . . . [where] what a man can be the next minute bears no relation to what he is or what he was the minute before."[7] Walker emerged from the desert committed to exploring the inner side of life through art. His Uncle Will had considered such a course at about the same age, but his sense of civic responsibility and his doubts about his own literary ability dissuaded him. Somewhere, perhaps in Kierkegaard, perhaps in the desert, perhaps in his indifference to success, Walker decided to make the necessary leap of faith.

Walker soon made two more decisions requiring a similar leap of faith. Like Will Barrett in *The Last Gentleman*, Will Percy had never decided whether love was "a sweetnesse or a wantonesse," so he had never married. When Walker returned from Sante Fe, he went to New Orleans and resumed his courtship of Mary Townsend, whom he had met while working at the Gamble clinic in Greenville. In November, 1946, they were married. By marrying, Walker enriched the personal life he aimed to explore and committed himself to overcoming the dilemma to which Will had succumbed. Walker and Bunt, as Mrs. Percy is called, moved to Will's summer home at Sewanee to read and study religion. In a few months they made another leap of faith by converting to Catholicism, coincidentally doing so in the same place that Will Percy had converted from Catholicism to uncertainty.

By this time Walker was firmly committed to becoming a writer. His brother visited him at Sewanee during the summer of 1947, and recalls seeing an eleven-hundred-page manuscript of a novel Walker had written called *The Charterhouse*. Phinizy was able to get through only about fifty pages, and some years later, after having it rejected by publishers and criticized to the tune of thirty pages by Caroline Gordon, Walker destroyed it. Toward the end of the summer Walker and Bunt moved to New Orleans. Walker refused to call himself a writer. When asked, he told people that he was a retired physician; but he continued to read intensively and work at his writing.[8]

After seven years of quietly living a life in New Orleans, Walker began publishing philosophical articles in various journals. These articles revealed his wide range of philosophic and linguistic interests, but like his Uncle Will's poetry, they were not the form best suited for his ideas. He was primarily interested in the alienation he found in everyday life, and to explore this problem fully he needed a form that would allow him to examine specific characters in concrete situations. In 1961 he brought out his first novel, *The Moviegoer*.

Walker's road to becoming a novelist was almost as long and circuitous as Will's road to writing *Lanterns on the Levee*. Both were strongly affected by the Percy tradition of leading an active, profitable, and useful life. Because the Percys placed a high value on leisure, Will was able to find time for a contemplative life as well as an active one. Walker has concentrated on writing, but even he made his bow to tradition by becoming a doctor, and could cite Colonel Percy's brothers, LeRoy Pope and John Walker, as precedents for not practicing his profession. Both Walker and Will felt pressure from within and without to devote themselves to something more respectable than simply living their lives; Walker was better able than Will to overcome this pressure, and this difference is apparent in their literary productivity.

If their family tradition of pursuing a respectable profession impeded Will's and Walker's literary careers, being a Percy also offered both men important advantages as writers. The first was financial security. Will was a good enough lawyer to make his career in a firm other than his father's, but he would have had trouble finding another senior partner as sympathetic to his frequent, lengthy vacations as LeRoy was, and some of his best poetry was written on these trips. Will's estate, in turn, has allowed Walker to devote his time to writing. Will could have retired from the law earlier than he did to write, but doing so during the depression might have compromised his family's financial security. Walker has been able to take better advantage of his family's resources in part because of his brothers. From the abolition of primogeniture and entail to the progressive inheritance tax, the American economy has demanded that prominent families produce at least one member in each generation who can do a little better than balance the books, and those that have not have ceased to be prominent.

Being a Percy also conferred other, less material advantages. Will and Walker received a good education and inherited the Percys' tradition of broad-ranging interests in the arts and sciences. Colonel Percy was a planter, soldier, lawyer, and politician; LeRoy combined law, engineering, and politics in advocating better levees, ran a plantation, and read *Ivanhoe* once a year. Such examples probably encouraged Will to pursue his literary and musical interests in addition to his career as an attorney. They may also have helped ease Walker's doubts about becoming a writer and encouraged him to use his scientific background in his novels, which he has done extensively.

Will and Walker also inherited an awareness of belonging to a family with a notable history. This consciousness of their past turned the family's habits into venerable traditions and provided Will and Walker with an ample supply of common stories and themes. There is a distinct philosophical difference between Will's and Walker's treatments of these themes and stories. Walker has used them to elaborate his Christian existentialism and to argue against his uncle's stoic philosophy. At other points, however, the differences are not so much antithetical as historical; Walker is a generation younger than Will, and his views on some issues, such as race, are more a sequel to Will's than a contradiction of them.

In his first novel, *The Moviegoer*, Walker stressed his rejection of Will's stoicism. Walker differentiates himself from Will by having Binx Bolling, the central character, reject his Aunt Emily's stoicism and, more positively, by describing Binx's search for a way to overcome his estrangement through the Kierkegaardian devices of ordeal, rotation, and repetition. The climax of the novel comes when Binx takes a train trip to Chicago with his cousin Kate, who shares his feeling of dislocation. They attempt to overcome their alienation by making love, and though they fail, the attempt is a clear violation of Aunt Emily's code of behavior. When Binx returns to New Orleans, he is summoned to his aunt's home for a thorough dressing down. Emily angrily defends the values of her family and class and attacks the morality of the modern world, assuming Binx has accepted the latter. Wondering where she went wrong raising him, she tells Binx: "More than anything I wanted to pass on to you the one heritage of the men of our family, a certain quality of spirit, a gaiety, a sense of duty, a nobility worn lightly, a sweetness, a gentleness with women—the only good things the South ever had and the only things that really matter in this life. Ah well. . . . But how did it happen that none of this ever meant anything to you?" But Binx is no more comfortable with the new morality than the old, and answers his aunt: "You say that none of what you said ever meant anything to me. That is not true. On the contrary, I have never forgotten anything you ever said. In fact I have pondered over it all my life. My objections, though they are not exactly objections, cannot be expressed in the usual way. To tell the truth, I can't express them at all."[9]

Although Binx is unable to formulate his objections to Aunt Emily's stoicism, *The Moviegoer* addressed several themes that Walker would use in his later novels to elaborate his "objections" to his Uncle Will. Aunt Emily suggests one of these themes when she tells Binx: "I'll make you a little confession. I am not ashamed to use the word class. I will also plead guilty to another charge. The charge is that people of my class think we're better than other people. You're damn right we're better. We're better because we do not shirk our obligations either to ourselves or to others." Will Percy held similar views on the nature and role of the South's upper class. In "Enzio's Kingdom" he imagined a civilization ruled by an aristocracy of merit, and in *Lanterns on the Levee* he used LeRoy as a representative of that class. LeRoy and his supporters, Will wrote, "were leaders of the people, not elected or self-elected, but destined, under the compulsion of leadership because of their superior intellect, training, character, and opportunity. And the people were willing to be led by them because of their desperate need of leadership in those troubled times." Will saw his father's defeat by Vardaman in the Senate race as a rejection of such leadership, and the experience set him on the road to the stoicism of a Roman watching the barbarians battering at his walls. "Since then," he recalled, "I haven't expected that what should be would be and I haven't believed that virtue guaranteed any reward except itself."[10]

The loss of society's deference and respect made Will wonder whether his class had degenerated from the example of its forebears. Young Enzio is not the leader his father Frederick was, just as, in *Lanterns*, Will is not the leader LeRoy was. In *Lanterns* LeRoy acted nobly by instinct. Will knew instinctively what was noble, but he had to muster his courage to do it. He knew that this difference was due in part to changes in the South. He wrote of his grandfather's career after the Civil War, "Those days you had to be a hero or a villain or a weakling—you couldn't be just middling ordinary."[11] Will could recall the values of his family and act accordingly; but his society no longer ratified his performance, and he could never be certain that he had performed his part properly.

The leading characters in Walker's novels take this degeneration and attendant uncertainty a step further. Binx Bolling confesses that he is not especially smart, though "my mother and my aunt think I am smart because I am quiet and absent-minded—and because my fa-

ther and grandfather were smart." Will Barrett, the major character of
Walker's second novel, *The Last Gentleman*, is more confused and
alienated than Binx. "Like many young men in the South," Walker
says of Barrett, "he became overly subtle and had trouble ruling out
the possible." The commonness of Barrett's malady among southerners suggests that it is due to social change, but Walker quickly adds
that in Barrett, the degeneration goes deeper: "It was more than being a
Southerner. For some years he had had a nervous condition and as a
consequence he did not know how to live his life."[12] This disclaimer is
probably due in part to Walker's reluctance to write a sociological
novel. It also suggests that the social changes that occurred while Will
Percy was growing up were internalized by Walker's generation, taking
the form in Barrett of mental instability.

It is worth noting, however, that Walker does not consider mental
instability a refutation of his characters' viewpoints. He recently told
an interviewer: "What I try to do is always pose the question 'Is this
man or woman more abnormal than the "normal society" around
them?' I want the reader to be poised between these two values, and I
want the question always to be raised as to who's crazy." Virtually all
of Walker's major characters undergo or have undergone some form of
psychiatric care, including Binx's cousin Kate, who Walker says may
be "closer to me than any of them."[13] Walker's viewpoint may have
been influenced by R. D. Laing, who also refuses to condemn a viewpoint simply because it is statistically abnormal, or "insane." It can
also be seen as a further tactical reduction of the Percy sphere of influence. By giving as much credence to the viewpoint of the deranged individual as to the "normal" viewpoint of modern society, Walker is in a
sense performing the intellectual equivalent of Will Percy's refusing to
mechanize operations at Trail Lake, except that now the walls of the
fortress encompass only the individual. In Walker's novels this constriction of sphere leads to estrangement from the world and to loneliness, which his characters try to overcome by reestablishing contact
with other isolated individuals. Walker's most successful evocation of
such intersubjectivity comes in his latest novel, *The Second Coming*,
and the two characters who achieve it are Will Barrett, now middle
aged and once again suffering mental lapses, and Allie, a young girl
who has recently escaped from an asylum.

In *The Last Gentleman* Walker gives us an updated version of *Lanterns on the Levee* that describes some of the changes in the South that make his characters unstable. The South is now "happy, victorious, Christian, rich, patriotic and Republican."[14] Instead of LeRoy Percy and his compatriots gathering on the veranda to sip juleps and discuss the delta's problems, Walker shows us Chandler Vaught, owner of the second largest Chevy dealership in the world, discussing world problems with Lamar Thigpen on the patio of a purple castle looking out onto a golf course. The South has become a grotesque parody of its past, peopled by businessmen whose wives decorate their homes in antebellum chic. If Walker's characters were not abnormal to begin with, they would, in such a society, have to become so in order to have any chance of living a life.

Lamenting the decline of the South is an old and honored custom among the Percys (and many other southerners). Even LeRoy, who believed in progress, bemoaned the decline after his defeat by Vardaman and during his fight against the Klan. Partly sour grapes, such lamentations also offered a therapeutic function, especially when they pointed toward impending disaster. During the Klan fight LeRoy traced the decline of Greenville's sense of community and predicted further decline if the Klan were allowed to stay, and he thereby encouraged his fellow citizens to act together as they had always done in times of disaster. During disasters people naturally look for leadership, and at such times the Percys were at their best. Colonel Percy emerged as a leader during what the white planters considered the disaster of Reconstruction. LeRoy won the confidence of his neighbors during the floods that plagued Greenville. He entered the Senate race because he and his supporters believed Vardaman threatened disaster. During and after the 1927 flood he naturally assumed a leading role representing the delta's interests in Washington, making dire predictions that the delta would become a wasteland without federal support for levees.

Disasters also held a certain appeal for Will, because they restored, at least temporarily, the sense of community he saw slipping away. He wrote of his experiences in the war: "That short period of my life spent in the line is the only one I remember step by step—as if it moved *sub specie aeternitatis*. Not that I enjoyed it; I hated it. Not that I was fitted for it by temperament or ability, I was desperately unfitted; but it, somehow, had meaning, and daily life hasn't: it was part of a common endeavor, and daily life is isolated and lonely." Will also admired the community spirit that the flood of 1927 temporarily restored to Greenville. "Those first few weeks the citizens of my little town were magnificent: they relearned friendliness; they re-established unity; they cleansed themselves of some of the venom and nastiness left by the Ku Klux Klan; they worked without pay for the general good, and no work was too hard and no hours too long."[15] Will also tried to get involved in the disaster of World War II, but his health prevented him from doing so.

Disasters have also played an important part in Walker's life and his novels. His career change from medicine to writing began during World War II and followed closely the twin disasters of his uncle's death and his own contraction of tuberculosis. In his novels Walker has used disasters in some of the traditional Percy ways. For him, as for Will, disasters offer a chance to overcome the boredom and estrangement of everyday life. In *The Moviegoer*, Kate tells Binx that the happiest moment of her life was a car wreck in which her fiancé died, and compares this to Binx's war experience. Binx does not share Kate's enthusiasm, but Will Barrett does, in *The Last Gentleman*. For Barrett, "It was not the prospect of the Last Day which depressed him but rather the prospect of living through an ordinary Wednesday morning. Though science taught that good environments were better than bad environments, it appeared to him that the opposite was the case." Barrett recalls two occasions when a disaster allowed him to overcome everydayness: once during a hurricane and again when a worker in a museum fell through a skylight, suddenly making it possible to understand the paintings.

Disasters allow Walker's characters to set aside their uncertainties and act. Kate tells Binx "how simple it would be to fight." For Barrett, war is a way of overcoming the problems he has "ruling out the possible. . . . What happens to a man to whom all things seem possible and every course of action open? Nothing of course. Except war. If a man lives in the sphere of the possible and waits for something to happen, what he is waiting for is war—or the end of the world. That is why Southerners like to fight and make good soldiers. In war the possible becomes actual through no doing of one's own." Walker's use of disasters to overcome everydayness combines his family history and his Christian existentialism. Gabriel Marcel, among others, prescribed "ordeal" as a way of overcoming alienation, and Walker has used this idea to interpret his family's history of flourishing during disasters from an existentialist viewpoint.[16]

A similar blend of family tradition and Christian existentialism underlies Walker's belief that the present age is passing away and a new age is dawning. Again setting a precedent for Walker, Will Percy wrote in *Lanterns*: "Under the southern Valhalla the torch has been thrust, already the bastions have fallen. Watching the flames mount, we, scattered remnant of the old dispensation, smile scornfully, but grieve in our hearts. A side-show Gotterdammerung perhaps, yet who shall inherit our earth, the earth we loved? The meek? The Hagens? In either event, we accept, but we do not approve." Will's vision of impending disaster strengthened his stoicism, a philosophy that not incidentally flourished during the historical gap between the old Roman civilization and the dawning age of Catholicism. Writing from a Christian rather than a stoic point of view, Walker has treated the prospect of an apocalypse more hopefully than Will did. In *The Moviegoer* Binx wonders: "Is it possible that—For a long time I have secretly hoped for the end of the world and believed with Kate and my aunt and Sam Yerger and many other people that only after the end could the few who survive creep out of their holes and discover themselves to be themselves and live merrily as children among the viny ruins."[17]

In his third novel, *Love in the Ruins*, Walker explores more extensively the possibilities offered by apocalypse. *Love in the Ruins* is, among other things, a reworking of the legend of Dr. Faust in an apocalyptic setting. Walker's Faust is Dr. Tom More, a dilapidated scion of Sir Thomas More, who has developed a device called a lapsometer to combat the malaise that is tearing society apart. The novel opens with Dr. More wondering: "Now in these dread latter days of the old violent beloved U.S.A. and of the Christ-forgetting Christ-haunted death-dealing Western world I came to myself in a grove of young pines and the question came to me: has it happened at last? Either I am right and a catastrophe will occur, or it won't and I'm crazy. In either case the outlook is not so good."[18]

As is his habit, Walker leaves considerable room for doubt about who is crazy. He describes a polarized, violent political atmosphere that is just similar enough to contemporary reality to be believable. On the other hand, Dr. More's behavior suggests that he might be imagining the apocalypse; he spends his evenings reading accounts of the battle of Verdun, looking for a way to use this disaster to overcome his own alienation. "It is possible," More suspects, "to be dying and alive at Verdun and alive and dying as a booster of the Nittany Lions."[19] This technique allows Walker to turn the self-doubts that his Uncle Will felt into an existential reevaluation of contemporary values.

Love in the Ruins reaches its climax when Art Immelmann, a Mephistophelian bureaucrat who has arranged the funding to produce More's lapsometers, distributes them to several medical students and then turns the lapsometers on the participants in a golf tournament. Dr. More finally vanquishes Immelmann by calling on the ghost of his great Catholic kinsman Sir Thomas More. The novel's apocalyptic setting has given him the fortitude to act resolutely, as his forebear did; but his science has not saved the world, as he had hoped it would.

The conclusion of *Love in the Ruins* is set five years further in the future. The threat of complete social breakdown has passed, though conditions have not improved. In the meantime the black revolutionaries who threatened Paradise Estates now own most of it because oil was discovered in their swamp. Dr. More has chosen between the four women he was in love with during the threatened apocalypse, and settled down to a quiet life with his former nurse, Ellen. The ordeal of rescuing Ellen from Art Immelmann gave Dr. More the fortitude to undertake the kind of life that Ellen represents—a life of "watching and waiting and thinking and working." The social inversion that occurred when blacks became wealthy has simplified his life. He now spends his time tending his garden and performing the few professional duties that the black majority deems within his competence. Ironically, his ostracism from public life has restored his sense of his own sovereignty. "I am a poor man but a kingly one," he declares. He continues working on his lapsometer, but his contentment in living his life with Ellen has dampened his enthusiasm for saving the world. His garden, unlike Will Percy's, is a private sanctuary; as Walker recently said of Dr. More, "He's a little like Candide who was cultivating his garden, a small garden." Unable to save the world, More has sealed himself off from it in order to save himself.[20]

Dr. More's simple, isolated life of "watching and waiting and thinking and working" is as close as Walker comes in his first four novels to prescribing a way to live a life in a time between ages. Walker uses two symbols in this prescription, blacks and women, that his uncle also used to criticize modern culture and describe the good life. The role of women and blacks in both Will's and Walker's writings has been determined primarily by their larger view of the world. Walker has given these symbols new meanings, because his prescription for the good life differs from his Uncle Will's.

Blacks have been important to the Percys since the first American members of the family bought slaves to work their plantations. After the slaves were freed, they remained an important factor in the delta's economy and, for a time, in politics. Colonel Percy fought to exclude blacks from politics during Reconstruction and adjusted to the economic effect of abolition by installing the sharecropping system on his plantation.

LeRoy inherited the sharecropping system from his father along with the old Percy Plantation, and also used it on his other plantations. Under this system blacks remained socially and economically subservient, and were highly vulnerable to unscrupulous planters. Their most substantial freedom was the right to move from one plantation to another if they believed they were being cheated, but even this right was impeded by the unspoken agreement among planters that prohibited hiring croppers who still owed a debt to their previous landlord. Many planters tried to tie blacks to the land indefinitely by never allowing their tenants to get out of debt. In the labor-hungry delta such agreements were not always enforceable, but planters did frequently pay off the debts of tenants moving onto their land, thus perpetuating what were often fraudulent debts.

In his dealings with the black croppers at Trail Lake, LeRoy tried to balance the business ethos of the New South with the paternalism of the Old. He expected his tenants to live up to the obligations of their contract and had no qualms about seizing their property if they did not. He refused, however, to impose debts that could never be paid off. In 1906 most of his tenants moved from Trail Lake because of the boll weevil, leaving behind a debt of twenty thousand dollars that was never collected. When tenants came to Trail Lake, LeRoy would pay off their debts to previous landlords only if they brought some supplies

of their own with them. This policy served as a rough-and-ready solution to a complex problem. It was economically feasible because croppers with their own equipment were worth the investment; and it demanded that blacks who owned property assume the responsibilities
that economic life entailed, while it prevented their inability to do so
from reenslaving them. LeRoy cooperated with other planters who had
legitimate grievances against blacks who cropped for him, but he stood
up for his tenants when he thought they were right, even if it meant
defying other planters. When a planter whose family was a longtime
friend of the Percys threatened a Negro who had left behind a debt of
forty dollars and moved onto Trail Lake, LeRoy wrote him that he did
not think it would be right to carry out these threats, and added, "I am
sure it would not be the wise thing."[21]

LeRoy's mixture of social Darwinism and paternalism extended beyond the fields of Trail Lake. He helped Dr. E. P. Brown build a factory
in Greenville to employ blacks; he wrote letters of recommendation
for, and otherwise encouraged, young blacks seeking a professional
life; he habitually checked land titles for black landowners who could
not pay for this service, and when he thought them deserving, lent
them money to forestall foreclosures. LeRoy encouraged blacks to
assume the economic responsibilities that came with emancipation,
but he doubted that many could do so successfully, and he retained a
strong measure of paternalism in his treatment of them. In a letter of
recommendation for his chauffeur, Ambrose Edgerton, LeRoy wrote
that Edgerton was a good driver and mechanic but that "he has one
defect. He has not very much sense and a great deal of vanity and
wants to be praised all of the time and does not like to be reproved or
corrected. . . . If anyone will take the trouble to give him a thrashing,
it will cure him of this fault." LeRoy's paternalism also led him to
favor a federal antilynching law and to oppose all mob efforts to take
blacks out of Greenville's jail before they were given a proper trial.[22]

LeRoy knew that in the short run blacks were vital to the delta's
prosperity. He tried without success to relieve this dependency by
bringing Italian laborers to Sunnyside Plantation. His fear that Vardaman would frighten blacks out of the delta was one of his major reasons for entering the Senate race; his fear that the Klan would have a
similar effect led him to oppose it; and his fear that many blacks
would never return to the delta dictated his decision to leave them on

the levee during the flood of 1927 and hope for good weather. LeRoy believed that the good life of the delta depended on economic success, and his view of the Negro's role in delta life was primarily economic.

LeRoy's belief in social Darwinism combined with his belief in the innate simplicity of blacks forced him to assign blacks a tragic role in the world. When a fellow Mississippian praised him for speaking out publicly for Negro education, LeRoy responded that he did not expect many blacks to advance beyond the rudiments, and predicted that those who did "will go elsewhere, and in course of time, under the inexorable working out of the 'survival of the fittest,' they will have to go to the wall." As George M. Frederickson has pointed out, the idea that blacks would inevitably lose out to whites in a Malthusian struggle for existence was widely held during the late nineteenth century and was usually used "to justify a policy of repression and neglect."[23] In his speech on black education, however, LeRoy reversed the rhetorical thrust of the argument, arguing that blacks should be educated so that the Darwinian process could complete its work sooner. He was thus able to argue for a benevolent policy toward blacks from the common premises of his times.

In similar fashion LeRoy reversed the implications of black stereotypes in the jokes that he told about blacks. As Kenneth Burke has pointed out, tragedy involves heroes and villains, while comedy juxtaposes the intelligent and fools. In LeRoy's jokes blacks possess a simple wisdom that makes fools of others. In a speech to the Senate opposing an investigation supposedly designed to help the cotton farmer, LeRoy identified himself with such wisdom, arguing the investigation would do more harm than good, and saying he felt like the Negro who was fighting a bear and prayed "Please, Lawd, if you won't help me, don't help the bear." In a speech opposing the direct election of senators, LeRoy told another story that contrasted such simple wisdom with the machinations of the white mind. "An ignorant negro presented himself to register and said to the registrar: 'I can neither read nor write, but I want to be tried on the understanding clause.' The officer, turning over the constitution to find some clause to question him on, said: 'Bill, what are constitutions made for anyway?' The answer, cheerful and immediate, was: 'Why, boss, they's made to keep negroes from voting.'"[24]

In a speech opposing the Klan, LeRoy took great delight in contrasting blacks with Klansmen and assigning the role of fool to the latter. Ridiculing the Klan's claim that blacks could trust its knights, LeRoy asked: "Can't you see sheriff Nicholson, if he wanted to arrest a negro for robbing a hen roost wiring to Nashville for a posse of klansmen, and going down the road with a gang of white robed men behind him to arrest the negro; you would have to advertise to find the negro after that parade." It was not the Negro who ran who was foolish; it was the Klansmen who expected him not to, and any planter, LeRoy added, who didn't realize this "hasn't as much sense as a string of live fish."[25] LeRoy believed that the simplicity of blacks protected them from white sophistry.

Will gave blacks a similar role in some of his stories. He recalled being at Trail Lake once and hearing a tenant ask whose car was parked outside the office. Another replied "Dat's *us* car." Will glowed with happiness, thinking "how sweet it was to have the relation between landlord and tenant so close and affectionate that to them my car was their car." Will's chauffeur, Ford, set him straight on the way home, explaining, "He meant that's the car *you* bought with *us* money."[26] In this story, as in LeRoy's, it is the blacks who see things clearly. The difference is that Will, more introspective than his father, aims the irony of the story at himself.

Will also accepted his father's notion that blacks were doomed in their confrontation with white civilization, giving the idea a new twist. Convinced that the commercialism of modern civilization stunted man's spiritual nature, Will argued that blacks and other "primitive" races lived a happier, more complete life than more "advanced" whites. His purest example of this idea was the Samoans he lived among for six months. American blacks, though somewhat corrupted by their contact with whites, still retained some of their innocence, and many of Will's stories contrast this innocence with the spiritual bankruptcy of the modern world. Will records one of Ford's stories in *Lanterns*, a story about a Negro whom God throws out of heaven for doing loop-the-loops with his new wings. He accepts his banishment philosophically, saying "Well, jest remember this, Lawd: while I wuz up here in yo' place I wuz the flyin'est fool you had." Will draws the story's moral himself, writing, "Since the thirteenth century no one except Ford and his kind has been at ease in heaven, much less confident enough of it to imagine an aeroplane stunt there." After a couple more of Ford's stories, Will added, "Ford is my fate, my Old Man of the Sea, who tells me of Martin and admonishing cooters and angels that do the loop-the-loop, my only tie with Pan and the Satyrs and all earth creatures who smile sunshine and ask no questions and understand."[27] Like LeRoy, Will located the wisdom of blacks in their simplicity and consequent invulnerability to the mental gyrations that troubled whites. The difference between the two Percys lay in Will's belief that the entire world, rather than just his specific political enemies, was the victim of such gyrations.

Walker's views on blacks are more liberal than Will's. He has endorsed the civil rights movement; he has rejected the idea that differences between the races are biologically caused, as LeRoy believed, or determined by enduring cultural differences, as Will thought; and he has accepted the idea that given the opportunity, blacks could overcome such differences in a relatively short time. These are the chief differences between Will and Walker on the race issue and the source of the irony in Walker's treatment of blacks in his novels.

In his first two novels Walker portrays several blacks who would all have felt at home working for Will Percy. He uses these characters chiefly to contrast the alienation of his major characters with the paternal involvement of their forebears. Binx Bolling says of his Aunt Emily's butler, "Mercer is uneasy that in threading his way between servility and presumption, his foot might slip."[28] In *The Last Gentleman* Walker gives his black characters last names, which Will seldom did, an addition that confers both dignity and distance.

In each of these novels there is one black character who does not fit the pattern, and each anticipates the more fully developed use of blacks in *Love in the Ruins*. In *The Moviegoer* Binx says of an unnamed black man, "He is more respectable than respectable; he is more middle-class than one could believe." Walker made the same point in an interview, saying that no one is more conventional than middle-class blacks who are trying to overcome their past. In *Love in the Ruins* Walker draws an ironic conclusion: Blacks, by becoming like whites, have become vulnerable to the malaise of modern civilization. Colley Wilkes, for example, is "one of those super-Negroes who speak five languages, quote the sutras, and are wizards in electronics as well." Wilkes performs brilliantly in the stereotypically white world of science, but in learning to do so he has lost his true self. Dr. More's lapsometer diagnoses Wilkes as "a self successfully playing at being a self that is not itself." After the blacks take over Paradise Estates, we find Wilkes driving an orange Toyota and listening to "a Treasury of the World's Great Music, which has the good parts of a hundred famous symphonies." He has become a thoroughly respectable middle-class philistine and now qualifies to play the fool in Walker's story. Will Percy believed that blacks must choose between being first-rate Negroes or second-rate whites; Walker acknowledges that blacks can become first-rate whites, but doubts that it will bring them the happiness they anticipate.[29]

Walker also uses blacks to represent simplicity. Most of the black characters in *The Last Gentleman* inhabit the suburban New South and share its grotesque quality. The exception is Merriam, hunting companion of Barrett's Uncle Fannin. Merriam is an old style Negro who lives with Uncle Fannin in Shut Off, Louisiana, and hunts quail with him at Sunnyside. Both men observe the old rituals governing relations between blacks and whites, but despite these restrictions, their relationship is a close and satisfying one. They are good friends in much the same way that LeRoy Percy and Holt Collier were good friends. Uncle Fannin and Merriam watch Captain Kangaroo in the morning, hunt all day, and watch television westerns at night. This simple life, though only sketchily developed, makes them perhaps the happiest, most contented characters in the novel.[30]

There is similar innocence in Val Vaught's pupils, a group of mute black children. She tells Barrett that these people are the only people she knows who still believe in religion. They are able to believe, because when they discover language, "they are like Adam on the First Day."[31] As mute black children, Val's pupils contain a triple dose of innocence, and this makes them ideally suited to escape everydayness and receive the values of a new age.

In the conclusion of *Love in the Ruins*, the blacks move into Paradise Estates and become the middle class, and Dr. More and Ellen move into the old slave quarters. Since Dr. More can no longer practice at the all-black hospital, he runs a fat clinic for middle-aged black women, who give him "Christmas gifs" and feed him at a segregated table at the country club. "My practice is small," he says, "but my health is better." The limitation of his economic and social prospects has freed Dr. More from his ambition to achieve goals. "Now while you work, you also watch and listen and wait. In the last age we planned projects and cast ahead of ourselves. We set out to 'reach goals.' We listened to the minutes of the previous meeting. Between times we took vacations."[32] His prospects for the future limited, Dr. More is now free to live with Ellen in the present and is prepared to receive any wondrous news that may happen to come his way. Walker uses the life blacks are leaving behind to suggest the innocence that modern man must recapture if he is to escape the malaise.

Dr. More's relegation to the social status of blacks is only one of the material changes in his life that allows him to lead a spiritual life of watching and waiting. The other is his marriage to Ellen, which has ended his philandering with a bevy of other women. Dr. More's choice of Ellen is another product of his ordeal, and it was the threat to Ellen during the climactic struggle with Art Immelmann that gave More the courage to triumph. Like the other women in Walker's first four novels, Ellen is significant primarily because of her relationship with the main character. Dr. More's relationship with Ellen is a clue to the nature of his new life, just as in *The Last Gentleman* Barrett's relationship with Kitty Vaught is a clue to the causes of his alienation and mental disturbances. As Walker explained in an interview, "I use sex as a symbol for something else. Sex here [in *The Last Gentleman*] is a symbol of failure on the existential level."[33]

When Aunt Emily listed the virtues of a gentleman in *The Moviegoer*, she included "a sweetness, a gentleness with women."[34] Part of being a gentleman is knowing how to treat a lady, and it is necessary to have a lady who is aware of the rules of the game and willing to play by them. LeRoy Percy had such a lady in his wife, Camille. She fit quite naturally into what has become the stereotype of the southern lady. She was charming, vivacious, and beautiful in the style of the day. She made the Percy home a delightful place to visit, and when she went to Washington with LeRoy, according to one society journalist, she "held a little court of her own beside her husband."[35] As lady of the Percy household, Camille was responsible for maintaining a religious atmosphere there, a task complicated by her husband, who was an Episcopalian largely because it left him free to hunt quail on Sunday mornings. Camille was a devout Catholic but never allowed religion to interfere with being a lady. LeRoy once wrote Will that Camille and a friend had recently gone to New Orleans to listen to sermons in their native French, but upon their return, her account of the trip included mostly car rides and dinners. However, LeRoy added, Camille did "introduce an innovation into the ancient practice of going around barefooted, with sack-cloth and ashes, in making their religious pilgrimage, and took in all the churches one morning in an auto."[36]

LeRoy treated Camille's religious impulses with the same amused tolerance with which he viewed her capacity for spending or giving away exorbitant sums of money even when cotton prices were low. He did so in part because Camille's foibles were those of a southern lady; she even suffered the traditional nervous condition common to southern ladies. Mostly, however, he tolerated Camille's excesses because he loved her deeply. He could not stand to be away from her for any length of time, and he died shortly after she did. LeRoy and Camille's relationship involved what psychologists would now call role playing, but both were content with their roles, and their love was made more meaningful by their mutual willingness to reinforce each other's self-image.

As he did with blacks, LeRoy found rhetorical uses for women. During the senatorial race between Vardaman and LeRoy's close friend John Sharp Williams, LeRoy wrote Williams about a speech Vardaman had made in which he described the rape of a white woman by a black man. LeRoy was furious. "He brings the shame of Southern women before a great audience, and depicts in vivid colors those things which we scarcely whisper to our wives at our own firesides, because they are so revolting to every instinct of decency, and he does so only to inflame the passions and gain a few paltry votes."[37] LeRoy was genuinely horrified, but not so horrified that he forgot the value of a few paltry votes. He advised Williams to use Vardaman's speech against him by pointing out that a true protector of southern ladies would never discuss such a subject in public.

As he had with blacks, Will Percy again took his father's political symbol and transformed it into an instrument of cultural analysis. The disjunction between the private, spiritual world and the public, material world that plagued Will created problems in his relationships with women. He was never able to find a woman who reconciled purity and sensuality, and he admired both qualities too greatly to settle for one or the other. This disjunction made women a key symbol in Will's thinking about what was wrong with Western civilization. Much of his essay "The White Plague" is devoted to describing the uninhibited sexual mores of the Samoans, and an entry in one of his notebooks explains the significance of the subject.

> Sex uninhibited results in Samoan sex, which is healthy but lacking in chivalry, romantic love. The south took the other path, sex inhibited, chivalry, women remote and in [illegible, one word]—all women either whores or heroines. This was itself a culture, a way of life, resulting in all the works of art from Tristan to [illegible, one word]. But today the custom falls between the two—there is promiscuity but it is forbidden and so stultifying, as good neither as Samoan nor the old magnolia south—it produces neither health nor art. It is neither clean romance nor clean sensuality, but something [illegible] and nasty only because there is no accepted convention of the good sex life.[38]

For Will the state of sexual relations was a symbol of civilization stuck between ages; the old values had lost their meaning, yet their shadow remained, preventing modern man from returning to the innocence and simplicity of the Samoans.

Walker Percy, in turn, began with the symbolic meaning Will attached to women and added to it from his experience living a generation later and from his viewpoint as a philosopher and linguist. In *The Moviegoer* two women are important symbols for Binx Bolling. His Aunt Emily represents the values of the family and South that Will represented for Walker. His cousin Kate is much like Binx; she has lost touch with the old values, and, unable to develop new ones of her own, does not know how to live her life. Binx tries to save Kate from her alienation by making love to her. This is a clear violation of his aunt's chivalric code, but because Kate has fallen victim to a malaise that gentlemen of old did not have to contend with, Binx's making love to her is the existential equivalent of a knight's saving a damsel in distress. Binx fails. "The burden was too great and flesh poor flesh, neither hallowed by sacrament nor despised by spirit . . . quails and fails."[39] Kate is neither whore nor heroine, while Binx cannot decide whether to emulate the proper Rory Calhoun or the rakish Rhett Butler. Binx and Kate are both victims of the dichotomy between lust and love that plagued Will Percy, but by viewing their situation from his existentialist position, Walker gives the story an ironic twist that distinguishes him from his uncle.

In *The Last Gentleman* Walker again attaches much the same meaning to sexual relations that Will did. Critic Panthea Broughton says of Walker, "Percy uses sexual matters as convenient illustrations of Cartesian dualism" throughout the novel by seeing Kitty Vaught as a lady and a whore. He hopes that marrying Kitty will allow him to reconcile the ideal and the material, but he is unable to decide whether to "court her henceforth in the old style" or to follow the example of her brother Sutter and "cultivate pornography in order to set it at naught." Kitty cannot help him choose, for she is as much a victim of the loss of the old standards as he is. "Love, she, like him, was obliged to see as a naked garden of stamens and pistils. . . . she was out to be a proper girl and taking every care to do the right wrong thing." Neither Barrett nor Kitty is able to reconcile lust and spiritual love.[40]

In *Love in the Ruins*, part of Dr. More's prescription for a way to live a life is suggested by his acceptance of the simple, innocent life of blacks. The other major element in the prescription is his choice of Ellen as a wife. Before making this choice, Dr. More considers three other women, each of whom represents a distinct way of living one's life.

Moira Schaffner represents a sexual attractiveness undiluted by idealism. Her simplicity is that of the simpleminded. She is interested in science only as a way of winning prizes, and her favorite poet is Rod McKuen. Moira's simplemindedness gives her promiscuity a veneer of innocence that increases her sexual appeal, but when the apocalypse draws near, she begins to act like a sniveling child. Moira's mindless sensuality is clearly too weak a foundation to build a life on in the ruins of a decaying civilization.

Lola Rhoades, whom More's mother hopes he will marry, offers him the option of a conventional life in the prosperous New South. Lola, the daughter and heiress of proctologist Dusty Rhoades, lives in an exact duplicate of the Tara Plantation used in *Gone with the Wind*. She offers Dr. More the chance to live as a New South aristocrat, puttering around the garden or laboratory and sitting on the porch at night drinking while the mad world goes its way. The problem with such a life is that the parody of the Old South in the New evokes in Dr. More "the intolerable tenderness of the past, the past gone and grieved over and never made sense of."[41] The life that Lola offers is secure from the madness of the present, but haunted by the past.

The third way of life that Dr. More foregoes is represented by Hester, who lives in a hippie commune in the swamp behind his home. Hester makes only a couple of brief appearances in the novel, but as Dr. More tells us himself, she is what he is looking for. "Hester is my type: post-Protestant, post-rebellion, post-ideology—reading Perry Mason here on a little ideological island!—reverted all the way she is, clear back to pagan innocence like a shepherd girl piping a tune on a Greek vase."[42] The problem is that Hester is much younger than Dr. More, much more a product of apocalyptic times, and she has already achieved the renewal of innocence that he seeks. She represents the life of simple waiting that Dr. More wants, but she cannot show the way to it.

Ellen, like Hester, represents a sort of innocence, but in Ellen this innocence takes a form more suitable for a middle-aged man whose ties to the past prevent him from completely entering the new age. Ellen has hardly entered it at all. She is a lady in the old style: dour and Presbyterian and chaste before marriage, dour and Presbyterian and lusty after. Unlike Hester, who comes as close as any of Walker's characters to living on the Kierkegaardian religious plane, Ellen's innocence is ethical. As Dr. More tells us, "Ellen is a Presbyterian who doesn't have much use for God but believes in doing right and does it."[43] This makes Dr. More's choice of Ellen more appropriate to Walker's limited purpose in the conclusion of *Love in the Ruins*. Ellen's strict moral code is not the way of the future; rather, it is a way for a man unable to completely escape the past to prepare himself and pass the time waiting for the new age. Ellen's Presbyterianism reinforces the limits of Walker's purpose: like all antinomians, including Kierkegaard, Walker is unwilling to posit a causal relationship between ethics and salvation.

In his fourth novel, *Lancelot*, the major character, Lancelot Lamar, is more violently deranged than Walker's other characters. When the novel begins, he has already blown up his home, killing his wife and several guests. He describes the events leading up to his act to his friend Harry from his cell in what is either a prison or mental ward. Lance was driven to murder when he discovered his wife's adultery. He does not regret his act: in fact, he hopes to lead a revolution that will restore the old values of chivalry, particularly the distinction between ladies and whores. He tells Harry: "I cannot tolerate this age. And I will not. . . . Make love not war? I'll take war rather than what this age calls love. Which is a better world, this cocksucking cuntlapping ass-holelicking fornicating Happyland U.S.A. or a Roman legion under Marcus Aurelius Antonius? Which is worse, to die with T. J. Jackson at Chancellorsville or to live with Johnny Carson in Burbank?" By promulgating such a philosophy through an obviously demented character, Walker disassociates himself from any attempt to reimpose the values of the past on others. Lancelot is a victim of the same dilemma that Will Percy's Enzio identified in his father Frederick: "To not hate wrong rubs out man's one distinction: / Ably to hate it saps the root of reason."[44]

Walker also uses blacks to argue the futility of good works. Shortly before he blows up his house and kills his wife, Lance gives Elgin, a young superblack in the mode of Colley Wilkes, enough money to marry a Jewish girl and move into a Massaschusetts suburb "which though a cradle of American liberty is unwilling to sell houses to blacks or Jews, especially blacks married to Jews."[45] Lance's participation in the civil rights movement at other points in the novel is equally cynical, although Walker himself has endorsed the movement. Lance's work for civil rights is admirable, but because his motives are flawed, his good works cannot save his soul. Will Percy would probably have agreed, but he would have insisted on performing good works anyway.

Walker recently traced his refusal to endorse specific political reforms to his existentialist outlook.

> I guess that it is a legacy of the existentialist tradition. Marcel always talked about being wary of mass movements or causes. There's always a danger of taking up a cause, of being too much identified with a cause. . . . Kierkegaard said himself, he said, "I am not an apostle." In the aesthetic phase you can talk about

how it is on the island, see, how it is in a certain time and a certain place in a certain culture, even a Christian culture, but what
you can't do is you can't speak with the authority of an apostle.[46]

Walker's refusal to propose solutions to the problems he diagnoses
in his novels has come under fire from Professor Cecil Eubanks. Eubanks argues that "the political relationship is primordial. It involves
more than ideology and protest movements, more than elections and
legislatures, more than a philosophy of order. Politics is an inevitable,
an inherent part of being-in-the-world." Eubanks denies that Walker's
Christian existentialism and apocalyptic expectations excuse him
from dealing with social and political issues. "If exile is the permanent
stance of the Christian, the attempt to build the kingdom must be
also."[47]

The clear, honest differences between Walker and Eubanks on this
issue spring ultimately from Walker's belief in Original Sin and Eubanks' rejection of it. However, even if we accept the Christian notion
that man is incapable of saving himself, there is still room to criticize
Walker's first four novels for concentrating on alienated individuals
rather than individuals interacting, for such interaction is part of life
in any age. This weakness is especially apparent in Walker's characters' relationships with women. Even in the conclusion of *Love in
the Ruins*, there is no evidence that Ellen shares Dr. More's stance of
watching and waiting. Walker has sound technical reasons for concentrating on a single individual: any extensive attempt to describe the
interrelationships between two abnormal characters might have obscured the contrast between the abnormal values of the major character and the values of normal society; at the very least, it would have
interrupted his efforts to evoke the major character's state of mind by
narrating the story through that mind. The purpose of Walker's first
four novels was to diagnose the ills of the world, and given his success
in doing so, it is easy to overlook his failure to do other things.

With the publication of his fifth novel, *The Second Coming*, Walker
takes up the theme of interpersonal relations in a world caught between ages. His entry into politics involves only politics in the most
basic sense of interaction with others. He proposes no programs, en-
dorses no causes. Such doings remain for Walker a form of death-in-
life. Will Barrett, several years older in this novel than in *The Last*

Gentleman, vows, "Death in the form of isms and asms shall not prevail over me, orgasm, enthusiasm, liberalism, conservatism, Communism, Buddhism, Americanism, for an ism is only another way of despairing of the truth."[48] Causes and programs remain abstractions which interfere with the search.

Communication and interaction between individuals is still possible, but it is exceedingly difficult because individuals speak, act, and think in abstractions, the acceptance of which mark the boundaries of the normal world. In *The Second Coming*, interaction between Barrett and Allison, the other major character, is made possible not by accepting these abstractions and working "within the system," so to speak, but by rejecting them at the most basic level through which they operate, language, and thereby rediscovering the ability to truly communicate. In *The Second Coming* the ability to communicate is confined to Barrett and Allison, but it should be remembered that Walker, like Will Percy, often uses sexual relations as a symbol for broader philosophical and cultural concerns, and this makes his latest novel more than a bizarre love story.

Barrett and Allison come to their relationship from opposite directions. Barrett, who suffered amnesiatic fits in *The Last Gentleman*, now remembers too much. He suffers spells that bring with them memories from his past, memories that revolve around a childhood hunting accident involving Barrett and his father, and his father's subsequent suicide. Gradually the memories come into focus, and Barrett understands the connection between them. The hunting accident, he discovers, was not an accident. His father had tried to shoot him for the same reason that he later killed himself: because death was preferable to the death-in-life of the modern world. Once Barrett understands his father's suicide, he is able to formulate a more hopeful alternative. He goes to a cave to await a sign that will prove the existence of God. To insure that the sign will be forthcoming if God does exist, he resolves to stay in the cave until he receives the sign or dies. The relationship between Barrett's experiment and his father's suicide mirrors the relationship between Walker's Christian existentialism and Will Percy's stoicism. Walker, like Barrett, accepts his uncle's vision of a world caught between ages, but he hopes that there is something beyond this world to justify life's despair. Barrett's experiment ends ambiguously, however, when he develops a toothache, and, crawling out of the cave, crashes into Allie's greenhouse.

Allison, on the other hand, remembers almost nothing because of the shock therapy she had been undergoing before her escape from a mental institution. One of the things that Allie cannot remember is how language works in daily life. She does not know the connotations and vernacular usages attached to words by normal society. As he does in his earlier novels, Walker contrasts her abnormality with normal society in a way that makes one appear as sensible as the other. "She reflected that people asked questions and answered them differently from her. She took words seriously to mean more or less what they said, but other people seemed to use words as signals in another code they had agreed upon."[49] After escaping from the asylum, Allie moves into an old greenhouse on her family's property and begins her life anew, keeping everything simple. Walker evokes her simplicity by describing her wonder and preoccupation with each step of the process of moving a large stove across the greenhouse, a process that takes a week. Her approach to language also evokes the wonder of innocence. She accepts new words as gifts, treating them as things in themselves; she forms sentences according to the relationships of the sounds of the words themselves, speaking in rhymes, rather than using the words to signify the worn-out abstractions of normal society.

Allie's innocent approach to language reflects Walker's interest in linguistic theory. Like Will Percy, who believed that teaching Samoan children the English language would infect them with the vices of Western civilization, Walker sees a strong relationship between the character of a culture and its language. Walker's technical work on linguistics has, in fact, been more therapeutic than his primarily diagnostic novels. J. P. Telotte has identified three benefits that the sovereign wanderer might hope to derive from the renewal of language Walker has proposed: the ability to "know" the world through language, and thereby "affirm his own existence or position in the world as the 'knower' of his domain"; the ability to charge the world with meaning and thus prevent further cultural disintegration; and a strengthening of "intersubjectivity" between individuals.[50]

Barrett derives all three of these benefits from his relationship with Allie. Their strengthened intersubjectivity takes the form of a marvelous love affair. Because she is linguistically innocent, Allie can be sexually bold without being whorish, and this makes her the most erotic woman in any of Walker's novels. Because Allie transcends the dichotomy between love and lust, she and Barrett are able to overcome their alienation by making love authentically.

Their love, in turn, enables Barrett and Allie to reclaim their sovereignty and restore order and meaning to their lives. After a couple of days of "intersubjectivity" at a local motel, "he now knew what needed to be done and could say so and she could heed him." Walker has argued that true communication requires both an *I* to speak and a *thou* to understand. Both are present here, and ability to communicate is directly linked to the ability to reclaim one's sovereignty and act.[51]

Barrett also believes that their love will allow them to restore meaning to the institution of marriage. When he proposes, Allie hesitates, fearing that "to marry might be to miscarry." Barrett, who is beginning to speak like Allie, reassures her. "It is possible that though marriage in these times seems for some reason to be a troubled, often fatal, arrangement, we might not only survive it but revive it."[52]

The bulk of *The Second Coming* focuses on the relationship between Barrett and Allie, yet there are strong indications at the end that their love might serve as a model for a further broadening of authentic communication with others. Once his sovereignty is restored, Barrett organizes a motley crew from the local rest home to build cabins, using their knowledge of old handicrafts to build stronger shelters than their modern counterparts, and providing the builders with simple, rewarding work. Barrett also finds such work for himself, reentering the legal profession even though he has already retired from a successful career on Wall Street. The life he plans with Allie is similar in its simplicity and humbleness to Dr. More's life with Ellen, but his cooperation with the cabin builders makes him more socially involved than Dr. More.

Walker also suggests that the love between Barrett and Allison might provide a clue for the Christian watcher and waiter. By having Barrett crash into Allie's greenhouse on his way out of the cave, Walker ambiguously suggests that she may be the sign that he was looking for. At the end of the novel Barrett wonders: "Is she a gift and therefore a sign of a giver? Could it be that the Lord is here, masquerading behind this simple silly holy face? Am I crazy to want both, her and Him? No, not want, must have. And will have."[53] The limits of this connection are strict: Barrett does not say that his relationship with Allison will lead him to God; he says only that the mysterious wonder of their love suggests the possibility of even more mysterious wonders. Walker remains an antinomian; he refuses to promise that works of any sort will lead to grace; but by connecting the material and spiritual worlds, he suggests the possibility of recharging the former with meaning.

The Second Coming marks the beginning of what promises to be an exciting new direction in Walker Percy's fiction. By taking a step back into the world, he has, temporarily at least, reversed the direction of his family's interests. Will Percy moved from his father's political and economic interests to the less mundane pursuit of poetry and culture. Walker, in his first four novels, took this withdrawal from everydayness to its ultimate conclusion by concentrating on abnormal individuals. Now he appears to be returning to the world in an attempt to find new meaning in the old ways. That he has taken such a roundabout route to his family legacy is not surprising; despite their similarities, the most important thing the Percys have in common is their uniqueness. This may yet prove to be the greatest attraction of being a Percy for Walker; the Percy family boasts enough eccentrics to fill one of his novels, and one of the greatest benefits of family life is the opportunity it offers for relationships with individuals like oneself. Walker has already tapped this resource by asking the questions and using the symbols of his forebears. As he continues to create, he may find even greater resources in the Percy past.

Notes

Chapter 1

1. John Hereford Percy, *The Percy Family of Mississippi and Louisiana* (Baton Rouge, 1943), 1–10, 48–53.
2. William Alexander Percy, *Lanterns on the Levee: Recollections of a Planter's Son* (1941; rpr. Baton Rouge, 1973), 39–40.
3. John Hereford Percy, *Percy Family*, 65, 74–75; Kathleen Moore Peacock, "William Alexander Percy: A Study in Southern Conservativism" (Master's thesis, Birmingham Southern College, 1958), 6–12.
4. LeRoy Percy to C. J. DuBuisson, June 25, 1908, in Percy Papers (on microfilm in the Louisiana State University Department of Archives and History), hereinafter cited as PP.
5. W. A. Percy, *Lanterns*, 11; Peacock, "William Alexander Percy," 9–11; LeRoy Percy to C. J. DuBuisson, June 25, July 3, 1908, in PP; William C. Sallis, "A Study of the Life and Times of LeRoy Percy" (Master's thesis, Mississippi State University, 1957), 4–5; Robert L. Brandfon, *Cotton Kingdom of the New South: A History of the Yazoo Mississippi Delta from Reconstruction to the Present* (Cambridge, Mass., 1967), 25; William D. McCain and Charlotte Capers (eds.), *Memoirs of Henry Tillinghast Ireys, Papers of the Washington County Historical Society, 1910–1915* (Jackson, Miss., 1954), 151, 257–58.
6. LeRoy Percy to C. J. DuBuisson, June 25, July 3, 1908, in PP; newspaper clippings, in PP; *The War of the Rebellion: A Compilation of the Official Records of the Union and Confederate Armies* (Washington, D.C, 1880–1901), Ser. I, Vol. VII, pp. 782–83. All citations are to Series I, hereinafter cited as *OR*.
7. LeRoy Percy to C. J. DuBuisson, June 25, July 3, 1908, and newspaper clippings, in PP; *OR*, XVII, 411–14, XXIX, 419; Brandfon, *Cotton Kingdom*, 36; Robert W. Harrison, *Levee Districts and Levee Building in Mississippi: A Study of the State and Local Efforts to Control Mississippi River Floods* (Stoneville, Miss., 1951), 27.
8. *OR*, XXIX, 419, XLII, Pt. 3, 1119–1201; T. Harry Williams, *Lincoln and His Generals* (New York, 1952), 299–300; Bruce Catton, *A Stillness at Appomattox* (Garden City, N. Y., 1953), 61–87, 153–80, 259–66.
9. *OR*, XLIX, Pt. 2, 1189, 1201–1202, 1211, 1225, 1256, 1262; Brandfon, *Cotton Kingdom*, 36; Harrison, *Levee Districts*, 27.
10. Harrison, *Levee Districts*, 27; LeRoy Percy to C. J. DeBuisson, June 25, July 3, 1908, and newspaper clippings, in PP; W. A. Percy, *Lanterns*, 273.
11. Memphis *Scimitar*, n.d., in PP.
12. Harrison, *Levee Districts*, 27; Walter Sillers, Sr., "Flood Control in Bolivar County, 1838–1924," *Journal Of Mississippi History*, IX (January, 1947), 3–20.
13. Harrison, *Levee Districts*, 29.
14. McCain and Capers, *Memoirs*, 310–24.
15. Harrison, *Levee Districts*, 43–44; Brandfon, *Cotton Kingdom*, 40–46; William C. Harris, *The Day of the Carpetbagger: Republican Reconstruction in Mississippi* (Baton Rouge, 1979), 295–300; James Wilford Garner, *Reconstruction in Mississippi* (New York, 1901), 311–16.
16. Harris, *Day of the Carpetbagger*, 297–98; Garner, *Reconstruction*, 311; Vernon Lane Wharton, *The Negro in Mississippi, 1865–1890* (Chapel Hill, 1947), 11–12, 27, 171; J. S. McNeilly, *Climax and Collapse of Reconstruction in Mississippi, 1874–1876*, 303.
17. McNeilly, *Climax and Collapse*, 303–304, 336–40; newspaper clippings, in PP.
18. McNeilly, *Climax and Collapse*, 363–75; newspaper clippings, in PP.
19. Albert D. Kirwan, *Revolt of the Rednecks: Mississippi Politics, 1876–1925* (Lexington, 1951), 27–28; Garner, *Reconstruction*, 311; McNeilly, *Climax and Collapse*, 378–80.

20. Harris, *Day of the Carpetbagger*, 660, 686, 690; Kirwan, *Revolt of the Rednecks*, 37–38; T. Harry Williams, *Romance and Realism in Southern Politics* (Baton Rouge, 1966), 50–51; David L. Smiley, "Cassius M. Clay and the Mississippi Election of 1875," *Journal of Mississippi History*, XIX (October, 1957): 234–51.

21. Harris, *Day of the Carpetbagger*, 692–97; Kirwan, *Revolt of the Rednecks*, 3; McNeilly, *Climax and Collapse*, 438–48.

22. Harris, *Day of the Carpetbagger*, 303; McNeilly, *Climax and Collapse*, 456–60.

23. McNeilly, *Climax and Collapse*, 460.

24. William W. White, "Mississippi Confederate Veterans in Public Office, 1875–1900," *Journal of Mississippi History*, XX (July, 1958), 147–56; LeRoy Percy to C. J. DuBuisson, June 25, July 3, 1908, and newspaper clippings, in PP.

25. LeRoy Percy to C. J. DuBuisson, June 25, July 3, 1908, and newspaper clippings, in PP.

26. Hodding Carter, *Southern Legacy* (Baton Rouge, 1950), 3–4.

Chapter 2

1. John Hereford Percy, *Percy Family*, 67; Memphis *Commercial Appeal*, December 25, 1929, in PP; *Biographical Directory of the American Congress, 1774–1971* (Washington D.C., 1971), 1529.

2. Memphis *Commercial Appeal*, December 25, 1929, and other clippings, in PP; Sallis, "LeRoy Percy," 30–32.

3. Hester S. Ware, "A Study of the Life and Works of William Alexander Percy" (Master's thesis, Mississippi State University, 1950), 8–10; W. A. Percy, *Lanterns*, 35–38; newspaper clippings, in PP.

4. LeRoy Percy to Prof. Echols, December 17, 1925, to Judge H. D. Minor, December 17, 1925, William H. Echols to LeRoy Percy, January 5, 1926, all in PP; Josephus Daniels, *The Life of Woodrow Wilson, 1856–1924* (Chicago, 1924), 56–57.

5. Greenville *Times*, December 3, 1881, and other newspaper clippings, in PP; Sallis, "LeRoy Percy," 29–33; Ware, "William Alexander Percy," 10–11.

6. Harrison, *Levee District*, iii, 69–71; Sallis, "LeRoy Percy," 33.

7. C. Vann Woodward, *Origins of the New South, 1877–1913* (Baton Rouge, 1951), 328–32, 346–47; Kirwan, *Revolt of the Rednecks*, 60–83; Wharton, *Negro in Mississippi*, 207–208; Sallis, "LeRoy Percy," 37.

8. Woodward, *Origins of the New South*, 332, 346–47; Kirwan, *Revolt of the Rednecks* 65–83, 136–39.

9. Harrison, *Levee Districts*, 116–17, 126; W. A. Percy, *Lanterns*, 242.

10. Brandfon, *Cotton Kingdom*, 65–66, 80, 103–12, 141; Woodward, *Origins of the New South*, 298; E. L. Langsford and R. H. Thibideaux, "Technical Bulletin, No. 682—Plantation Organization in the Yazoo Mississippi Delta," *Technical Bulletins, Nos. 676–700* (Washington D.C., 1940), 12–13.

11. William F. Holmes, "William Alexander Percy and the Bourbon Era in the Yazoo-Mississippi Delta," *Mississippi Quarterly*, XXVI (Winter, 1972–73), 71–88; W. A. Percy, *Lanterns*, 70–73; Kirwan, *Revolt of the Rednecks*, 109–110.

12. Kirwan, *Revolt of the Rednecks*, 109–110; Holmes, "William Alexander Percy," 81–86.

13. Vicksburg *Herald*, June 11, July 12, 1898; William F. Holmes, *The White Chief: James Kimble Vardaman* (Baton Rouge, 1970), 64; Kirwan, *Revolt of the Rednecks*, 103; W. A. Percy, *Lanterns*, 66–67.

14. Vicksburg *Herald*, June 11, 14, 1898; Edward Mayes, *Lucius Q. C. Lamar: His Life, Times, and Speeches, 1825–1893* (Nashville, 1896), 331.

15. Vicksburg *Herald*, May 25, 1889; Holmes, *Vardaman*, 63–67.

16. Vicksburg *Herald*, January 11, 16, 19, 25, 27, February 8, March 24, April 5, 1898; Brandfon, *Cotton Kingdom*, 186.

17. Vicksburg *Herald*, May 8, 28, June 4, 7, 1898; Holmes, *Vardaman*, 71–72; Kirwan, *Revolt of the Rednecks*, 112–13.

18. Vicksburg *Herald*, June 6, 1898.

19. Vicksburg *Herald*, June 11, 1898; Greenville *Times*, reprinted *ibid.*, June 14, 1898.

20. Vicksburg *Herald*, June 6, 1898.

21. *Ibid.*, July 12–19, 21, 24, 28, 1898; Holmes, *Vardaman*, 72.

22. Vicksburg *Herald*, July 22, 28, 1898; Holmes, *Vardaman*, 72.

23. Kirwan, *Revolt of the Rednecks*, 117–21, 140.

24. Jackson *Daily Clarion-Ledger*, July 3, 7, 10, August 1, 4, 6, 8, 19, 23, 27, 28, 30, September 1, 4, 8–13, 15–20, 22–23, October 1, 13, 18, 1902.

25. *Ibid.*, May 21, 31, November 12–14, 17, 20, 1902; Brandfon, *Cotton Kingdom*, 169–70.

26. Jackson *Daily Clarion-Ledger*, November 12–15, 17, 20, 1902; Interview with Brodie S. Crump, by the author, Greenville, Miss., October 22, 1976 (Transcript in Louisiana State University Department of Archives and History, Baton Rouge).

27. Holmes, *Vardaman*, 112.

28. *Ibid.*, 110–28; Kirwan, *Revolt of the Rednecks*, 146–54; Eugene E. White, "Anti-Racial Agitation in Politics: James Kimble Vardaman in the Mississippi Gubernatorial Campaign of 1903," *Journal of Mississippi History*, VII (April, 1945), 91–131; Heber Ladner, "James Kimble Vardaman, Governor of Mississippi, 1904–1908," *Journal of Mississippi History*, II (October, 1940), 175–205.

29. Jackson *Daily Clarion-Ledger*, January 6, 1910.

30. *Ibid.*, July 4, September 1, 1902; Vicksburg *Herald*, January 18, 1898; Woodward, *Origins of the New South*, 207–208; Wharton, *Negro in Mississippi*, 95–96, 106–15; Brandfon, *Cotton Kingdom*, 114–15; Alfred H. Stone, *Studies in the American Race Problem* (New York, 1908), 235–72.

31. Jackson *Daily Clarion-Ledger*, May 27, July 1, 14, 15, August 6, 8, 16, 25, September 8, October 24, November 17, 21, 1902; Brandfon, *Cotton Kingdom*, 56, 93–94, 99, 141–43; Wharton, *Negro in Mississippi*, 104–105.

32. Lee J. Langly, "Italians in the Cotton Fields," *Manufacturer's Record*, XLV (April 7, 1904), quoted in Brandfon, *Cotton Kingdom*, 148.

33. LeRoy Percy to H. P. Trezevant, March 27, 1907, to D. A. McGregor, December 26, 1907, both in PP; Brandfon, *Cotton Kingdom*, 144–48; Stone, *American Race Problem*, 180–98; *Senate Documents*, 61st Cong., 2nd Sess., No. 633, Pt. 24, pp. 307–34.

34. Brandfon, *Cotton Kingdom*, 148–56; LeRoy Percy to Baron Des Planches, February 14, 1907; Charles Scott to LeRoy Percy, February 8, 1907, both in PP.

35. Brandfon, *Cotton Kingdom*, 161–64; *Senate Documents*, 61st Cong., 2nd Sess., No. 633, Pt. 24; Stone, *American Race Problem*; Senator Augusto Pierantoni, "Italian Feeling on American Lynching," *Independent*, LV (August 27, 1903), 2040–42; LeRoy Percy to John T. Savage, March 6, 1907, J. T. Savage to LeRoy Percy, March 8, 1907, LeRoy Percy to George S. Edgell, March 25, 1907, to Charles Scott and others, April 3, 1907, to Capt. J. S. McNeilly, April 3, 1907, and to Boltin Smith, October 8, 1907, The Consolate to Guiseppe Augusto Catalani, n.d., all in PP.

36. LeRoy Percy to Baron des Planches, February 14, 1907, and to Geo. S. Edgell, February 14, 1907, Geo. S. Edgell to LeRoy Percy, February 20, 26, 1907, and to Luigi Villari, February 6, 1907, LeRoy Percy to John Savage, March 6, 1907, J. T. Savage to LeRoy Percy, March 8, 1907, LeRoy Percy to Geo. S. Edgell, March 9, 1907, to John Savage, March 9, 1907, and to W. A. Percy, April 19, 1907, all in PP.

37. LeRoy Percy to W. A. Percy, April 19, 1907, to Charles Scott and others, April

3, 1907, Memphis *Commercial Appeal*, clipping, n.d., dateline April 15, 1907, all in PP; Brandfon, *Cotton Kingdom*, 159–60.

38. LeRoy Percy to S. Moroni, May 30, 1908, in PP.

39. LeRoy Percy to Boltin Smith, October 8, 1907, to Geo. C. Wartenburg, October 8, 1907, to J. T. Savage, October 8, 1907, and to G. Garibaldi, November 30, 1907, in PP.

40. LeRoy Percy to Gov. X. O. Pindall, July 27, 1907, in PP.

41. LeRoy Percy to Chs. Scott, August 21, 1907, in PP; Pete Daniels, *The Shadow of Slavery* (Urbana, 1972), 83, 102–103.

42. LeRoy Percy to Raymond Patterson, January 5, 1908, in PP.

43. LeRoy Percy to Walker Percy, November 18, 1907, to Capt. J. S. McNeilly, November 19, 20, 27, 1907, to John M. Parker, November 27, 28, 1907, to W. P. Dawson, December 14, 1907, to John Sharp Williams, November 30, 1907, to Capt. J. S. McNeilly, December 31, 1907, to J. M. F. Erwin, January 6, 1908, to Geo. S. Edgell, January 17, 1908, to Allen Gray, February 21, 1908, and to M. V. Richards, April 3, 1908, Boltin Smith to LeRoy Percy, May 19, 1908, LeRoy Percy to Dodds-Meade and Company, November 28, 1908, to Geo. S. Edgell, January 1, 1909, to W. A. Percy, May 16, 1908, all in PP; Brandfon, *Cotton Kingdom*, 164–65.

44. LeRoy Percy to John G. Jones, December 1, 1908, in PP.

45. LeRoy Percy to Chas. H. Starling, November 10, 1908, to Boltin Smith, December 31, 1908, and to Will Hardie, January 11, 1909, all in PP; Woodward, *Origins of the New South*, 410–12.

46. LeRoy Percy to John Sharp Williams, June 22, 1907, and to Capt. J. S. McNeilly, June 22, 1907, both in PP; Kirwan, *Revolt of the Rednecks*, 178–84; Holmes, *Vardaman*, 177–83.

47. LeRoy Percy to John Sharp Williams, June 22, 1907, in PP.

48. George C. Osborn, *John Sharp Williams: Planter-Statesman of the Deep South* (Baton Rouge, 1943), 7–14, 135–37; Frank E. Smith, *The Yazoo River* (New York, 1954), 265.

49. LeRoy Percy to Charles Scott, March 6, 25, 1907, to Gen. Frank C. Armstrong, March 9, 1907, to Col. E. H. Woods, March 28, 1907, and to Col E. H. Woods, April 25, 1907, all in PP; Kirwan, *Revolt of the Rednecks*, 185–87; LeRoy Percy, "A Southern View of Negro Education," *Outlook*, LXXXVI (August 3, 1907), 730–32.

50. LeRoy Percy, "Negro Education," 730–32.

51. Theodore Roosevelt to J. M. Dickinson, May 22, 1907, J. M. Dickinson to LeRoy Percy, May 17, 1907, and to The President, May 17, 1907, Theodore Roosevelt to J. M. Dickinson, May 22, 1907, Victor S. Clark to LeRoy Percy, May 22, 1907, Richard Edmons to LeRoy Percy, May 23, 1907, LeRoy Percy to Judge J. M. Dickinson, August 10, 1907, and to President Roosevelt, August 10, 1907, Washington *Times*, clipping, August 6, 1907, *Colliers*, clipping, August 21, 1907, all in PP; LeRoy Percy, "Negro Education," 730.

52. LeRoy Percy to W. A. Percy, July 16, 1907, to Capt. E. H. Woods, July 9, 15, 1907, to S. B. Paxton, July 15, 1907, and to Judge C. C. Moody, July 16, 1907, all in PP.

53. LeRoy Percy to W. M. Hemingway, July 8, 1907, to Ben Wells, July 12, 1907, to Walter Sillers, July 13, 1907, to Dr. Spivey, July 16, 1907, and to C. H. Williams, July 20, 1907, all in PP; Holmes, *Vardaman*, 185–89.

54. LeRoy Percy to W. A. Percy, October 8, 1907, and Percy to President Roosevelt, August 10, 1907, both in PP; Kirwan, *Revolt of the Rednecks*, 184–87; Holmes, *Vardaman*, 190–91; Osborn, *Williams*, 174.

55. LeRoy Percy to W. A. Percy, October 8, 1907, and to Walker Percy, October 23, 1907, Jos. E. Ransdell to LeRoy Percy, December 14, 1907, all in PP.

56. LeRoy Percy to Capt. J. S. McNeilly, March 26, 1908, November 8, 1907, to Charles Scott, October 8, October 19, 1907, January 4, 16, 21, February 10, 1908, and

to E. F. Noel, November 19, 1907, January 6, 25, 31, 1908, and other correspondence, all in PP.

57. LeRoy Percy to E. E. Richardson, March 26, 1908, and to Boltin Smith, March 26, 1908, C. G. Elliott to LeRoy Percy, March 22, 1907, all in PP.

58. LeRoy Percy to Walker Percy, June 14, 1908, to Alex Y. Scott, May 20, 1908, to John R. Gage, May 20, 1908, to B. L. Lee, May 20, 1908, to S. Castleman, May 23, 1908, and to Capt. J. S. McNeilly, June 6, 1908, all in PP.

59. LeRoy Percy to Capt. J. S. McNeilly, May 19, 1908, to Mrs. R. L. McLaurin, March 27, 1908, and to President Theodore Roosevelt, March 27, 1908, W. K. Mc-Laurin to LeRoy Percy, April 1, 1908, LeRoy Percy to The President, c/o Senator A. J. McLaurin, telegram, April 1, 1908, and to J. B. Hebron, November 5, 1908, all in PP.

60. LeRoy Percy to President Theodore Roosevelt, March 4, 1909, in PP.

Chapter 3

1. Jackson *Daily Clarion-Ledger*, December 23, 24, 25, 1909; New York *Times*, clipping, February 4, 1910, in PP; Kirwan, *Revolt of the Rednecks*, 191–92; Holmes, *Vardaman*, 201–202.

2. Jackson *Daily Clarion-Ledger*, December 25, 29, 1909, January 2, 5, 1910; Kirwan, *Revolt of the Rednecks* 191–94; Holmes, *Vardaman*, 201–205.

3. Jackson *Daily Clarion-Ledger*, December 25, 29, 1909; W. A. Percy to LeRoy Percy, May 29, 1910, in PP; *Congressional Record*, 62nd Cong., 2nd Sess., 227.

4. Jackson *Daily Clarion-Ledger*, January 2, 5, 1910; Sallis, "LeRoy Percy" 63–64; newspaper clippings, n.d., dateline Jackson, January 1, in PP; Adwin Wigfall Green, *The Man Bilbo* (Baton Rouge, 1963), 24–29.

5. Jackson *Daily Clarion-Ledger*, January 5, 1910; Holmes, *Vardaman*, 202–206; Kirwan, *Revolt of the Rednecks*, 192–93; Sallis, "LeRoy Percy," 63–65.

6. Jackson *Daily Clarion-Ledger*, January 7, 8, 1910; Sallis, "LeRoy Percy," 67–69.

7. Jackson *Daily Clarion-Ledger*, January 13, 14, 26, 28, 29, 1910.

8. *Ibid.*, February 1, 2, 1910; Holmes, *Vardaman*, 212–13.

9. Jackson *Daily Clarion-Ledger*, February 5, 1910; Interview with Brodie S. Crump, by the author; Sallis, "LeRoy Percy," 78.

10. Jackson *Daily Clarion-Ledger*, February 5, 6, 10, 11, 12, [1910].

11. *Ibid.*, February 16, 17, 18, 22, 23, 1910; Sallis, "LeRoy Percy," 81; Holmes, *Vardaman*, 214.

12. Jackson *Daily Clarion-Ledger*, February 23, 1910; Holmes, *Vardaman*, 214–15; Sallis, "LeRoy Percy," 80–83; Kirwan, *Revolt of the Rednecks*, 196–97.

13. Jackson *Daily Clarion-Ledger*, February 26, 1910; newspaper clippings, in PP; Sallis, "LeRoy Percy," 86, 90–98.

14. Holmes, *Vardaman*, 215; Kirwan, *Revolt of the Rednecks*, 197; LeRoy Percy to John Brunini, March 1, 1910, and to Ben Exum, March 1, 1910, both in PP.

15. New York *Times*, February 24, 1910, and other newspaper clippings, n.d., all in PP.

16. St. Louis *Globe Democrat*, clipping, n.d., newspaper clipping, March 15, 1910, newspaper clipping, n.d., miscellaneous invitations, LeRoy Percy to W. A. Percy, March 6, 1910, all in PP.

17. W. A. Percy to LeRoy Percy, April 5, 1910, in PP; Kirwan, *Revolt of the Rednecks*, 197–206; Holmes, *Vardaman*, 215–28; Sallis, "LeRoy Percy," 102.

18. *Speeches of Senator LeRoy Percy Before the Mississippi Legislature*, pamphlet, W. A. Percy to Senator LeRoy Percy, May 2, 1910, to Eugene Gerald, April 29, 1910, J. C. Walker to Senator LeRoy Percy, April 17, 1910, all in PP; Holmes, *Vardaman*, 230–34.

19. *Congressional Record*, 61st Cong., 2nd Sess., 5315–18.

20. Holmes, *Vardaman*, 40–41, 184–85.

21. *Speeches of Senator LeRoy Percy Before the Mississippi Legislature*, pamphlet, Theodore Roosevelt to LeRoy Percy, June 29, 1910, both in PP.

22. *Congressional Record*, 61st Cong., 2nd Sess., 8628–32.

23. W. A. Percy, *Lanterns*, 149–50; Holmes, *Vardaman*, 240–41; Sallis, "LeRoy Percy," 127.

24. Vicksburg *Daily Herald*, clipping, July 3, 1910, and unidentified clipping, n.d., both in PP; W. A. Percy, *Lanterns*, 150–51; Holmes, *Vardaman*, 241; Kirwan, *Revolt of the Rednecks*, 220.

25. Holmes, *Vardaman*, 253; Green, *The Man Bilbo*, 39; newspaper clipping, n.d., in PP.

26. Jackson *Daily News*, July 5, 1910, June 10, 1911; Harry N. Ball to LeRoy Percy, July 10, n.y., in PP; Holmes, *Vardaman*, 237–39.

27. LeRoy Percy to Camille Percy, August 29, September 1, 3, 1910, all in PP.

28. LeRoy Percy, *Speech of United States Senator LeRoy Percy Delivered at the State Fair*, Jackson, Miss., October 31, 1910, Memphis *Commercial Appeal*, October 17, 1910; Greenville *Daily Democrat*, November 11, 1910, newspaper clippings, n.d., W. A. Percy, Diary, all in PP.

29. W. A. Percy, Diary, W. A. Percy to Senator LeRoy Percy, November 24, December 2, 5, 1910, all in PP; Kirwan, *Revolt of the Rednecks*, 2207–2209; Sallis, "LeRoy Percy," 115–17.

30. LeRoy Percy to W. A. Percy, December 1, 1910, newspaper clipping, n.d., both in PP; *Congressional Record*, 61st Cong., 3rd Sess., 2128–31, 3539–42, 3862–69.

31. Holmes, *Vardaman*, 249–52; Kirwan, *Revolt of the Rednecks*, 214, 222–25; Jackson *Daily News*, June 10, 1911, Jackson *Daily Clarion-Ledger*, June 10, 1911, Greenville *Times-Democrat*, June 20, 1911, Memphis *Commercial Appeal*, n.d., New Orleans *Times-Picayune*, n.d., Macon *Beacon*, n.d., and other newspaper clippings, A. T. McIlwain to C. C. Anderson, July 29, 1911, Robert N. Somerville to W. A. Percy, April 7, 1911, W. A. Percy to William Crump, May 27, 1911, LeRoy Percy to S. R. Smith, January 18, 1909, W. A. Percy to Capt. J. S. McNeilly, August 4, 1910, all in PP.

32. Osborn, *Williams*, 420; Kirwan, *Revolt of the Rednecks*, 242–43; W. A. Percy to William Crump, February 8, 1911, May 3, 1911, to Carter Percy, May 15, 1911, Walter Sillers to W. A. Percy, March 15, 1911, W. A. Percy to Walter Sillers, March 23, 1911, William Crump to Thos. Owen, June 17, 1911, all in PP.

33. Jackson *Daily News*, April 19, 1911; newspaper clippings, in PP.

34. W. A. Percy to Senator LeRoy Percy, February 3, 1911, to Judge C. C. Moody, February 6, 1911, to Senator LeRoy Percy, April 6, 1911, to William Crump, May 6, 1911, all in PP; Holmes, *Vardaman*, 236, 256.

35. Natchez *Daily Democrat*, June 25, 1911; Kirwan, *Revolt of the Rednecks*, 222; newspaper clippings, in PP.

36. Kirwan, *Revolt of the Rednecks*, 228–31; Holmes, *Vardaman*, 254–55.

37. Vicksburg *Post*, clipping, August 4, 1911; Jackson *Daily Clarion-Ledger*, clipping, August 22, 1911, Charlotte, N.C. *Observer*, clipping, August 6, 1911, LeRoy Percy to John Sharp Williams, August 5, 1911, and to C. H. Williams, August 5, 1911, all in PP.

38. E. F. Noel to LeRoy Percy, August 3, 1911, August 7, 1911, Dunbar Rowland to LeRoy Percy, August 3, 1911, John Sharp Williams to LeRoy Percy, August 9, 1911, Senator J. W. Bailey to LeRoy Percy, August 12, 1911, other letters, New York *Evening Post*, August 11, 1911, and other newspaper and magazine clippings, all in PP; W. A. Percy, *Lanterns*, 154.

39. George Creel, "What Are You Going To Do About It? The Carnival of Corrup-

tion in Mississippi," *Cosmopolitan*, II (November, 1911), 725–35; E. F. Noel to W. A. Percy, October 13, 18, 1911; to LeRoy Percy, October 13, 1911, W. A. Percy to E. F. Noel, October 16, 1911, W. D. Anderson to W. A. Percy, October 17, 1911, John Sharp Williams to LeRoy Percy, October 28, 1911, Frederick Sullens to LeRoy Percy, December 11, 1911, several letters to LeRoy Percy, all in PP.

40. Walker Percy to Capt. J. S. McNeilly, October 19, 1911, LeRoy Percy to E. W. Stewart, November 2, 1911, Typescript interview with LeRoy Percy, n.d., F. W. Pettibone to LeRoy Percy, December 20, 1911, all in PP.

41. *Congressional Record*, 62nd Cong., 2nd Sess., 226–30.

42. LeRoy Percy to Capt. Mac (McNeilly), February 10, 1912, in PP; Kirwan, *Revolt of the Rednecks*, 232; Holmes, *Vardaman*, 261.

43. LeRoy Percy to Capt. J. S. McNeilly, May 5, 1913, to Senator J. A. Ransdell, May 5, 1913, both in PP; *Congressional Record*, 62nd Cong., 2nd Sess., 4843, 5091, 5248–49, 5311–16, 6115–23; 62nd Cong., 3rd Sess., 2683, 3501, 3570–79, 3764, 4367, 4372.

44. LeRoy Percy to Senator F. M. Stone, June 20, 1912, to J. S. Williams, June 20, 1912, to R. G. Backus, June 21, 1912, and to M. B. Trezvant, December 26, 1913, all in PP; *Congressional Record*, 61st Cong., 2nd Sess., 3227, 4034, 4968–69, 9047, 10394–95; 61st Cong., 3rd Sess., 2080, 2088.

45. LeRoy Percy to H. J. Gensler, May 28, 1913, Springfield *Republican*, August 10, 1912, clipping, both in PP; Osborn, *Williams*, 312; *Congressional Record*, 62nd Cong., 3rd Sess., 4033, 4299, appendix, 184–90.

Chapter 4

1. W. A. Percy to Wm. Stanley Braithwaite, October 11, 1922, in PP; W. A. Percy, *Lanterns*, 35–81; Ware, "William Alexander Percy," 10–12.

2. W. A. Percy to William Stanley Braithwaite, October 11, 1922, "Night," in scrapbook, both in PP; W. A. Percy, *Lanterns*, 56–57, 81–83.

3. W. A. Percy, *Lanterns*, 83–93.

4. Newspaper clippings, n.d., in PP; Ware, "William Alexander Percy," 16–21; Phinizy Spalding, "William Alexander Percy: His Philosophy of Life as Reflected in His Poetry" (Master's thesis, University of Georgia, 1957), 22.

5. Camille Percy to W. A. Percy, August 14, 1902, LeRoy Percy to W. A. Percy, August 14, 1902, *Pathfinder*, n.d., and other newspaper clippings, n.d., all in PP.

6. W. A. Percy to Prof. Frederick Hard, November 2, 1922, and to Wm. Stanley Braithwaite, October 11, 1922, W. A. Percy, untitled poem, "An ocean sigh . . . ," *The Sewanee Purple*, clipping, January 30, 1942, all in PP.

7. W. A. Percy, *Lanterns*, 92–95; Ware, "William Alexander Percy," 25–27.

8. W. A. Percy to Camille Percy, September 29, November 15, December 22, 1904, to Camille Percy, October 6, n.y., to Carrie Stern, April 21, 1907, to Dr. Geo. M. Baker, March 12, 1926, and to LeRoy Percy, November 11, n.y., all in PP; W. A. Percy, *Lanterns*, 105–13.

9. W. A. Percy to Camille Percy, January 9, 17, 28, February 4, April 10, 14, August 11, 19, 1905, and to LeRoy Percy, January 2, March 30, November 11, n.y., all in PP.

10. LeRoy Percy to W. A[rmstrong]. Percy, July 16, 1907, W. A. Percy to LeRoy Percy and Percy to Camille Percy, several letters, all in PP.

11. W. A. Percy to Miss Carrie Stern, April 21, 1907, the S. S. McClure Company to W. A. Percy, February 15, 1908, both in PP; William Alexander Percy, *The Collected Poems of William Alexander Percy* (New York, 1943), 35, 76.

12. W. A. Percy to Miss Helen Campbell, May 2, 1923, and several letters to LeRoy Percy and to Camille Percy, all in PP.

13. W. A. Percy, *Collected Poems*, 66–68; Benjamin Willis Dickey, "William Alexander Percy: An Alien Spirit in the Twentieth Century" (Master's thesis, Alabama Polytechnic Institute, 1951), 56.

14. W. A. Percy to Camille Percy, March 26, 1906, and June 27, 1908, both in PP.

15. W. A. Percy to Camille Percy, June 27, 1908, LeRoy Percy to Walker Percy, June 14, 1908, to Thomas Cook and Sons, July 3, 1908, to West Publishing Company, September 29, 1908, and to F. C. Armstrong, Nov. 3, 1908, W. A. Percy to Miss Carrie [Stern], Tuesday, n.d., and to Camille Percy, September 13, 1909, newspaper clippings, n.d., all in PP.

16. W. A. Percy to LeRoy Percy, May 29, 1910, to LeRoy Percy, February 3, 1911, and to LeRoy Percy, April 20, 1912, LeRoy Percy to W. A. Percy, February 27, 1909, W. A. Percy to Dear Judge [Moody], August 23, 1910, to Theo. McKnight Jr., January 10, 1912, to W. S. Zimmerman, May 7, 1911, and to W. H. Clements, May 7, 1911, W. A. Percy, Diary, miscellaneous legal correspondence, all in PP.

17. W. A. Percy to LeRoy Percy, April 21, May 2, 1910, to Oscar Johnson, June 17, 1910, to Capt. J. S. McNeilly, August 25, 1910, to LeRoy Percy, January 9, 17, 23, February 17, April 6, 1911, and to William Crump, May 6, 1911, all in PP.

18. W. A. Percy, Diary, in PP; Holmes Adams, "Writers of Greenville, Mississippi, 1915–1950," *Journal of Mississippi History*, XXXII (Fall, 1970), 229–43.

19. Witter Bynner to W. A. Percy, September 1914, W. A. Percy to Yale University Press, September 12, 1915, Byrne Hackett to W. A. Percy, May 28, 1915, all in PP.

20. W. A. Percy, *Collected Poems*, 12–28.

21. *Ibid.*, 43–53.

22. *Ibid.*, 64, 79–82, 86–88, Spalding, William Alexander Percy," 33.

23. *Dial*, clipping, n.d., Chicago *Evening Post*, review by Llewellyn Jones, December 10, 1915, Llewellyn Jones to W. A. Percy, December 11, 1915, William Stanley Braithwaite to W. A. Percy, January 10, 1916, miscellaneous clippings, all in PP.

Chapter 5

1. LeRoy Percy to Senator John Sharp Williams, February 4, May 4, 1914, to W. H. Negus, February 14, 1914, and to D. A. Scott, June 22, 1914, W. A. Percy to Mrs. Jas. E. Negus, September 9, 1914, all in PP; W. A. Percy to Dearest Coz [Janet Dana], Sunday, n.d., in Janet Percy Dana Longcope Papers, Louisiana State University, Department of Archives and History, Baton Rouge.

2. Leroy Percy to B. G. Humphries, October 23, 1914, and to Mrs. Lucy E. Maitland, April 8, 1915, both in PP.

3. LeRoy Percy to Capt. J. S. McNeilly, May 17, 1915, in PP.

4. W. A. Percy to Janet Percy Dana, November 20, 1914, in Longcope Papers.

5. J.P.D. [Janet Percy Dana] to W. A. Percy, December 11, [1914], in PP; W. A. Percy to Janet Percy Dana, December 17, 1914, in Longcope Papers; W. A. Percy to Bishop Thos. Gailor, January 27, 1915, in PP.

6. W. A. Percy to Janet [Dana], Tuesday, n.d., and to Janet Percy Dana, January 23, October 2, 1915, all in Longcope Papers.

7. W. A. Percy to Janet Percy Dana, May 28, 1915, in Longcope Papers; Janet Dana to W. A. Percy, February 28, June 9, 23, July 14, August 22, September 14, 22, October 5, 29, 1915, all in PP.

8. W. A. Percy to Carrie Stern, February 16, 1916, Janet Dana to W. A. Percy, August 3, 9, 1916, all in PP; W. A. Percy to This, coz dear. [Janet Dana], Friday night, n.d., to Dearest Coz [Janet Dana], Tuesday, n.d., and to Mrs. Warfield [Janet Dana] Longcope, September 3, 1916, all in Longcope Papers; Hudean Windham, "A Study of William Alexander Percy's Life and Poetry" (Master's thesis, George Peabody College for Teachers, 1939), 21, 41.

9. W. A. Percy to Mrs. Warfield Longcope, November 10, 1916, in Longcope Papers; W. A. Percy to Miss Carrie Stern, December 10, 1916, "Grandpere," in envelope addressed to Carrie Stern, from Rotterdam, 1916, W. A. Percy, "Dice Throwers?" December 18, Rotterdam, and "Grandfather," all in PP.

10. W. A. Percy, *Lanterns*, 156–68; Certificate, awarded to W. A. Percy by the Belgian government, n.d., in PP; Ware, "William Alexander Percy," 121.

11. LeRoy Percy to Senator John Sharp Williams, June 5, 1915, to Hon. Jos. W. Bailey, August 10, 1915, to Col. Theodore Roosevelt, January 20, 1916, and to Judge J. M. Dickinson, May 22, 1916, all in PP.

12. LeRoy Percy to Hon. B. G. Humphries, January 19, April 28, 1916, to Capt. J. S. McNeilly, April 28, 1916, to A. H. Stone, March 23, 1916, and to Congressman B. G. Humphries, January 2, 1917, all in PP; Harrison, *Levee Districts*, 226; Holmes, *Vardaman*, 327.

13. LeRoy Percy to Capt. J. S. McNeilly, February 15, 1917, LeRoy P. Percy to LeRoy Percy, April 21, 1917, LeRoy Percy to LeRoy P. Percy, April 26, 1917, to Senator John Sharp Williams, April 24, 1917, to Col. Theodore Roosevelt, n.d., to Col. Theodore Roosevelt, May 22, 1917, to John Sharp Williams, May 23, 1917, and to General Leonard Wood, June 30, 1917, all in PP.

14. W. A. Percy to Miss Carrie Stern, April 2, 1917, W. A. Percy, Poetry notebook, Paris, April 1917, LeRoy Percy to Belgium Relief Commission, May 5, 1917, to C. M. Davis, May 5, 1917, to W. A. Percy, April 28, 1917, to Mrs. C. J. McKinney, April 3, 1917, and to Capt. J. S. McNeilly, April 3, 14, 1917, all in PP.

15. W. A. Percy to Mrs. Warfield Longcope, July 7, 1917, in Longcope Papers; LeRoy Percy to Capt. J. S. McNeilly, June 12, July 9, 1917, Flyer, Vicksburg *Herald*, n.d., Aberdeen *Examiner*, July 13, 1917, Greenville *Daily Democrat*, June 18, 1917, *Delta Lighthouse*, July 7, 1917, and other clippings, n.d., Bertha McGee Scales to W. A. Percy, July 3, 1917, D. W. Houston to LeRoy Percy, July 10, 1917, all in PP.

16. W. A. Percy to Henry A. Bellows, June 4, 1917, Samuel McCoy to W. A. Percy, July 17, 1917, H. A. Bellour to W. A. Percy, July 17, 1917, W. A. Percy to William Stanley Braithwaite, August 11, 1917, all in PP; W. A. Percy, *Collected Poems*, 139, 164.

17. Greenville *Daily Democrat*, clipping, June 18, 1917, LeRoy Percy to Capt. J. S. McNeilly, April 25, 1917, to Hon. B. G. Humphreys, May 26, 1917, and to A. B. Blanton, June 16, 1917, all in PP.

18. LeRoy Percy to W. H. Negus, August 7, 1917, to Kenneth G. Price, September 18, 1917, to LeRoy P. Percy, September 21, 1917, to Frank W. Williams, September 7, 1917, and to Dear Will [Percy], October 26, 1917, W. A. Percy to Carrie Stern, October 7, 1917, Geo. L. Leftwich to Mrs. LeRoy Percy, October 25, 1917, "Special Orders," No. 158, Camp Stanley, November 27, 1917, all in PP; W. A. Percy, *Lanterns*, 169–83.

19. LeRoy Percy to W. A. Percy, October 6, 15, 26, 1917, to LeRoy P. Percy, October 26, 1917, to G. P. Clark, November 10, 1917, to R. B. Anderson, November 26, 1917, to W. H. Powell, November 23, 1917, W. H. Powell to LeRoy Percy, November 14, 1917, Governor Theodore G. Bilbo to LeRoy Percy, November 26, 1917, LeRoy Percy to Gov. Theodore G. Bilbo, November 27, 1917, Alex. Y. Scott to LeRoy Percy, December 3, 1917, all in PP.

20. MMF to Stone Deavours, February 18, 1918, miscellaneous newspaper clippings, n.d., LeRoy Percy to W. A. Percy, June 30, 1918, Percy and Percy to Harris Dickson, December 10, 1917, LeRoy Percy to Dear Charlie, February 1, 1918, and to Judge W. B. Parker, June 17, 1918, H. O. Pate to LeRoy Percy, July 6, 1918, LeRoy Percy to Hugh T. Kerr, September 19, 1918, H. C. Lodge to LeRoy Percy, October 12, 1918, all in PP.

21. LeRoy Percy to LeRoy P. Percy, December 14, 1917, W. A. Percy, "To C. P.," "Our Generation," "To Mother," "This Generation," "Poppy Fields," all in PP; W. A.

Percy, *Collected Poems*, 188, 190, 192–93; Ware, "William Alexander Percy," 102.

22. LeRoy Percy to W. A. Percy, December 22, 29, 1917, both in PP.

23. LeRoy Percy to Dear Charlie, February 1, 1918, Janet Longcope to W. A. Percy, March 24, 1918, W. A. Percy to Carrie Stern, May 2, 1918, MMF to Stone Deavours, February 18, 1918, W. A. Percy to Mother Dear, June 16, 1918, and to B., August 16, 1918, PP; W. A. Percy, *Lanterns*, 195–200.

24. W. A. Percy to Mother Dear, August 7, 1918, in Percy, "Lanterns on the Levee," typescript, Chap. 17, in PP.

25. W. A. Percy to Mother dear, August 11, 18, September 7, 1918, in Percy, "Lanterns on the Levee," typescript, Chap. 17, W. A. Percy to Mother dear, September 13, 1918, and to LeRoy Percy, August 31, 1918, all in PP.

26. Edward M. Coffman, *The War to End All Wars* (New York, 1968), 299–356; Laurence Stallings, *The Doughboys* (New York, 1963), 222–36; U.S. Department of the Army, Historical Division, *Meuse-Argonne Operations of the American Expeditionary Forces* (Washington D.C., 1948), 129–34. Vol. IX of *United States Army in the World War, 1917–1919.*

27. Coffman, *War to End All Wars*, 308–11; U.S. Department of the Army, Historical Division, *Meuse-Argonne Operations*, 163–65, 169–70.

28. Stallings, *The Doughboys*, 306–309; W. A. Percy to Dear Father, October 25, 1918, in PP.

29. Ernest Hemingway, *A Farewell to Arms* (New York, 1929), Chap. 27; Frederick J. Hoffman, *The Twenties* (New York, 1949).

30. Paul Fussell, *The Great War and Modern Memory* (New York, 1975), 156–59.

31. *Ibid.*, 170–85; W. A. Percy to Dear Father, October 25, 1918, and to LeRoy Percy, November 15, 1918, W. A. Percy, field message book, all in PP.

32. Fussell, *The Great War*, 232–43; W. A. Percy, *Lanterns*, 202; W. A. Percy, *Collected Poems*, 197; W. A. Percy, "Waiting the Offensive," W. A. Percy to Mother dear, August 11, 1918, and to W. S. Lewis, April 20, 1920, all in PP.

33. David M. Kennedy, *Over Here* (New York, 1980), 205–15.

34. W. A. Percy to LeRoy Percy, February 17, 1919, to Master William A. Percy, January 11, 1919, to Jean S. Milner, April 16, 1919, and to Bishop Albion V. Knight, April 17, 1919; Walter Hullikan to W. A. Percy, January 20, 1919, LeRoy Percy to Capt. W. A. Percy, August 19, 1919, all in PP; W. A. Percy, *Lanterns*, 223–26.

35. W. A. Percy to G. G. Wyant, June 25, 1919, and to Carrie Stern, September 1, 1919, [Janet Longcope] to W. A. Percy, December 18, 1919, all in PP.

36. W. A. Percy to Miss Medora Hambough, April 13, 1929, and W. A. Percy, Diary, 140–48, both in PP.

37. W. A. Percy, *Collected Poems*, 91–128.

Chapter 6

1. LeRoy Percy to Lawrence D. McMeekin, September 17, 1917, in PP.

2. LeRoy Percy to W. A. Percy, July 30, 1920, to Mrs. W. A[rmstrong]. Percy, October 19, December 23, 1920, to J. W. McGrath, February 13, 1922, to A. H. Stone, February 20, 1922, and to Senator Jos. E. Ransdell, March 9, 1922, Alfred H. Stone, "As to Senator Percy," pamphlet, Dunleith, Miss., June, 1923, all in PP; Vicksburg *Herald*, March 1, 1922; Sallis, "LeRoy Percy," 164–65; George Brown Tindall, *The Emergence of the New South, 1913–1945* (Baton Rouge, 1967), 113.

3. The best introduction to the Ku Klux Klan of the twenties is Robert Moats Miller, "The Ku Klux Klan," in John Braeman, Robert H. Bremmer, and David Brody (eds.), *Change and Continuity in Twentieth-Century America: The 1920's* (Columbus, Ohio, 1968), 215–56.

4. LeRoy Percy to A. H. Stone, February 27, 1922, in PP; W. A. Percy, *Lanterns*, 232.

5. Vicksburg *Herald*, March 4, 1922; LeRoy Percy, "Address by Senator LeRoy Percy," reprinted from Houston *Chronicle*, March 19, 1922, in PP; W. A. Percy, *Lanterns*, 232–33;

6. Vicksburg *Herald*, clipping, March 2, 4, 1922, Jackson *Daily Clarion-Ledger*, clipping, March 2, 1922, LeRoy Percy, *Ku Klux Klan Unnecessary*, pamphlet, LeRoy Percy, *Address by Senator LeRoy Percy, Greenville, Miss.*, pamphlet, all in PP; W. A. Percy, *Lanterns*, 232–33; Sallis, "LeRoy Percy," 151–53.

7. Clippings from New York *World*, New York *Evening Post*, Memphis *Commercial Appeal*, New Orleans *Times-Picayune*, Vicksburg *Herald*, and others, William Bell to LeRoy Percy, March 6, 1922, see also Perry W. Howard to LeRoy Percy, March 27, 1922, James A. Michell to LeRoy Percy, March 28, 1922, D. J. Foreman to LeRoy Percy, March 21, 1922, Rev. O. H. Hall to LeRoy Percy, March 9, 1922, Wallace A. Battle, Okolona, Miss., to LeRoy Percy, March 4, 1922, and J. M. Williamson to LeRoy Percy, March 7, 1922, for editorials condemning the speech, see clippings from Columbus *Dispatch* and Rolling Fork *Pilot*, the latter a Klan newspaper, all in PP.

8. Hugh B. McCormick to LeRoy Percy, March 2, 1922, W. L. Evans to LeRoy Percy, March 2, 1922, J. D'Antoni to LeRoy Percy, March 20, 1922, J. T. Savage to LeRoy Percy, March 29, 1922, William J. McGinley to LeRoy Percy, June 2, 1922, LeRoy Percy to William J. McGinley, June 5, 1922, S. S. Coleman to LeRoy Percy, March 28, 1922, R. W. Colomb to LeRoy Percy, March 2, 1922, Lewis Stein to LeRoy Percy, March 6, 1922, Aaron Sapiro to LeRoy Percy, March 27, 1922, Institute Franco-Anglais to LeRoy Percy, March 13, 1922, Lea Beaty to LeRoy Percy, March 20, 1922, all in PP.

9. Ralph W. McGee to LeRoy Percy, March 2, 1922, Dick Cox to LeRoy Percy, March 5, 1922, J. G. McGuire to LeRoy Percy, March 13, 1922, C. M. McKinnon to LeRoy Percy, March 25, 1922, I.D. Bensen to LeRoy Percy, March 27, 1922, P. S. Calvern to LeRoy Percy, March 27, 1922, Hamilton A. Long to LeRoy Percy, March 29, 1922, all in PP.

10. W. A. Percy, *Lanterns*, 230–31; U.S. Department of Commerce and Labor, Bureau of the Census, Special Reports, *Religious Bodies, 1906* (Washington, D.C., 1910), I, 330; U.S. Department of Commerce, Bureau of the Census, *Religious Bodies, 1916* (Washington D.C., 1919), I, 279.

11. Leland *Enterprise*, clipping, March 18, 1922, in PP; Sallis, "LeRoy Percy," 155; W. A. Percy, *Lanterns*, 234.

12. LeRoy Percy to H. M. Garwood, March 10, 22, 1922, and to Marcellus E. Foster, March 22, 30, 1922, Hiram M. Garwood to LeRoy Percy, March 3, 20, 30, April 5, 1922, Marcellus E. Foster to LeRoy Percy, March 16, 27, 1922, LeRoy Percy to R. H. Hill, March 30, 1922, all in PP.

13. LeRoy Percy to C. P. Mooney, March 20, 30, 1922, and to Ellery Sedgwick, March 20, 28, April 27, May 1, 1922, Ellery Sedgwick to LeRoy Percy, April 7, 21, May 4, 1922, LeRoy Percy to W. A. Percy, April 8, 1922, all in PP; LeRoy Percy, "The Modern Ku Klux Klan," *Atlantic Monthly*, CXXX (July, 1922), 122–28.

14. LeRoy Percy to Ellery Sedgwick, April 27, 1922, in PP.

15. Charles C. Alexander, *The Ku Klux Klan in the Southwest* (Lexington, Ky., 1965), 68.

16. Alexander, *Klan in the Southwest*, 68–73.

17. G. K. Rutledge to LeRoy Percy, July 21, 1922, Patrick O'Donnell to LeRoy Percy, telegram, February 16, 1923, LeRoy Percy to Patrick O'Donnell, telegram, February 19, 1923, and to Governor John M. Parker, February 19, 1923; *Tolerance*, clipping, February 25, 1923, all in PP; Kenneth T. Jackson, *The Ku Klux Klan in the City, 1915–1930* (New York, 1967), 93–110.

18. Jackson, *Klan in the City*, 105–106; Vicksburg *Herald*, February 27, 1923.

19. *Extract from Speech of LeRoy Percy Delivered in Chicago on February 26, 1923,* in PP.

20. Patrick H. O'Donnell to LeRoy Percy, February 28, 1923, LeRoy Percy to Patrick H. O'Donnell, March 5, 1923, and to Gov. John M. Parker, March 5, 1923, all in PP; Vicksburg *Herald,* March 4, 1923.

21. LeRoy Percy to Leon Moyse, January 11, 1923, to J. Speed Elliott, March 28, 1923, to W. P. McKinney, April 2, 1923, and to A. P. Wilkey, January 20, 1923, all in PP.

22. Greenville *Daily Democrat,* clipping, March 21, 1923, in PP.

23. Arnold S. Rice, *The Ku Klux Klan in American Politics* (Washington, D.C., 1962), 8–11; John Higham, *Strangers in the Land: Patterns of American Nativism, 1860–1925* (New York, 1963), 297–98.

24. "A Manly Letter from Dr. Smythe," Greenville *Daily Democrat,* clipping, n.d., *Speech of Ex-United States Senator LeRoy Percy,* Greenville, Miss., April 23, 1923, both in PP; W. A. Percy, *Lanterns,* 234–35; Interview with Brodie S. Crump, by the author.

25. "A Manly Letter from Dr. Smythe," Greenville *Daily Democrat,* clipping, n.d., in PP.

26. *Speech of Ex-United States Senator LeRoy Percy,* Greenville, Miss., April 23, 1923, untitled speech, May 9, 1923, both in PP.

27. J. K. Skipwith to LeRoy Percy, May 3, 1923, in PP.

28. LeRoy Percy to J. K. Skipwith, May 5, 1923, Greenville *Daily Democrat,* clipping, May 7, 1923, both in PP.

29. Unsigned, letterhead H. G. Vaught to LeRoy Percy, May 7, 1923, LeRoy Percy to H. G. Vaught, May 8, 1923, and to Fred Hudson, May 19, 1923, Memphis *Tri-State American,* clipping, May 9, 1923, all in PP.

30. Untitled speech, May 9, 1923, in PP.

31. LeRoy Percy to Wm. Ray Toombs, May 13, 1923, in PP; Memphis *Commercial Appeal,* May 18, 1923; W. A. Percy, *Lanterns,* 235–36.

32. LeRoy Percy to Wm. Ray Toombs, May 13, 1923, in PP; Memphis *Commercial Appeal,* May 18, 1923.

33. J. B. Hebron to LeRoy Percy, May 17, 1923, W. C. Winter to LeRoy Percy, May 15, 1923, F. V. Brahan to LeRoy Percy, May 15, 1923, J. M. Perkins to LeRoy Percy, May 13, 1923, A. D. Pan to LeRoy Percy, May 15, 1923, Bill Hebron to SP, May 16, 1923, LeRoy Percy to J. B. Hebron, May 17, 1923, W. A. Percy to B. O. McGee, May 31, 1923, LeRoy [Pratt] Percy to LeRoy Percy, May 18, 1923, LeRoy Percy to Dr. J. T. Atterbury, June 15, 1923, all in PP; W. A. Percy, *Lanterns,* 236.

34. W. A. Percy to Elliot Cage, May 21, 1923, LeRoy Percy to B. B. Harper, May 15, 1923, LeRoy Percy to Sen. Jos. W. Bailey, May 14, 1923, to J. A. Davenport, May 19, 1923, to L. H. Gaines, May 14, 1923; to Mayor R. L. Wade, May 16, 1923, and others, with pamphlets enclosed; to Dr. J. T. Atterbury, June 15, 1923, and to Gov. John M. Parker, August 23, 1923, "To the Voters of Washington County," all in PP; Sallis, "LeRoy Percy," 159–60.

35. LeRoy Percy to Gov. John M. Parker, August 23, 1923, and to John M. Mecklin, September 26 1923, both in PP; W. A. Percy, *Lanterns,* 237; Interview with Brodie S. Crump, by the author; Interview with Don R. Baker, by the author, Leland, Mississippi, October 23, 1976 (Transcript in Louisiana State University Department of Archives and History, Baton Rouge).

36. LeRoy Percy to John M. Mecklin, September 26, 1923, and to Chief Justice William Howard Taft, September 25, 1923, both in PP; W. A. Percy, *Lanterns,* 237–41.

37. Interview with Brodie S. Crump, by the author.

38. William H. Taft to LeRoy Percy, August 30, 1923, in PP.

39. LeRoy Percy to Chief Justice William Howard Taft, September 25, 1923, and to Alice D. Jenkins, July 19, 1922, both in PP.

40. LeRoy Percy to LeRoy Pratt Percy, June 16, 1924, to W. A. Percy, June 16, 1924, to Judge J. M. Dickinson, June 17, 1924, Judge Ben Lindsey to LeRoy Percy, April 24, 1925, W. A. Percy to Camille Percy, June 17, 1924, all in PP.

Chapter 7

1. James E. West to W. A. Percy, February 28, 1922, T. C. Catchings to Mrs. LeRoy Percy, June 2, 1922, Emma D. Welk to Mrs. LeRoy Percy, June 1, 1922, Reginald Herbert Smith to W. A. Percy, March 30, 1922, W. A. Percy to Chalmers Potter, March 7, 1922, to Boltin Smith, March 10, 1922, and to Geo. J. Leftwich, February 10, 1922, all in PP; W. A. Percy, *Collected Poems*, 142.

2. W. A. Percy, *Lanterns*, 222–24.

3. H. M., "A Misguided Poet," *Poetry* (July, 1917), clipping, William Stanley Braithwaite, "A Poet Comes Out of Mississippi," Boston *Evening Transcript*, clipping, January 2, 1916, Llewellyn Jones, Review of *Sappho in Levkas*, Chicago *Evening Post*, clipping, December 10, 1915, all in PP.

· 4. W. A. Percy to S. T. Clover, November 1, 1920, Llewellyn Jones, "Beauty and Insight," Chicago *Evening Post*, clipping, November 25, 1921, both in PP; Dickey, "William Alexander Percy," 14–15.

5. Stirling Bowen, Review of *In April Once*, Detroit *News*, clipping, September 19, 1920, W. A. Percy to S. T. Clover, November 1, 1920, and to W. S. Lewis, September 29, October 4, 1920, all in PP.

6. Stuart P. Sherman to My Dear Painter, November 7, 1920, W. A. Percy to L. G. Painter, April 16, 1921, both in PP.

7. W. A. Percy to C. McD. Puckette, March 17, 1921, in PP; Hoffman, *The Twenties*, 165–80.

8. W. A. Percy to James Robert Peery, September 3, 1921, and to Ellery Sedgwick, November 10, 1920, both in PP.

9. W. A. Percy, "Greenville Trees," typescript, includes "The Crepe Myrtles," in PP; W. A. Percy, *Collected Poems*, 275–80.

10. W. A. Percy to Miss Jennie Q. Whelan, May 13, 1921, in PP.

11. DuBose Heyward to W. A. Percy, July 3, 1923, W. A. Percy to DuBose Heyward, July 14, 1923, both in PP.

12. W. A. Percy to *The Double Dealer*, September 6, 1921, to J. R. Moreland, November 15, December 9, 1921, to DuBose Heyward, December 15, 1921, to Botticelli's Primavera, December 9, 1921, to George Herbert Clark, November 16, 1921, to Miss Alice R. Smith, March 27, 1922, to John McClure, March 25, 1922, Rex G. Fuller to W. A. Percy, December 4, 1922, W. A. Percy to John Moreland, November 25, 1922, all in PP; for the bibliography and texts of W. A. Percy's magazine poetry, see Dickey, "William Alexander Percy."

13. Allen Tate to W. A. Percy, September 28, October 16, 1922, W. A. Percy to Allen Tate, October 11, 1922, Allen Tate to W. A. Percy, November 27, [1922], John C. Ransom to W. A. Percy, May 8, [1922], Allen Tate to W. A. Percy, July 21, 26, 1923, W. A. Percy to Alex Tate, July 23, 1923, all in PP.

14. W. A. Percy to J. R. Moreland, December 9, 1921, and to Alice R. Smith, March 27, 1927, both in PP.

15. W. A. Percy to *The Double Dealer*, September 6, 1921, in PP; W. A. Percy, "In Black and White," *Double Dealer*, (June, 1921), cited in Spalding, "William Alexander Percy."

16. W. A. Percy to Ellery Sedgwick, December 10, 1921, in PP; W. A. Percy, *Collected Poems*, 291–97.

17. W. A. Percy to Rev. A. R. Grey, April 5, 1922, in PP; W. A. Percy, *Lanterns*, 238; Harold Speakman, *Mostly Mississippi* (New York, 1927), 258–59.

18. W. A. Percy to Rev. A. R. Gray, April 5, 1922, to Major McKellar, May 4, 1922, and to Ben Finney, October 12, 1922, all in PP.

19. W. A. Percy to George Herbert Clark, April 26, 1922, to Yale University Press, April 28, May 11, 1922, and to Wilson Follett, May 12, 24, June 14, 1922, Wilson Follett to W. A. Percy, May 19, June 6, July 19, 1922, all in PP; William Alexander Percy (ed.), *Poems of Arthur O'Shaughnessy* (New Haven, 1923), 5–6.

20. Percy (ed.), *Poems of Arthur O'Shaughnessy*, 2–3, 5–6.

21. W. A. Percy to Camille Percy, July 24, August 8, 25, 1922, all in PP.

22. W. A. Percy to Wilson Follett, June 28, 1923, and to Bernard H. Knowll, September 5, 1929, both in PP; W. A. Percy, *Collected Poems*, 340.

23. Janet Dana to W. A. Percy, June 3, 1918, January 7, 1919, Janet Longcope to W. A. Percy, March 1, 1920, all in PP.

24. James Truslow Adams, Introduction to *The Education of Henry Adams*, by Henry Adams (New York, 1931), vi-vii.

25. W. A. Percy to Charles Scribner's Sons, November 18, 1922, January 4, 1923, to Wilson Follett, February 27, 1923, June 28, July 26, 1923, all in PP.

26. Dickey, "William Alexander Percy," 17–18; Spalding, "William Alexander Percy," 137.

27. W. A. Percy, *Collected Poems*, 281; Spalding, "William Alexander Percy," 66.

Chapter 8

1. LeRoy Percy to Editor of *Commercial Appeal*, May 19, 1923, to R. O. Purdy, May 14, 1923, to Judge J. M. Dickinson, May 14, 1923, to C. M. Davis, May 18, 1923, all in PP; Vicksburg *Herald*, May 3, August 1, 1923; Higham, *Strangers in the Land*, 313–21.

2. LeRoy Percy to Lieut-Gov. Dennis Murphree, October 4, 1926, to J. B. Gully, January 20, 1925, to W. T. Wynn, January 9, 1926, to Walton Shields, January 9, 1926, and to W. M. Whittington, March 4, 1927, all in PP.

3. LeRoy Percy to James Sexton, January 15, 1926, to Mrs. C. J. McKinney, January 25, 1926, to Stephen M. Weld and Co., March 1, 1926, to Wm. T. Wynn, March 1, 1926, to Frank B. Hayne, March 2, 1926, to Senator Pat Harrison, June 14, 1926, to LeRoy Pratt Percy, July 8, 13, 1926, to Messrs. Fenners & Bean, October 14, 1926, to W. B. Roberts, October 9, 1926, to L. M. Pool, October 12, 1926, to B. W. Hirsh, October 14, 1926, to W. B. Snowden, October 12, 1926, and to W. M. Whittington, March 25, 1927, all in PP.

4. V. A. Griffith to LeRoy Percy, May 5, 1923, LeRoy Percy to Gen. T. C. Catchings, May 8, 1923, to Ned Sayford, December 16, 1925, to Judge C. C. Moody, January 9, 1926, to Judge J. M. Dickinson, January 18, 1926, and to Wm. McMartin, January 19, 1927, all in PP.

5. LeRoy Percy to W. A. Percy, January 23, May 8, 1924, to Oscar Johnston, June 14, 1924, to N. Picard, November 25, 1924, to Geo. B. Alexander, October 30, 1924, to Mrs. C. J. McKinney, October 30, 1924, to Senator John Sharp Williams, November 3, 1925, to F. V. Brahan, November 9, 1925, to Frank Williams, January 18, 1926, to Judge J. M. Dickinson, January 18, 1926, to Mrs. C. J. McKinney, January 25, 1926, W. A. Percy to LeRoy Pratt Percy, May 20, 1926, LeRoy Percy to LeRoy Pratt Percy, August 11, September 28, 1926, and to Miss Dana Sexton, November 2, 1926, all in PP.

6. W. A. Percy to Camille Percy, February 3, 1925, J. L. [Janet Longcope] to W. A.

Percy, June 15, 1925, W. A. Percy to Huger Jervey, May 15, 1925, to H. W. Jervey, June 3, 1926, to W. H. Griffin, October 1, 1926, to Bernard Flexner, October 5, 1926, and to Dear Miss Wright, May 25, 1926, LeRoy Percy to Mrs. C. J. McKinney, April 4, 1927, W. A. Percy, "We are not sown . . .," untitled poem, all in PP.

7. W. A. Percy, "The University of the South," booklet reprinted from *Sewanee Review* (April, 1927), in PP; Robert M. Crunden, *The Superfluous Men: Conservative Critics of American Culture, 1900–1945* (Austin, 1977); Joseph Blotner, *Faulkner: A Biography* (New York, 1974) 323.

8. LeRoy Percy to E. E. Grant, October 6, 1908, in PP; W. A. Percy, *Collected Poems*, 351–52; Spalding, "William Alexander Percy," 102; Blotner, *Faulkner*, 288.

9. Mrs. George Parmly Day to W. A. Percy, March 14, 25, April 17, 1925; W. A. Percy to Mrs. George Parmly Day, March 20, 31, April 14, 1925, to Countee Cullen, April 20, 1925, to L. P. Soule, April 15, 1926, and to Henri Faust, November 12, 1926, all in PP.

10. Mary C. Booze to LeRoy Percy, March 17, 1926, W. A. Percy to Mary C. Booze, April 8, 1926, to Dr. Hugh Gamble, January 11, 1926, Dr. Hugh Gamble to W. A. Percy, January 29, 1926, W. A. Percy to Francis Harmon, February 4, 1926, to National Red Cross, March 18, 1926, and to Herbert Hoover, October 4, 1926, all in PP.

11. Brandfon, *Cotton Kingdom*, 22–23; LeRoy Percy, *Mississippi River Floods*, House Committee on Flood Control, 64th Cong., 1st Sess., Microform (Westport, Conn., n.d.), 43.

12. W. A. Percy, *Lanterns*, 247–54.

13. W. A. Percy, Typescript of *Lanterns on the Levee*, Chap. 19, in PP.

14. W. A. Percy, *Lanterns*, 255–56.

15. LeRoy Percy to Judge J. M. Dickinson, August 7, 20, 1927, in PP; W. A. Percy, *Lanterns*, 256–58.

16. W. A. Percy, *Lanterns*, 257–58.

17. W. A. Percy, Typescript of *Lanterns on the Levee*, Chap. 19, in PP; W. A. Percy, *Lanterns*, 258; Daniels, *Shadow of Slavery*, 157; Richard H. King, *A Southern Renaissance* (New York, 1980), 94.

18. W. A. Percy, unidentified clipping, n.d., "Relief Chairman Pays Tribute to Colored People," unidentified clipping, n.d., both in PP; W. A. Percy, *Lanterns*, 265–68.

19. "Mississippi Poet Busy . . .," unidentified clipping, dateline Greenville, October 4, LeRoy Percy to G. L. Rawls, June 28, 1927, to Garner Green, n.d., to L. A. Downs, September 10, 1927, all in PP.

20. LeRoy Percy to Ned Rice, May 31, 1927, in PP.

21. Charles G. Dawes to LeRoy Percy, June 23, 1927, LeRoy Percy to LeRoy Pratt Percy, July 11, 1927, J. M. Dickinson to LeRoy Percy, August 1, 1927, Charles G. Dawes to LeRoy Percy, August 6, 1927, LeRoy Percy to Miss Lady Percy, October 7, 1927, and to Dear Will [Percy], October 28, 1927, Greenville *Democrat Times*, clipping, June 6, 1927, New Orleans *Item*, clipping, n.d., all in PP.

22. W. A. Percy to Camille Percy September 13, 1927, to Geo. Parmly Day, August 31, 1927, and to Miss E. Holliday, November 26, 1927, LeRoy Percy to W. A. Percy, October 11, 1927, W. A. Percy, "Lyric," all in PP; Spalding, "William Alexander Percy," 46; W. A. Percy, *Collected Poems*, 358–59.

23. LeRoy Percy to L. O. Crosby, September 10, 1927, to L. A. Downs, September 10, 1927, to Dr. W. M. Clack, October 4, 1927, to Mrs. Archie Barkley, October 12, 1927, and to Miss Lady Percy, October 7, 1927, all in PP.

24. LeRoy Percy to Miss Lady Percy, October 7, 1927, and to Dear Will [Percy], October 28, 1927, both in PP.

25. Percy, *Mississippi River Floods*, 43–49.

26. *Ibid.*, 46–49; LeRoy Percy to LeRoy Pratt Percy, May 26, 1928, and estimate from F. V. Ragsdale Company, both in PP.

27. LeRoy Percy to Hubert K. Reese, November 26, 1927, George Gordon Battle to

LeRoy Percy, December 9, 1927, LeRoy Percy to F. B. Keech and Co., December 19, 1927, to Jas. McConkey, December 19, 1927, to Mrs. W. A. Percy, December 20, 1927, and to Gov. Dennis Murphree, December 21, 1927; all in PP.

28. W. A. Percy to LeRoy Percy, February 9, 1928, LeRoy Percy to Mrs. W. A. Percy, February 22, 1928, both in PP; LeRoy Percy, *Flood Control*, Senate Committee on Commerce, 70th Cong., 1st Sess., Microform (Westport, Conn., n.d.), 99–101.

29. LeRoy Percy, *Flood Control*, 99–112.

30. LeRoy Percy to Mrs. W. A. Percy, February 22, 1928, in PP; Harrison, *Levee Districts*, 56, 235; Tindall, *Emergence*, 240.

31. Janet Longcope to W. A. Percy, January 8, February 20, April 11, November 5, 1928, W. A. Percy to LeRoy Percy, February 9, 1928, LeRoy Percy to LeRoy Pratt Percy, October 13, 1928, George Parmly Day to W. A. Percy, April 8, 1929, W. A. Percy to Henry Smith, June 26, 1929, all in PP.

32. W. A. Percy, "Cadenza on a Popular Theme," typescript in PP; Spalding, "William Alexander Percy," 194–96.

33. LeRoy Percy to George Gordon Battle, January 12, 1928, to Wrenn Bros. & Co., April 4, 1928, to James Stone, June 29, 1928, to H. C. Hamblen, October 11, 1928, to Dear Willie [Percy], June 30, 1928, to Sen. Pat Harrison, August 24, 30, September 22, 1928, and Pat Harrison to LeRoy Percy, September 18, 25, 1928, LeRoy Percy to Hon. Hubert D. Stephens, August 24, 1928, and to Senator John Sharp Williams, September 22, 1928, John Sharp Williams to LeRoy Percy, September 26, 1928, all in PP.

34. LeRoy Percy to LeRoy Pratt Percy, May 26, 1928, October 13, 1928, to Roger Generelly, November 3, 1928, to H. K. Reese, November 10, 1928, to LeRoy Pratt Percy, April 27, 1929, and to Miss Lady Percy, May 3, 1929, all in PP.

35. LeRoy Percy to Walter Sillers, Sr., April 3, 1929, and to Lester Fant, August 12, 1929, both in PP.

36. LeRoy Percy to LeRoy Pratt Percy, June 20, 1929, H. C. Hamblen to LeRoy Percy, August 1, 1929, LeRoy Percy to H. C. Hamblen, August 3, 1929, all in PP.

37. LeRoy Percy to Judge George Ethridge, May 4, 1929, to Mrs C. Y. Percy, May 25, 1929, and to Wm. C. Bitting, June 29, 1929, all in PP.

38. LeRoy Percy to Arthur E. Morgan, July 1, 1929, and to Mrs. LeRoy Pratt Percy, August 13, 1929, both in PP.

39. MMF to W. A. Percy, October 19, 1929, and to Franklin Simon & Co., October 19, 1929, W. A. Percy to E. L. Rogers, October 18, 1929, all in PP; Sallis, "LeRoy Percy," 166.

40. W. A. Percy to Malcolm Davis, December 2, 1929, Secretary to Jas. G. McConkey, November 11, 1929, John Sharp Williams to LeRoy Percy, November 21, 1929, all in PP.

41. Herbert Hoover to LeRoy Percy, November 12, 1929, W. A. Percy to Malcolm Davis, December 2, 1929, Greenville *Daily Democrat-Times*, clipping, n.d., all in PP.

42. Memphis *Commercial Appeal*, clipping, November 4, 1933, other obituaries and testimonials, all in PP.

Chapter 9

1. W. A. Percy to H. B. Williams, January 14, 1930, in PP; Spalding, "William Alexander Percy," 47.

2. W. A. Percy to Mrs. W. A. Percy, March 11, 1930, and to W[illie]. A. Percy, January 15, 1930, both in PP.

3. LeRoy Percy to Mrs. Harriet S. Turner, February 15, 1917, in PP; Spalding, "William Alexander Percy," 49.

4. John Hereford Percy, *Percy Family*, 67–68; Robert Coles, *Walker Percy: An American Search* (Boston, 1969), 59; Carlton Cremeens, "Walker Percy, The Man and the Novelist: An Interview," *Southern Review* IV (April, 1968), 287.

5. W. A. Percy, *Lanterns*, 312; Spalding, "William Alexander Percy," 50; John Carr, "An Interview with Walker Percy," *Georgia Review*, XXV (Fall, 1971), 317–32.

6. Greenville High School *Pica* (The interviewer may have been Walker, who wrote a column for the *Pica*), clipping, W. A. Percy to Norman V. Donaldson, March 13, 1931, Norman V. Donaldson to W. A. Percy, March 16, 1931, miscellaneous reviews, clippings, all in PP; Norman Douglas, *Birds and Beasts of the Greek Anthology* (New York, 1929), i–vi.

7. W. A. Percy to Donald Davidson, May 31, 1930, quoted in Spalding, "William Alexander Percy," 81.

8. W. A. Percy to John Chapman, July 3, 1930, quoted in Spalding, "William Alexander Percy," 81.

9. Spalding, "William Alexander Percy," 48–49; Ware, "William Alexander Percy," 122–23.

10. Hodding Carter, *Where Main Street Meets the River* (New York, 1952), 68.

11. Carter, *Main Street*, 67–69; Ware, "William Alexander Percy," 123; Raymond McClinton, "A Social-Economic Analysis of a Mississippi Delta Plantation," (Master's thesis, University of North Carolina, 1938).

12. McClinton, "Delta Plantation," 6, 48–52.

13. Carter, *Main Street*, 68; Hortense Powdermaker, *Stranger and Friend* (New York, 1966), 142.

14. Speakman, *Mostly Mississippi*, 258–61; W. A. Percy, *Lanterns*, 303–304; Ware, "William Alexander Percy," 112–13; Jonathan Daniels, *A Southerner Discovers the South* (New York, 1938), 174; Hodding Carter, *Lower Mississippi* (New York, 1942), 403; Interview with B. Phinizy Percy, by John Jones, New Orleans, La., April 17, 1980 (Transcript in Mississippi Department of Archives and History, Jackson).

15. Daniels, *Southerner*, 173; Roark Bradford, "Kansas Brown," *Colliers*, XVII (December, 1938), 102–12.

16. Daniels, *Southerner*, 173–75.

17. Powdermaker, *Stranger and Friend*, 191.

18. Windham, "Percy's Life and Poetry," 101–103.

19. Carol Malone, "William Alexander Percy: Knight to His People, Ishmael to Himself, and Poet to the World" (Master's thesis, University of Mississippi, 1961), 51–52.

20. W. A. Percy, "The White Plague," in PP.

21. *Ibid.*

22. W. A. Percy to Mark Clifton, March 7, 1930, Delta *Democrat-Times*, clipping, January 22, 1942, in PP.

23. W. A. Percy, *Lanterns*, 334; Windham, "Percy's Life and Poetry," 160–63; Carter, *Main Street*, 76.

24. W. A. Percy to The Delta Democrat, n.d., Hodding Carter, "For Will," Delta *Democrat-Times*, clipping, January 22, 1942, both in PP; Powdermaker, *Stranger and Friend*, 138–42; Carter, *Southern Legacy* (Baton Rouge, 1950), 5; Carter, *Main Street*, 69–95; W. A. Percy, *Lanterns*, 334; Windham, "Percy's Life and Poetry," 24, 28; Spalding, "William Alexander Percy, 49; David L. Cohn, *God Shakes Creation* (New York, 1935), xi–xvi; Richard H. King, "Mourning and Melancholia: Will Percy and the Southern Tradition," *Virginia Quarterly Review*, LIII (Spring, 1977), 148.

25. W. A. Percy to Miss E. Holliday, September 30, 1929, W. A. Percy to Yale Press, miscellaneous correspondence, Greenville *Daily Democrat-Times*, clipping, May 4, 1935, all in PP; Malone, "William Alexander Percy," 68–69; Carter, *Lower Mississippi*, 404.

26. Worcester *Sunday Telegram*, clipping, February 20, 1938, in PP; Carter, *Lower*

Mississippi, 401–404; Blotner, *Faulkner,* 130–32, 144–45, 323, 606; Coles, *Walker Percy,* 58; Windham, "Percy's Life and Poetry," 163; Malone, "William Alexander Percy," 68; Spalding, "William Alexander Percy," 52; Mary Joan Lueckenbach, "William Alexander Percy and Walker Percy: The Progeny of a Brooding Knight," (Master's thesis, University of Mississippi, 1973), 3; Ashley Brown, "An Interview with Walker Percy," *Shenandoah,* XVIII (Spring, 1967) 3–12.

27. Coles, *Walker Percy,* 58; Carter, *Lower Mississippi,* 402–404; Malone "William Alexander Percy," 68; Lueckenbach, "Progeny," 8; Dickey, "William Alexander Percy," 47; Windham, "Percy's Life and Poetry," 27.

28. Memphis *Commercial Appeal,* clipping, May 21, 1939, in PP; Windham, "Percy's Life and Poetry," 21–27; Spalding, "William Alexander Percy," 51–52; Malone, "William Alexander Percy," 34; Ware, "William Alexander Percy," 124.

29. W. A. Percy to Mr. George Vaughn, February 15, 1935, quoted in Spalding, "William Alexander Percy," 108.

30. W. A. Percy to Walker Percy, May 3, 1938, cited in Spalding, "William Alexander Percy," 108.

31. Vicksburg *Sunday Post-Herald,* clipping, January 15, 1939, in PP; W. A. Percy, "Loyalty," quoted in Spalding, "William Alexander Percy," 254.

32. W. A. Percy, Poetry notebook, W. A. Percy, "For the Younger Generation," typescript, both in PP.

33. Will's application quoted in Spalding, "William Alexander Percy," 231–32; Dickey, "William Alexander Percy," 160–62; Malone, "William Alexander Percy," 98.

34. Burton Rascoe, "Percy and his 'Lanterns,'" Chicago *Sun,* clipping, February 1, 1942, in PP; Spalding, "William Alexander Percy," 53–54; Malone, "William Alexander Percy," 128; Dickey, "William Alexander Percy," 31.

35. W. A. Percy, Diary, in PP; Spalding, "William Alexander Percy," 54; Malone, "William Alexander Percy," 128.

36. Tupelo *Daily Journal,* clipping, March 21, 1939, in PP.

37. [W. A. Percy], Manuscript, untitled chapter, [W. A. Percy], "1914–1916," typescript, [W. A. Percy] Chap. 17, typescript, all in PP.

38. Crunden, *Superfluous Men.*

39. LeRoy Percy to Chas. S. Petrie, June 7, 1929, in PP; W. A. Percy to Huger Jervey, June 14, 1940, quoted in Spalding, "William Alexander Percy," 57.

40. Spalding, "William Alexander Percy," 58.

41. W. A. Percy to Mrs. Warfield Longcope, August 28, 1940, quoted in Spalding, "William Alexander Percy," 59; Malone, "William Alexander Percy," 128.

42. W. A. Percy, "Apologia," typescript, in PP; Malone, "William Alexander Percy," 130; Dickey, "William Alexander Percy," 31; Spalding, "William Alexander Percy," 60.

43. New York *Herald Tribune,* April 4, 11, August 8, October 10, 31, November 21, December 12, 1941, New York *Times,* March 23, 1942, *Publisher's Weekly,* September 13, 1941, Syracuse *Herald-American,* July 5, 1942, all clippings in PP; Dickey, "William Alexander Percy," 31–32; Malone, "William Alexander Percy," 129.

44. Atlanta *Constitution,* March 28, 1941, Richmond *Times-Dispatch,* March 16, 1941, Charlotte *Observer,* March 16, 1941, all clippings in PP.

45. Edwin Tribble, Review, in Washington *Star,* March 30, 1941, Charlotte Becker, Review, in Buffalo *News,* March 15, 1941, Review, *Time,* March 24, 1941, Hirschell Brickell, "The Revealing Memoirs of a Southern Planter," New York *Times,* March 23, 1941, *New York Times Book Review,* May 18, 1941, Lawrence Olsen, Review, in New York *Herald-Tribune,* March 9, 1941, and other reviews and clippings, all in PP. See also Dickey, "William Alexander Percy," 31–36.

46. William Jay Gold, Review, in *Saturday Review of Literature,* April 5, 1941, James Orrick, "Eheu! Fugaces," *Virginia Quarterly Review,* VII (Summer, 1941), 446–48, George Steater, Review, in *Commonweal,* May 30, 1941, Review, in *Na-*

tion, May 31, 1941, George C. Osborn, Review, in *Journal of Southern History*, VII (August, 1941), all clippings in PP.

47. A. J. Nock, Review of *Lanterns*, in *Atlantic Monthly*, CLXVII (May, 1941), clipping, in PP; Crunden, *Superfluous Men*, 27; Albert Jay Nock, *Memoirs of a Superfluous Man* (Chicago, 1964), xi-xii.

48. W. J. Cash, Review of *Lanterns*, in Charlotte *News*, May 10, 1941, reprinted in Joseph Morrison, *W. J. Cash* (New York, 1967), 290–94.

49. W. A. Percy to Hester Ware, June 2, 1941, in Ware, "William Alexander Percy," 127.

50. "News of Borzoi Books," clipping, August 5, 1941, in PP; Malone, "William Alexander Percy," 98; Spalding, "William Alexander Percy," 59–61.

51. Malone, "William Alexander Percy," 44.

52. Delta *Democrat-Times*, January 22, 1942, New Orleans *Times*, January 22, 1942, both clippings, in PP; Malone, "William Alexander Percy," 98–99; Interview with Walker Percy, by John Jones, April 17, 1980 (Transcript in Mississippi Department of Archives and History, Jackson).

53. "The Poetry Society of America," March, 1942, *Saturday Review of Literature*, April 18, 1942, both clippings in PP; Spalding, "William Alexander Percy," vi, 62.

54. Caroline Gordon, Review of *Collected Poems*, in *New York Herald Tribune Weekly Book Review* January 9, 1944, quoted in Dickey, "William Alexander Percy," 24–25.

Chapter 10

1. Walker Percy, Introduction to *Lanterns on the Levee: Recollections of a Planter's Son*, by William Alexander Percy (Baton Rouge, 1973), xvi.

2. W. A. Percy, *Lanterns*, 152, 54.

3. Interview with Walker Percy, by John Jones.

4. Coles, *Walker Percy*, 62; Scott Byrd, "Mysteries and Movies: Walker Percy's College Articles and *The Moviegoer*," *Mississippi Quarterly*, XXV (Spring, 1972) 165–81.

5. Coles, *Walker Percy*, 63–64; Interview with Walker Percy, by John Jones; Martin Luschei, *The Sovereign Wayfarer: Walker Percy's Diagnosis of the Malaise* (Baton Rouge, 1972), 4.

6. Interview with Walker Percy, by John Jones.

7. Walker Percy, *The Last Gentleman* (New York, 1966), 356.

8. Interview with B. Phinizy Percy, by John Jones; Luschei, *The Sovereign Wayfarer*, 11–12.

9. Walker Percy, *The Moviegoer* (New York, 1961), 244–45.

10. *Ibid.*, 222–23; W. A. Percy, *Lanterns*, 69, 154.

11. W. A. Percy, *Lanterns*, 273.

12. Walker Percy, *The Moviegoer*, 51; Walker Percy, *The Last Gentleman*, 10–11.

13. Interview with Walker Percy, by John Jones.

14. Walker Percy, *The Last Gentleman*, 185.

15. W. A. Percy, *Lanterns*, 223, 258.

16. Walker Percy, *The Last Gentleman*, 23; Luschei, *The Sovereign Wayfarer*, 42.

17. W. A. Percy, *Lanterns*, 63; Walker Percy, *The Moviegoer*, 231.

18. Walker Percy, *Love in the Ruins* (New York, 1971), 3.

19. *Ibid.*, 190.

20. *Ibid.*, 382; Interview with Walker Percy, by John Jones.

21. Unsigned [LeRoy Percy] to Whom It May Concern, December 27, 1915, in PP.

22. LeRoy Percy to President of the State Medical Board, March 24, 1908, to Dr. E. P. Brown, January 26, 1909, to Boltin Smith, June 19, 1918, and to W. H. Hardie, June 22, 1919, Mary C. Booze to Dr. J. C. Overton, January 22, 1926, all in PP; Dickey, "William Alexander Percy," 149n.

23. LeRoy Percy to J. M. Taylor, May 20, 1907, in PP; George M. Frederickson, *The Black Image in the White Mind* (New York, 1971), 228–55.

24. *Congressional Record*, 61st Cong., 2nd Sess., 5316–18; 3rd Sess., 3541.

25. *Speech of Ex-United States Senator LeRoy Percy*, Greenville, Miss., April 23, 1923, in PP.

26. W. A. Percy, *Lanterns*, 291.

27. *Ibid.*, 293, 296.

28. Walker Percy, *The Moviegoer*, 22.

29. *Ibid.*, 233; Cremeens, "Walker Percy," 276; Walker Percy, *Love in the Ruins*, 29, 112.

30. Walker Percy, *The Last Gentleman*, 337–47.

31. *Ibid.*, 301.

32. *Ibid.*, 381–82.

33. Carr, "An Interview with Walker Percy," 330. See also Coles, *Walker Percy*, 205–208.

34. Walker Percy, *The Moviegoer*, 224.

35. Unidentified clipping, n.d., in PP.

36. LeRoy Percy to W. A. Percy, April 28, 1908, in PP.

37. LeRoy Percy to John Sharp Williams, June 22, 1907, in PP.

38. W. A. Percy, Prose and poetry notebook, n.d., in PP.

39. Walker Percy, *The Moviegoer*, 200.

40. Panthea Reid Broughton, "Gentlemen and Fornicators: *The Last Gentleman* and a Bisected Reality," in Broughton, ed., *The Art of Walker Percy: Stratagems for Being* (Baton Rouge, 1979); Walker Percy, *The Last Gentleman* 166, 281, 167.

41. Walker Percy, *Love in the Ruins*, 339.

42. *Ibid.*, 49.

43. *Ibid.*, 384.

44. Walker Percy, *Lancelot* (New York, 1977), 158; W. A. Percy, "Enzio's Kingdom," in *Collected Poems*, 331.

45. Walker Percy, *Lancelot*, 198.

46. Interview with Walker Percy, by John Jones.

47. Cecil L. Eubanks, "Walker Percy: Eschatology and the Politics of Grace," *Southern Quarterly*, XVIII (Spring, 1980), 121–36.

48. Walker Percy, *The Second Coming* (New York, 1980), 273.

49. *Ibid.*, 38–39.

50. J. P. Telotte, "Charles Peirce and Walker Percy: From Semiotic to Narrative," *Southern Quarterly*, XVIII (Spring, 1980), 65–79.

51. Walker Percy, *The Second Coming*, 342; Walker Percy, *The Message in the Bottle*, (New York, 1975), 281.

52. Walker Percy, *The Second Coming*, 341, 343.

53. *Ibid.*, 360.

Bibliography

I. Primary Sources

A. MANUSCRIPTS

Louisiana State University Department of Archives and History, Baton Rouge
    Ferguson, Percy, Papers, April 25–May 3, 1912.
    Longcope, Janet Percy Dana, Papers, 1911–1917.
    * Percy, LeRoy and Family, Papers, 1894–1930.
    * Percy, William Alexander, Papers, 1902–1941.

B. PUBLIC DOCUMENTS

Biographical Directory of the American Congress, 1774–1971. Washington, D.C., 1971.
Congressional Record. 61st Cong., 2nd Sess.; 61st Cong., 3rd Sess.; 62nd Cong., 1st Sess.; 62nd Cong., 2nd Sess.; 62nd Cong., 3rd Sess.
Langsford, E. L. and R. H. Thibideaux. "Technical Bulletin, No. 682—Plantation Organization and Operation in the Yazoo Mississippi Delta." *Technical Bulletins, Nos. 676–700.* Washington, D. C., 1940.
Leavell, R. H., *et al. Negro Migration in 1916–17.* Washington, D.C., 1919.
Percy, LeRoy. *Flood Control.* Senate Committee on Commerce. 70th Cong., 1st Sess. Microform. Westport, Conn., n.d.
————. *Hearings . . . on the Control of Destructive Flood Waters of the United States.* House Committee on Flood Control. 70th Cong., 1st Sess. Microform. Westport, Conn., n.d.
————. *Mississippi River Floods.* House Committee on Flood Control. 64th Cong., 1st Sess. Microform. Westport, Conn., n.d.
Senate Documents, 61st Cong., 2nd Sess., No. 633, Pt. 24.
U.S. Department of the Army, Historical Division. *Meuse-Argonne Operations of the American Expeditionary Forces.* Washington, D.C., 1948. Vol. IX of *United States Army in the World War, 1917–1919.*
U.S. Department of Commerce and Labor. Bureau of the Census. *Special Reports: Religious Bodies, 1906.* Washington, D.C., 1910.
U.S. Department of Commerce. Bureau of the Census. *Religious Bodies, 1916.* Vol. I of 2 vols. Washington, D.C., 1919.
The War of the Rebellion: A Compilation of the Official Records of the Union and Confederate Armies. 70 vols., Washington, D.C., 1880–1901.

* Author's note: Subsequent to my research, the collection herein referred to as the Percy Papers was reclassified and reorganized as the LeRoy Percy and Family Papers and the William Alexander Percy Papers, and was placed on microfilm.

C. NEWSPAPERS

Jackson *Daily Clarion-Ledger*, May 21–November 22, 1902; June, 1909–January, 1911; December 21, 1921–July 8, 1922; February 28–September 7, 1923.
Jackson *Daily News*, July 5, 1910–June 10, 1911.
Memphis *Commercial Appeal*, March 1–May 31, 1923.
Natchez *Daily Democrat*, June 25, 1911.
Vicksburg *Herald*, January 1–August 7, 1898; January, 1919–November, 1923.

D. PAMPHLETS

Percy, LeRoy. *Address by Senator LeRoy Percy, Greenville, Miss., March 8, 1922.* Knights of Columbus, 1922.
———. *Ku Klux Klan Unnecessary.*
———. *The Payne-Aldrich Tariff Law Responsible for the High Price of Food-Investigation of Gambling in Cotton Futures.* Washington, D.C., 1910.
———. *Speech of Ex-United States Senator LeRoy Percy.* Greenville, Miss., April 23, 1923.
———. *Speech of United States Senator LeRoy Percy Delivered at the State Fair.* Jackson, Miss., October 31, 1910.

E. BOOKS

Adams, Henry. *The Education of Henry Adams.* New York, 1931.
Carter, Hodding. *Southern Legacy.* Baton Rouge, 1950.
———. *Lower Mississippi.* New York, 1942.
———. *Where Main Street Meets the River.* New York, 1952.
Cohn, David L. *God Shakes Creation.* New York, 1935.
Daniels, Jonathan. *A Southerner Discovers the South.* New York, 1938.
Douglas, Norman. *Birds and Beasts of the Greek Anthology.* New York, 1929.
Hemingway, Ernest. *A Farewell to Arms.* New York, 1949.
McCain, William D. and Charlotte Capers, eds. *Memoirs of Henry Tillinghast Ireys, Papers of the Washington County Historical Society, 1910–1915.* Jackson, Miss., 1954.
Morison, Elting E., ed. *The Letters of Theodore Roosevelt.* Cambridge, Mass., 1954.
Morrison, Joseph. *W. J. Cash.* New York, 1967.
Nock, Albert Jay. *Memoirs of a Superfluous Man.* Chicago, 1964.
Percy, Walker. *The Message in the Bottle.* New York, 1975.
———. *The Moviegoer.* New York, 1961.
———. *The Last Gentleman.* New York, 1966.
———. *Love in the Ruins.* New York, 1971.
———. *Lancelot.* New York, 1977.
———. *The Second Coming.* New York, 1980.
Percy, William Alexander. *Lanterns on the Levee.* 1941; rpr. Baton Rouge, 1973.
———. *The Collected Poems of William Alexander Percy.* New York, 1943.
———, ed. *Poems of Arthur O'Shaughnessy.* New Haven, 1923.
Powdermaker, Hortense. *Stranger and Friend.* New York, 1966.

F. PERIODICALS

Bradford, Roark. "Kansas Brown." *Colliers*, XVII (December, 1938), 102–12.

Creel, George. "What Are You Going To Do About It? The Carnival of Corruption in Mississippi," *Cosmopolitan*, II (November, 1911), 725–35.

Percy, LeRoy. "The Modern Ku Klux Klan." *Atlantic Monthly*, CXXX (July, 1922), 122–28.

———. "A Southern View of Negro Education." *Outlook*, LXXXVI (August 3, 1907), 730–32.

Percy, William Alexander. "Cadenza on a Popular Theme." *Southwest Review*, XIII (Fall, 1928).

Pierantoni, Augusto. "Italian Feeling on American Lynching." *Independent*, LV (August 27, 1903), 2040–42.

G. INTERVIEWS

Baker, Don R., by the author, Leland, Miss., October 23, 1976. Transcript in Louisiana State University Department of Archives and History, Baton Rouge.

Carter, Hodding, by T. H. Baker, New Orleans, La., November 8, 1968. Transcript in Lyndon Baines Johnson Library, Oral History Collection, Austin, Tex.

Crump, Brodie S., by the author, Greenville, Miss., October 22, 1976. Transcript in Louisiana State University Department of Archives and History, Baton Rouge.

Foote, Shelby, by John Jones, Memphis, Tenn., August 16, 1979. Transcript in Mississippi Department of Archives and History, Jackson.

Percy, B. Phinizy, by John Jones, New Orleans, La., April 17, 1980. Transcript in Mississippi Department of Archives and History, Jackson.

Percy, Walker, by John Jones, Covington, La., April 17, 1980. Transcript in Mississippi Department of Archives and History, Jackson.

II. Secondary Sources

A. BOOKS

Alexander, Charles C. *The Ku Klux Klan in the Southwest*. Lexington, Ky., 1965.

Blotner, Joseph. *Faulkner: A Biography*. New York, 1974.

Brandfon, Robert L. *Cotton Kingdom of the New South: A History of the Yazoo Mississippi Delta from Reconstruction to the Present*. Cambridge, Mass., 1967.

Catton, Bruce. *A Stillness at Appomattox*. Garden City, N. Y., 1953.

Coffman, Edward M. *The War to End All Wars*. New York, 1968.

Coles, Robert. *Walker Percy: An American Search*. Boston, 1969.

Crunden, Robert M., ed. *The Superfluous Men: Conservative Critics of American Culture, 1900–1945*. Austin, 1977.

Daniels, Josephus. *The Life of Woodrow Wilson, 1856–1924*. Chicago, 1924.

Daniels, Pete. *The Shadow of Slavery*. Urbana, 1972.

Frederickson, George M. *The Black Image in the White Mind*. New York, 1971.

Fussell, Paul. *The Great War and Modern Memory*. New York, 1975.

Garner, James Wilford. *Reconstruction in Mississippi*. New York, 1901.

Green, Adwin Wigfall. *The Man Bilbo*. Baton Rouge, 1963.

Harris, William C. *The Day of the Carpetbagger: Republican Reconstruction in Mississippi*. Baton Rouge, 1979.

Harrison, Robert W. *Levee Districts and Levee Building in Mississippi: A Study of the State and Local Efforts to Control Mississippi River Floods*. Stoneville, Miss., 1951.

Higham, John. *Strangers in the Land: Patterns of American Nativism, 1860–1925*. New York, 1963.

Hoffman, Frederick J. *The Twenties*. New York, 1929.

Holmes, William F. *The White Chief: James Kimble Vardaman*. Baton Rouge, 1970.

Jackson, Kenneth T. *The Ku Klux Klan in the City, 1915–1930*. New York, 1967.

Kennedy, David M. *Over Here*. New York, 1980.

King, Richard H. *A Southern Renaissance*. New York, 1980.

Kirwan, Albert D. *Revolt of the Rednecks: Mississippi Politics, 1876–1925*. Lexington, 1951.

Luschei, Martin. *The Sovereign Wayfarer: Walker Percy's Diagnosis of the Malaise*. Baton Rouge, 1972.

McNeilly, J. S. *Climax and Collapse of Reconstruction in Mississippi, 1874–1876*.

Mayes, Edward. *Lucius Q. C. Lamar: His Life, Times, and Speeches. 1825–1893*. Nashville, 1896.

Osborn, George C. *John Sharp Williams: Planter-Statesman of the Deep South*. Baton Rouge, 1943.

Percy, John Hereford. *The Percy Family of Mississippi and Louisiana*. Baton Rouge, 1943.

Rice, Arnold S. *The Ku Klux Klan in American Politics*. Washington, D.C., 1962.

Smith, Frank E. *The Yazoo River*. New York, 1954.

Speakman, Harold. *Mostly Mississippi*. New York, 1927.

Stallings, Laurence. *The Doughboys*. New York, 1963.

Stone, Alfred H. *Studies in the American Race Problem*. New York, 1908.

Tindall, George Brown. *The Emergence of the New South, 1913–1945*. Baton Rouge, 1967.

Wharton, Vernon Lane. *The Negro In Mississippi, 1865–1890*. Chapel Hill, 1947.

Williams, T. Harry. *Lincoln and His Generals*. New York, 1952.

———. *Romance and Realism in Southern Politics*. Baton Rouge, 1966.

Woodward, C. Vann. *Origins of the New South 1877–1913*. Baton Rouge, 1951.

B. ARTICLES AND ESSAYS

Adams, Holmes. "Writers of Greenville, Mississippi, 1915–1950." *Journal of Mississippi History*, XXXII, no. 3, (Fall, 1970), 229–43.

Broughton, Panthea Reid. "Gentlemen and Fornicators: *The Last Gentleman* and a Bisected Reality." In *The Art of Walker Percy: Stratagems for Being*, edited by Panthea Reid Broughton, Baton Rouge, 1979.

Brown, Ashley. "An Interview with Walker Percy." *Shenandoah*, XVIII (Spring, 1967), 3–12.

Byrd, Scott. "Mysteries and Movies: Walker Percy's College Articles and *The Moviegoer*." *Mississippi Quarterly*, XXV (Spring, 1972), 165–81.

Carr, John. "An Interview with Walker Percy." *Georgia Review*, XXV (Fall, 1971), 317–32.

Cremeens, Carlton. "Walker Percy, the Man and the Novelist: An Interview." *Southern Review*, IV (April, 1968), 271–90.

Eubanks, Cecil L. "Walker Percy: Eschatology and the Politics of Grace." *Southern Quarterly*, XVIII (Spring, 1980), 121–36.

Holmes, William F. "William Alexander Percy and the Bourbon Era in the Yazoo-Mississippi Delta." *Mississippi Quarterly*, XXVI (Winter, 1972–73), 71–88.

King, Richard H. "Mourning and Melancholia: Will Percy and the Southern Tradition." *Virginia Quarterly Review*, LIII (Spring, 1977), 248–64.

Ladner, Heber. "James Kimble Vardaman, Governor of Mississippi, 1904–1908." *Journal of Mississippi History*, II (October, 1940), 175–205.

Miller, Robert Moats. "The Ku Klux Klan." In *Change and Continuity in Twentieth-Century America: The 1920's*, edited by John Braeman, Robert H. Bremmer, and David Brody. Columbus, Ohio, 1968.

Sillers, Walter, Sr. "Flood Control in Bolivar County, 1838–1924." *Journal of Mississippi History*, IX (January, 1947), 3–20.

Smiley, David L. "Cassius M. Clay and the Mississippi Election of 1875." *Journal of Mississippi History*, XIX (October, 1957), 234–51.

Telotte, J. P. "Charles Peirce and Walker Percy: From Semiotic to Narrative." *Southern Quarterly*, XVIII (Spring, 1980), 65–79.

White, Eugene E. "Anti-Racial Agitation in Politics: James Kimble Vardaman in the Mississippi Gubernatorial Campaign of 1903." *Journal of Mississippi History*, VII (April, 1945), 91–131.

White, William W. "Mississippi Confederate Veterans in Public Office, 1875–1900." *Journal of Mississippi History*, XX (July, 1958), 147–56.

C. MASTER'S THESES

Dickey, Benjamin Willis. "William Alexander Percy: An Alien Spirit in the Twentieth Century." Alabama Polytechnic Institute, 1951.

Lueckenbach, Mary Joan. "William Alexander Percy and Walker Percy: The Progeny of a Brooding Knight." University of Mississippi, 1973.

Malone, Carol. "William Alexander Percy: Knight to his People, Ishmael to Himself, and Poet to the World." University of Mississippi, 1961.

McClinton, Raymond. "A Social-Economic Analysis of a Mississippi Delta Plantation." University of North Carolina, 1938.

Peacock, Kathleen Moore. "William Alexander Percy: A Study in Southern Conservatism." Birmingham Southern College, 1958.

Sallis, William C. "A Study of the Life and Times of LeRoy Percy." Mississippi State University, 1957.

Spalding, Phinizy. "William Alexander Percy: His Philosophy of Life as Reflected in His Poetry." University of Georgia, 1957.

Ware, Hester S. "A Study of the Life and Works of William Alexander Percy." Mississippi State University, 1950.

Windham, Hudean. "A Study of William Alexander Percy's Life and Poetry." George Peabody College for Teachers, 1939.

Index